# IRISH RAIL TRACTION & TRAVEL

## Fourth Edition

Peter Jones
&
Andrew Marshall

ISBN 0-9521496-1-3

Published by the Irish Traction Group.
Registered as a charity in England & Wales, No. 1000382.
Registered address: 31 Hayfield Road, Bredbury, Stockport, Cheshire, SK6 1DE.

© Copyright 2004. Irish Traction Group, 31 Hayfield Road, Bredbury, Stockport, SK6 DE

All rights reserved. No part of this publication may be reproduced in any form by any means electronic, mechanical, photocopying, recording or otherwise without the prior permission of the publisher.

# INTRODUCTION

Since the publication of the third edition of "Irish Railways, Traction & Travel" in October 1994, and "Irish Locomotives and Rolling Stock" in 1996, much has changed on the Irish railway scene. Demand by enthusiasts for greater information relating to the Irish locomotive and rolling stock fleets continues to grow, and the purpose of this fourth edition is to update the reader with current events and to expand on areas not previously covered in the earlier editions. Information is updated to that available at the beginning of September 2004.

# GENERAL NOTES AND CONTENTS

The current Irish railway network is operated by two companies, Iarnród Éireann in the Irish Republic and Translink NI Railways (formerly Northern Ireland Railways) in Northern Ireland. Iarnród Éireann is a subsidiary company of Córas Iompair Éireann, the Irish transport holding company which itself operated the service in the Republic via its railway division from 1st January 1945 until 2nd February 1987. Translink NI Railways is a subsidiary company of Northern Ireland Transport Holding Co. Ltd. Translink NI Railways operate all internal passenger services within Northern Ireland and share the cross border passenger services with Iarnród Éireann. Iarnród Éireann operate all internal passenger and freight services within the Irish Republic. Included in this edition are:

(1): A full list of all classes of diesel locomotives owned by CIE/IE, NIR/Translink NI Railways and the UTA. Individual locomotive details (where available records permit) are given, including notes regarding final disposal where a locomotive is no longer in traffic. Photographs are included of most of the classes of locomotives described in the text. Locomotives owned by the UTA are shown in Appendix 1.

(2): A full list of all IE, CIE, NCC, GNR(I), UTA, NIR and Translink NI Railways diesel and petrol driven multiple units, railbuses and railcars built since 1906, together with individual vehicle details (where available records permit), including notes regarding final disposal (where known) where a vehicle no longer exists.

(3): Similar details to (2) above for the push/pull sets to which many of the former CIE railcars were subsequently converted.

(4): A full current coaching stock fleetlist for both IE and Translink NI Railways, together with brief technical details.

(5): A current fleet list of track machines and engineers' vehicles for both IE and Translink NI Railways, together with brief details of type, builder, use and location.

(6): A list of all preserved coaching stock registered to run on both IE and Translink NI Railways tracks (all are owned or operated by the Railway Preservation Society of Ireland (RPSI)).

(7): Details of tram vehicles operating the new LUAS system, together with distance tables for the first two lines to be constructed.

(8): A full list of all current freight train workings, giving days of operation and departure times, together with usual motive power and type of wagons in the train consist. Notes are given in relation to the traffic flows.

(9): Distance tables are included for all routes which are still open to either passenger or freight traffic on both systems. Also included are distance tables for routes which, although closed, may still see very occasional traffic. Details of permanent speed restrictions and their locations are quoted in order to assist readers whose interest lies in the field of train timing. Also included are details of the signalboxes and Method of Operation information, which is included in the distance tables where appropriate.

# GENERAL TRAVEL INFORMATION

## ROVER TICKETS

Enthusiasts may find Rover Tickets very useful for travel in Ireland. At the time of writing the following are available (prices as at May 2004, but subject to revision).

## Iarnród Éireann

### 5 Day IE Explorer Ticket
Cost €115.50 Adult, €58.50 Child, Standard class only. 5 days unlimited travel on all IE services within a fixed 15 day period. Boundary on cross border services is Dundalk.

### 1 Day DART & Dublin Bus Rover
Cost €7.70 Adult, €11.60 Family. Standard class only. One day's unlimited travel in the Dublin Suburban area bounded by Balbriggan, Kilcoole, Howth, Maynooth and Hazelhatch & Celbridge.

### 1 Day DART Rover (short hop zone)
Cost €6.50 Adult, €11.00 Family, €3.00 Child, Standard class only. As above but valid on rail services only.

### 3 Day DART & Dublin Bus Rover
Cost €15.00 Adult, Standard class only. One day's unlimited travel in the Dublin suburban area bounded by Balbriggan, Kilcoole, Howth, Maynooth and Hazelhatch & Celbridge.

### 3 Day DART Rover (short hop zone)
Cost €13.00 Adult, Standard class only. As above but valid on rail services only.

## Translink NI Railways

### 7 Day All-Line Ticket
Cost £47.00 Adult, £23.50 Child. Seven days unlimited travel on all Translink NI Railways services. Boundary on cross border services is Newry.

### 3 Day All-Line Ticket
Cost £32.00 Adult, £16.00 Child. Three days unlimited travel on all Translink NI Railways services. Boundary on cross border services is Newry.

### 1 Day All-Line Ticket
Cost £13.00 Adult, £6.50 Child. one day unlimited travel on all Translink NI Railways services. Boundary on cross border services is Newry.

### Sunday 1 Day All-Line Ticket
Cost £4.50 Adult, £2.25 Child. Unlimited travel on all Translink NI Railways Sunday services. Boundary on cross border services is Newry.

## Both Systems

### 5 Day Irish Explorer Ticket
Cost £90.00 / €143.00 Adult, £45.00 / €71.50 Child. Standard class only. 5 days unlimited travel on both IE and Translink NI Railways rail networks within a fixed 15 day period.

### 8 Day Emerald Card Ticket
Cost £124.00 / €198.00 Adult, £62.00 / €99.00 Child. Standard class only. 8 days unlimited travel within a fixed 15 day period on all IE and Translink NI Railways services and those of Bus Éireann, Ulsterbus, Dublin Bus and Belfast Citybus.

### 15 Day Emerald Card Ticket
Cost £214.00 / €341.00 Adult, £107.00 / €170.50 Child, Standard class only. 15 days unlimited travel within a fixed 30 day period on all IE and Translink NI Railways services and those of Bus Éireann, Ulsterbus, Dublin Bus and Belfast Citybus

The above tickets cannot be obtained in mainland UK, and are only available directly from the relevant operators.

### Euro-Domino Tickets

Valid on all IE services. These tickets are a 3 day pass, with an option for purchasing up to five extra days of travel. Boundary on cross border services is Dundalk. The 2004 Adult prices, which are for standard class tickets, are laid out below. First class tickets are approximately 50% dearer. Youth ED passes cost 25% less and Child fares are half of the Adult fare.

|       | 3 days            | Extra days        |
|-------|-------------------|-------------------|
| Adult | £48.00 / €70.00   | £10.00 / €14.00   |

## TRAVEL ENQUIRY OFFICES

Note: For dialing local numbers within the Irish Republic, do not dial 00353, and place a 0 in front of the rest of the number.

### Translink NI Railways

Travel & Information Centre, Central Station, Belfast, BT1 3PB.
Travel Centre, Great Northern Mall, Gt. Victoria Street, Belfast, BT1 7GN.
Telephone: 028 9024 2420. Bus & Train enquiries: 028 9066 6530.

### Iarnród Éireann

Passenger Enquiries Dublin Area, Connolly Station, Amiens Street, Dublin 1.
00 353 1 8366222  or  00 353 1 8365418.

Heuston Station, Dublin 8.
00 353 1 8365420/1

Travel Centre, 35 Lower Abbey Street, Dublin 1.
00 353 1 8366222 (enquiries).
Travel Centre, 65 Patrick Street, Cork.

00 353 1 7034070 (reservations).
00 353 21 504888 (enquiries and reservations).

## Bus Éireann

Busaras (Bus Station), Dublin  00 353 1 8302222
Travel Information  00 353 1 8366111

## SHIPPING SERVICES

The following is a list of shipping services, and their operators, between the UK and Ireland. Further details may be obtained directly from the operators at the web sites/telephone numbers given below, or from Travel Agents. (N.B. Sailing's marked * do not convey foot passengers).

| Route | Operator | Scheduled Crossing Time |
|---|---|---|
| Cairnryan - Larne | P&O Irish Sea | 1 hour (SuperStar Express) |
|  |  | 1 hour 45 mins (Ship) |
| Fishguard - Rosslare | Stena Line | $3^{1}/_{2}$ hours (Ship) |
|  |  | 1hour 50 mins (Sea Lynx) |
| Fleetwood - Larne * | P&O Irish Sea | 8 hours (Ship) |
| Holyhead - Dún Laoghaire | Stena Line | 1 hour 39 mins (HSS) |
| Holyhead - Dublin * | Stena Line | 3 hours (Ship) |
| Holyhead - Dublin | Irish Ferries | $3^{1}/_{4}$ hours (Ship) |
|  |  | 1 hour 49 mins (Swift) |
| Liverpool - Belfast * | Norse Merchant Ferries | 8 hours (Ship) |
| Liverpool - Dublin * | P&O Irish Sea | $7^{1}/_{2}$ hours (Ship) |
| Liverpool - Dublin * | Norse Merchant Ferries | 7 hours (Ship) |
| Liverpool - Dublin | Isle of Man Steam Packet | 3 hours 55 mins |
| Mostyn - Dublin * | P&O Irish Sea | 6 or $7^{1}/_{2}$ hours (Ship) |
| Pembroke - Rosslare | Irish Ferries | $3^{3}/_{4}$ hours (Ship) |
| Stranraer - Belfast | Stena Line | $3^{1}/_{4}$ hours (Ship) |
|  |  | $1^{1}/_{2}$ hour (HSS) |
| Stranraer - Belfast | SeaCat Scotland | $1^{3}/_{4}$ hours (SeaCat) |
| Swansea - Cork | Swansea Cork Ferries | 10 hours (Ship) |
| Troon - Larne * | P&O Irish Sea | 4 hours (Ship) |

## Contact Details For Shipping Companies

**Swansea Cork Ferries**  (www.directferries.com/swanseacork.htm)
Great Britain: 01792 456116.  Republic of Ireland: 021 427 1166.

**Norse Merchant Ferries**  (www.norsemerchant.com)
Great Britain: 0870 6004321.  Republic of Ireland: 01 8192999

**Stena Line**  (www.stenaline.com)
All bookings are now directed through the central reservations office. Some of the individual port telephone numbers listed below automatically divert to the central office outside of normal office hours. The telephone number of the central reservation office is 0990 70 70 70.

A recorded information line, updated hourly, is also available on 08705 755 755. This information line can be used to obtain information on sea conditions, departures times, delays and road conditions en-route to the ports, by selecting the appropriate recorded message. A 24 hour recorded information line, giving details of delays etc. on all Stena Line Irish departures, is available by dialling (Dublin) 01 204 7799.

*Stena Line Travel Centres:*

| | | | |
|---|---|---|---|
| Belfast: | 028 9088 4089. | Stranraer: | 01776 802121. |
| Fishguard: | 01348 404404. | Rosslare: | 053 33997. |
| Dublin: | 01 204 7744. | Holyhead: | 01407 606733. |
| Dún Laoghaire: | 01 204 7777. | | |

**Irish Ferries** (www.irishferries.com)
All bookings are now directed through the central reservations office at Liverpool. Some of the individual port telephone numbers automatically divert to the central office outside of normal office hours. The telephone number of the central reservation office at Liverpool is 0345 17 17 17 (for firm bookings only). All other enquiries should be made to 0990 17 17 17. Republic of Ireland 0870 5171717.

*Irish Ferries Travel Centres:*

| | |
|---|---|
| Dublin: | 01 661 0715 (24 hour answering information service). |
| Rosslare: | 053 33158. |
| Holyhead: | 0870 5329129. |
| Pembroke: | 0870 5329543. |

**P&O Irish Sea** (www.poirishsea.com)
Great Britain: 0870 2424 777.          Republic of Ireland: 1800 409 049.

**SeaCat Scotland** (www.seacat.co.uk)
Great Britain: 08705 523 523.          Republic of Ireland: 1800 805055.

## FLIGHTS

Several companies offer competitively priced flights between mainland UK and Ireland. The best way of checking routes, availability, and fares is via the Internet. Some useful website addresses are listed below:

www.aerlingus.com          www.easyjet.co.uk
www.aerarran.com           www.flybmi.com
www.britishairways.com     www.ryanair.com

## TELEPHONE DIALLING CODES

Dialling the Republic of Ireland from the UK (including Northern Ireland)
The International dialling code for the Republic of Ireland is 00 353.
To dial a Dublin number, i.e. 01 1234567 from the UK, dial 00 353 and omit the leading "0" from the local dialling code, i.e. 00 353 1 1234567.

Dialling the UK from the Republic of Ireland
The International dialling code for the UK is 00 44.
To dial a UK number, i.e. 01234 567890 from the Republic of Ireland, dial 00 44 and delete the leading "0" from the local dialling code i.e. 00 44 1234 567890.

Dialling Northern Ireland from the Republic of Ireland
To dial a Northern Ireland number, i.e. 028 12345678 from the Republic of Ireland, change the dialling code from 028 to 048, i.e. 048 12345678. This applies to all 028 numbers.

## PASSPORTS

Passports are not required by United Kingdom citizens to visit the Republic of Ireland, but some form of identification must be carried by travellers to satisfy security checks.

## CURRENCY

The Euro ( ) is the unit of currency in the Republic of Ireland. £ Sterling is the currency of Northern Ireland.

## ACCOMMODATION

Unlike the rest of Europe, there are no overnight rail passenger services in Ireland, and overnight accommodation must be found for those who wish to visit Ireland for longer than a day. A list of reasonably priced Bed & Breakfast accommodation, which are situated near to main railway stations, is included as an appendix at the rear of this book (see Appendix 5)

# NOTES APPLICABLE TO ALL ROLLING STOCK

Notes of a non general nature are given under the appropriate company and type of stock.

## GENERAL

Class details and dimensions are shown in imperial units with the metric equivalents (with the exception of weights, 1 ton = 1.016 tonnes) given in parentheses.
All maintenance work, other than daily servicing, is done at Inchicore (IE), Fairview (IE for DART vehicles), Drogheda (IE for DMU vehicles) or York Road (Translink NI Railways).

## DATES TO TRAFFIC

The date shown is the date or month the vehicle was officially accepted into traffic. This should not be confused with the arrival/delivery date, as each vehicle can be subject to a series of test runs and examinations over a period of time prior to final acceptance. Depending on the success or otherwise of these tests/examinations and other factors e.g. holidays, industrial disputes etc., the time interval between delivery and acceptance could run into weeks or months. Information is given as far as available official records permit, especially in the case of the older vehicles, where few, if any, records still exist.

## DATE STOPPED

The date shown is the date that the locomotive was stopped for maintenance purposes. In some cases, certain operational "stopped" locomotives have continued to be used on restricted duties until either withdrawn or repaired.

## DATE WITHDRAWN

This is the date or month that each vehicle was finally written off the railway's books and sanctioned for scrapping. This date may be several years after the vehicle was stopped (see above), or only a few days, depending on the circumstances. e.g. A vehicle may succumb to a major failure, and then be used as a source of spare parts. Such a vehicle would still be shown as officially "in stock" until such time as it is deemed to be of no further value, when it would then be sanctioned for scrap. If this occurs on the first few vehicles to be stopped within a class, then the withdrawal date will be significantly later than the stopped date, but if it should occur on the final few vehicles of a class, then the spare parts value would be considerably less, and hence the withdrawal date will be much nearer the stopped date. In a few isolated cases, vehicles have been withdrawn whilst still in traffic, e.g. It may have been decided to eliminate the final few vehicles of a particular class as surplus to requirements. In such cases a vehicle may not have been taken out of traffic until it suffered a failure, which may be several days after the official withdrawal date.

In some instances vehicles have been stopped following failure, but kept reasonably intact so that they may be repaired for further service should the need arise at some future date. This occurred with the 101(B) class locomotives of CIE, which were stopped over the period 1969 to 1978, but retained "in stock" until sanctioned for withdrawal in 1984 as locomotives of 201 (C) class were then surplus to requirements and were set aside for this purpose. During 1986, many 071 class locomotives were found to have serious bogie defects which meant that virtually the whole fleet was taken out of traffic for repairs. This resulted in several 201 (C) class locomotives being temporarily returned to traffic to cover the resultant shortage of locomotives.

## LOCOMOTIVE FITTINGS AND DETAILS

Individual locomotive fittings are shown against each locomotive number. For a locomotive no longer in traffic, the fittings shown are as at the date the locomotive was finally stopped. This is because certain fittings have been removed from redundant locomotives for further use in serviceable locomotives, and is particularly true with regard to the CAWS and train radio equipment fitted in each locomotive cab. As all IE/CIE and NIR/Translink NI Railways' locomotives except CIE D301-5 and G601-3 were fitted with vacuum brakes when new, this is not shown as an individual characteristic against each locomotive.

Only the newer 201 class locomotives built in 1994-95 are still fitted with operational electric train supply equipment, (referred to as "Head End Power" or "HEP"). The electric supply on these locomotives is only used in conjunction with the cross border De-Dietrich coaches. All other passenger trains continue to be heated by means of an electric generator van or a steam generator van in the train formation.

The following abbreviations are used to denote the various fittings:

| | |
|---|---|
| A | Train air brakes in addition to vacuum brakes. |
| E | Electric train supply equipment (NIR 101 and 111 class locomotives only). |
| H | Three-phase electric train supply equipment "Head End Power" (HEP) for use with cross border De-Dietrich coaches only. |
| M | Multiple working facility (see locomotive class headings for restrictions). |
| N | Push/pull facility (former CIE system with converted AEC 2600 series railcar vehicles). |
| O | Push/pull facility (former NIR system, with suitably equipped Mark 2 vehicles only). |
| P | Mark 3 push/pull facility. (with IE vehicles 6101-05/6301-19/6402 only). |
| R | NIR train radio. |
| S | CAWS (Continuous Automatic Warning System) for operating over the CTC (Centralised Traffic Control) system and IE train radio. |
| X | Engine bonnet extension. |

## CUT UP / DISPOSAL DATE

This is the approximate date, given to the nearest month, that a vehicle was finally broken up for scrap or disposed of for a reason other than further use. (e.g. many multiple units were consigned to a tip for burial due to asbestos contamination). Certain information on this front has eluded the authors and any information that readers may possess would be welcome. Such missing information is denoted by a ? symbol in the vehicle tables. Withdrawn vehicles shown in the text with this column blank are currently stored awaiting disposal.

## CUT UP / STORE / DISPOSAL LOCATION

This is the last known location at the time of going to press of a stopped/withdrawn vehicle. In the case of a vehicle no longer in existence (or buried due to asbestos contamination) a date is shown in the previous column, and the location given is the location where the vehicle was cut up or buried. In other cases the vehicle is still extant at the location shown. Certain information on this front has eluded the authors and any information that readers may possess would be welcome. Such missing information is denoted by a ? symbol in the vehicle tables. Preserved locomotives are shown at their current location and are indicated by (P).

## DIESEL RAILCAR & MULTIPLE UNIT STOCK

All railcar and multiple unit details relate to their original configuration as railcars/multiple units unless otherwise stated. All third class vehicles were re-designated standard class from June 1956 following the UIC decision to abolish the erstwhile second class. All vehicles are to be assumed to be of open seating layout unless otherwise stated. All vehicle superstructure dimensions are given over body unless otherwise stated. Details of modifications and dates when carried out, are given as notes where appropriate. In all subsections power cars are listed first, followed by trailers. This is relevant where duplication of numbers between power cars and trailers exists.

## ACKNOWLEDGEMENTS

The authors would like to thank both IE and Translink NI Railways for their help in the production of this book, as well as many enthusiasts for their help and encouragement. In particular we would like to thank the following for their help in preparing this particular edition:

Martin Baumann, Ken Manto, Jimmy Doody, Philip Clampett, Derek Byrne and Damien Farrel.

## ABBREVIATIONS

The following abbreviations are used throughout this book:

| | | | |
|---|---|---|---|
| AEC | Associated Engine Company. | F | First Class seats. |
| ACV | Associated Commercial Vehicles. | S | Standard Class seats. |
| B&CDR | Belfast & County Down Railway. | T | Third Class seats. |
| BR | British Rail. | (A) | Asbestos contaminated vehicle, buried rather than cut up. |
| BREL | British Rail Engineering Limited. | | |
| BUT | British United Traction. | (P) | preserved. |
| CIE | Córas Iompair Éireann. | hp | horsepower. |
| DART | Dublin Area Rapid Transit. | k/hr | kilometres per hour. |
| GSR | Great Southern Railway. | kN | kilo newtons. |
| GNR(B) | Great Northern Railway (Board). | kW | kilowatts. |
| GNR(I) | Great Northern Railway (Ireland). | lb/hr | pounds per hour. |
| IE | Iarnród Éireann. | lbf | pounds force. |
| NIR | Northern Ireland Railways. | mph | miles per hour. |
| LMS(NCC) | London Midland & Scottish Railway (Northern Counties Committee). | oou | out of use. |
| | | rpm | revolutions per minute. |
| SCG | Self Changing Gears Ltd. | | |
| UTA | Ulster Transport Authority. | | |

## BIBLIOGRAPHY

35 Years of NIR 1967 to 2002 by Jonathan M Allen.
Diesel Dawn by Colm Flanagan.
Irish Steam Loco Register by Peter Rowledge.
Locomotives of the GNR(I) by Norman Johnston.
Journal of the Irish Railway Record Society.
Irish Railway News (website).

# SECTION 1 - IARNRÓD ÉIREANN STOCK LIST

## BRIEF HISTORY

IE came into existence on 2nd February 1987 when the original state owned national transport authority, CIE, was split up into three subsidiary companies. Of these three, IE took over responsibility for the operation of all rail services within the Irish Republic, Bus Atha Cliath became responsible for Dublin bus services and Bus Éireann for provincial bus services. CIE was itself formed on 1st January 1945 when the former GSR and the Dublin United Transport Company (DUTC) were amalgamated under the terms of the 1944 Transport Act. CIE was then nationalised under the 1950 Transport Act, and absorbed the lines south of the border of the former GNR(B) in 1958 when this was divided between CIE and the then UTA by the Great Northern Railway Act of that year.

## LOCOMOTIVE CLASSIFICATION

The diesel locomotive fleet of CIE was formerly classified by letters which prefixed locomotive numbers. This letter also gave an indication of the power output of the locomotive (A being the highest, and so on), but was eventually dropped in 1972 in favour of the present number only scheme. However, many departments within Iarnród Éireann still refer to certain types of locomotives by their former letter classifications, and therefore these are shown in brackets in class headings following the current classification. 071 class and the newer 201 class locomotives never received a letter classification as they were delivered after the scheme was discontinued.

# LOCOMOTIVES

## 001 (A) CLASS                                                           Co-Co

**Built:** 1955-56 by Metropolitan Vickers at Dukinfield Works, Manchester.
**Original Engine:** Crossley HSTV8 of 1200 hp (896 kW) at 625 rpm.
**Rebuilt:** 1968-71 by CIE at Inchicore Works, Dublin.
**Replacement Engine:** General Motors 12-645E of 1325 hp (989 kW) at 800 rpm.
**Transmission:** Electric.
**Traction Motors:** Metropolitan Vickers MV137CW.
**Maximum Tractive Effort:** 46000 lbf (205 kN).
**Continuous Tractive Effort:** 18000 lbf (80 kN) at 21.5 mph.
**Power At Rail:** 1032 hp (770 kW).
**Weight:** 82 tons.
**Length Over Buffers:** 51 ft (15.54 m).
**Wheel Diameter:** 3 ft 2 in (965 mm).
**Maximum Speed:** 75 mph.
**Multiple Working:** Not fitted (two were temporarily fitted for trials).

**Works Numbers:** 887-946 in order. All works plates show built 1955.
**Notes:** Originally numbered A1 to A60, renumbered A1R to A60R when re-engined, and later 001 to 060.

| Loco No. | Fittings | Date to Traffic | Date Rebuilt | Date Stopped | Date Withdrawn | Month Cut | Cut up/Preservation/ Store Location |
|---|---|---|---|---|---|---|---|
| 001 | S | 27.09.55 | 30.03.71 | 17.08.94 | 06.09.95 | 11.95 | Inchicore Works |
| 002 | S | 29.09.55 | 17.12.70 | 19.12.90 | 18.11.92 | 06.94 | Inchicore Works |
| 003 | S | 27.09.55 | 10.03.71 | 05.04.95 | 06.09.95 | - | Inchicore Works (P) |
| 004 |   | 01.10.55 | 19.02.71 | 23.07.79 | 13.04.84 | 09.84 | Inchicore Works |
| 005 | S | 06.10.55 | 21.09.71 | 09.01.95 | 01.03.95 | 06.95 | Inchicore Works |
| 006 |   | 03.10.55 | 12.11.71 | 09.09.83 | 05.10.84 | 08.92 | Inchicore Works |
| 007 | S | 14.10.55 | 06.07.71 | 14.10.90 | 18.11.92 | 05.94 | Inchicore Works |
| 008 |   | 18.10.55 | 30.07.70 | 23.10.73 | 05.10.77 | ? | Inchicore Works |
| 009 | S | 18.10.55 | 08.10.70 | 06.07.93 | .93 | 06.94 | Inchicore Works |
| 010 |   | 20.10.55 | 26.10.70 | 20.12.78 | 13.04.84 | 09.84 | Inchicore Works |
| 011 | S | 24.10.55 | 01.02.71 | 23.12.94 | 06.09.95 | 11.95 | Inchicore Works |
| 012 | S | 28.02.56 | 10.06.71 | 04.04.95 | 06.09.95 | 11.95 | Inchicore Works |
| 013 | S | 30.11.55 | 13.01.71 | 06.10.92 | 18.11.92 | 05.94 | Inchicore Works |
| 014 | S | 06.12.55 | 11.02.71 | 19.05.92 | 02.11.94 | 03.95 | Inchicore Works |
| 015 | S | 24.12.55 | 20.05.71 | 04.04.95 | 06.09.95 | - | Inchicore Works |
| 016 | S | 20.12.55 | 02.12.70 | 27.08.93 | 06.09.95 | 11.95 | Inchicore Works |
| 017 | S | 07.01.56 | 04.11.70 | 29.09.93 | 02.11.94 | 02.95 | Inchicore Works |
| 018 | S | 16.01.56 | 16.07.71 | 28.10.92 | 01.03.95 | 06.95 | Inchicore Works |
| 019 | S | 26.01.56 | 28.09.70 | 01.06.93 | 01.03.95 | 05.95 | Inchicore Works |
| 020 | S | 01.02.56 | 31.08.70 | 21.09.92 | 02.11.94 | 02.95 | Inchicore Works |
| 021 | S | 05.02.56 | 01.04.71 | 18.08.92 | 18.11.92 | 06.94 | Inchicore Works |
| 022 | S | 19.02.56 | 19.05.70 | 07.02.92 | 02.11.94 | 03.95 | Inchicore Works |
| 023 | S | 19.02.56 | 18.06.71 | 30.10.91 | 18.11.92 | 06.94 | Inchicore Works |
| 024 | S | 23.02.56 | 01.09.71 | 25.04.86 | 28.01.87 | 07.92 | Inchicore Works |
| 025 | S | 03.03.56 | 17.07.70 | 27.08.93 | 01.03.95 | 06.95 | Inchicore Works |
| 026 | S | 10.03.56 | 25.11.71 | 04.08.94 | 01.03.95 | 05.94 | Inchicore Works |
| 027 | S | 06.03.56 | 24.06.70 | 09.06.92 | 02.11.94 | 03.95 | Inchicore Works |
| 028 |   | 16.03.56 | 04.05.70 | 09.02.84 | 05.10.84 | 09.92 | Inchicore Works |
| 029 | SA | 23.03.56 | 24.04.70 | 13.07.88 | 18.11.92 | 05.94 | Inchicore Works |
| 030 | S | 19.03.56 | 30.01.70 | 09.02.93 | 02.11.94 | 03.95 | Inchicore Works |
| 031 | S | 11.04.56 | 22.09.71 | 03.01.91 | 18.11.92 | 07.94 | Inchicore Works |
| 032 |   | 29.03.56 | 06.02.70 | 12.03.83 | 05.10.84 | 09.92 | Inchicore Works |
| 033 | S | 29.03.56 | 13.03.70 | 04.10.91 | 18.11.92 | 05.94 | Inchicore Works |
| 034 | S | 29.03.56 | 09.12.69 | 25.06.86 | 28.01.87 | 09.92 | Inchicore Works |
| 035 | S | 15.04.56 | 20.08.69 | 27.08.93 | 02.11.94 | 03.95 | Inchicore Works |
| 036 | S | 17.04.56 | 01.12.69 | 19.12.94 | 06.09.95 | 11.95 | Inchicore Works |
| 037 |   | 28.04.56 | 02.03.70 | 15.11.83 | 05.10.84 | 08.92 | Inchicore Works |
| 038 | S | 24.04.56 | 17.04.71 | 23.11.93 | 01.03.95 | 06.95 | Inchicore Works |
| 039 | S | 14.05.56 | 23.07.69 | 23.09.95 | 06.09.95 | - | Inchicore Works (P) |
| 040 | S | 30.04.56 | 28.10.69 | 02.06.88 | 18.11.92 | 05.94 | Inchicore Works |
| 041 |   | 08.05.56 | 22.07.69 | 18.01.83 | 05.10.84 | 08.92 | Inchicore Works |
| 042 |   | 19.05.56 | 20.07.69 | 09.10.92 | 18.11.92 | 07.94 | Inchicore Works |
| 043 | S | 06.06.56 | 15.09.71 | 17.06.88 | 18.11.92 | 06.94 | Inchicore Works |
| 044 |   | 19.05.56 | 29.05.70 | 31.10.83 | 05.10.84 | 08.92 | Inchicore Works |
| 045 |   | 30.05.56 | 04.11.69 | 08.03.84 | 05.10.84 | 09.92 | Inchicore Works |

| | | | | | | | |
|---|---|---|---|---|---|---|---|
| 046 | | 31.05.56 | 10.04.70 | 21.04.79 | 14.01.80 | ? | Inchicore Works |
| 047 | S | 15.06.56 | 24.10.69 | 05.11.93 | 02.11.94 | 03.95 | Inchicore Works |
| 048 | S | 23.06.56 | 01.10.69 | 24.05.94 | 01.03.95 | 06.95 | Inchicore Works |
| 049 | S | 23.06.56 | 10.09.69 | 22.12.93 | 01.03.95 | 06.95 | Inchicore Works |
| 050 | S | 31.07.56 | 28.09.71 | 20.09.86 | 28.01.87 | 10.92 | Inchicore Works |
| 051 | S | 16.06.56 | 04.10.69 | 08.02.95 | 06.09.95 | 11.95 | Inchicore Works |
| 052 | S | 12.07.56 | 06.12.69 | 02.01.92 | 18.11.92 | 06.94 | Inchicore Works |
| 053 | S | 26.06.56 | 18.08.71 | 02.12.92 | 01.03.95 | 05.95 | Inchicore Works |
| 054 | S | 23.06.56 | 04.11.71 | 28.07.93 | 02.11.94 | 02.95 | Inchicore Works |
| 055 | S | 01.08.56 | 01.07.70 | 11.03.95 | 06.09.95 | - | Hell's Kitchen (P) |
| 056 | S | 23.08.56 | 10.11.69 | 29.10.92 | 18.11.92 | 05.94 | Inchicore Works |
| 057 | S | 08.09.56 | 27.03.70 | 02.01.92 | 02.11.94 | 03.95 | Inchicore Works |
| 058 | S | 20.09.56 | 12.05.68 | 12.04.91 | 01.03.95 | 06.95 | Inchicore Works |
| 059 | S | 20.10.56 | 22.07.68 | 29.04.86 | 28.01.87 | 08.92 | Inchicore Works |
| 060 | S | 09.01.57 | 15.01.70 | 09.12.83 | 05.10.84 | 09.92 | Inchicore Works |

002, 027, 035, 036, 046, 054, 056 and 059 had their engines up-rated to 1650 hp (1231 kW) at 900 rpm and their maximum speed increased to 80 mph. Power at rail was 1295 hp (966 kW). Their traction motors were also rewound to cope with extra power. All were either down-rated or withdrawn by the late 1980's.
003 has been preserved by the Irish Traction Group as A3R. 003 was used to haul a railtour from Limerick Check to Limerick and back on 07.10.95.
004 was hijacked, derailed and burnt out at Goraghwood on 23.07.79.
008 suffered bomb damage at Meigh on 23.10.73.
010 collided with NIR vehicles 69, 768 and 742 at Lisburn whilst working the 11:00 Belfast Central to Dublin Connolly "Enterprise Express" on 20.12.78.
015 has been retained by Iarnród Éireann.
032 ran away into Cork Yard on 12.03.83 whilst working the previous day's 23:30 North Wall to Cork liner train. The damaged bodyshell was repaired but never fitted out.
039 has been preserved by the Irish Traction Group as A39. 039 (as A39) was retained after its official withdrawal date to work a farewell railtour on 23.09.95.
040 was withdrawn following collision damage sustained in a shunting accident at Heuston Station on 02.06.88.
046 suffered bomb damage at milepost 65¼ (Killeen Bridge) between Dublin and Belfast on 21.04.79.
055 (as A55) has been incorporated into a museum at the Hell's Kitchen public house, Castlerea, Co. Roscommon. The engine room has been fitted out as a seating area.
057 was used for local trips and pilot work in the Dublin area until January 1993.

# 071 CLASS                                                                                    Co-Co

**Built:** 1976 by General Motors, La Grange, Illinois, USA.
**Engine:** General Motors 12-645E3C of 2475 hp (1845 kW) at 900 rpm.
**General Motors Designation:** JT22CW.
**Transmission:** Electric.
**Traction Motors:** General Motors D77B.
**Maximum Tractive Effort:** 55100 lbf (245 kN).
**Continuous Tractive Effort:** 46850 lbf (209 kN) at 15.1 mph.
**Power At Rail:** 1823 hp (1360 kW).
**Weight:** 99 tons.
**Length Over Buffers:** 57 ft (17.37 m).
**Wheel Diameter:** 3 ft 4 in (1016 mm).
**Maximum Speed:** 90 mph.

**Multiple Working:** With any IE / NIR GM built locomotive (except 201 class). However, the use of this facility is prohibited.
**Works Numbers:** 713736 - 713753 in order.

| Loco No. | Fittings | Date to Traffic |
|---|---|---|
| 071 | SAM | 30.05.77 |
| 072 | SAM | 01.06.77 |
| 073 | SAM | 02.06.77 |
| 074 | SAM | 04.06.77 |
| 075 | SAM | 02.06.77 |
| 076 | SAM | 24.05.77 |
| 077 | SAM | 06.06.77 |
| 078 | SAM | 30.05.77 |
| 079 | SAM | 25.05.77 |
| 080 | SAM | 30.05.77 |
| 081 | SAM | 27.05.77 |
| 082 | SAM | 23.05.77 |
| 083 | SAM | 29.05.77 |
| 084 | SAM | 30.05.77 |
| 085 | SAM | 25.05.77 |
| 086 | SAM | 14.06.77 |
| 087 | SAM | 26.05.77 |
| 088 | SAM | 06.07.77 |

**Name:**

082    CUMANN NA nINNEALTOIRI
       THE INSTITUTION OF ENGINEERS OF IRELAND

All locomotives when built were fitted with General Motors 12-645E3B power units, but all were modified in the 1990's to 12-645E3C power units. 076 received a second hand reconditioned 12-645E3 power unit during 2001, after its original power unit was damaged beyond repair. The refurbished power unit was purchased from Sweden and is believed to originate from a former SJ class T44 locomotive.
All 071 Class locomotives were fitted with a power reduction system (similar to Slow Speed Control) when new, but this has since been removed.

## 101 (B) CLASS                                              A1A-A1A

**Built:** 1956-57 by The Birmingham Railway Carriage & Wagon Co at Smethwick.
**Engine:** Sulzer 6LDA28 of 960 hp (716 kW) at 710 rpm.
**Transmission:** Electric.
**Traction Motors:** Metropolitan Vickers MV137.
**Maximum Tractive Effort:** 41800 lbf (186 kN).
**Continuous Tractive Effort:** 16900 lbf (76 kN) at 16 mph.
**Power At Rail:**
**Weight:** 75.45 tons.
**Length Over Buffers:** 47 ft 8 in (14.53 m).
**Wheel Diameter:** 3 ft 1$^1/_2$ in (953 mm).
**Maximum Speed:** 75 mph.
**Works Numbers:** DEL20-31 in order.
**Notes:** Originally numbered B101 to B112.

| Loco No. | Date to Traffic | Date Stopped | Month Withdrawn | Month Cut | Cut Up/ Preservation Location |
|---|---|---|---|---|---|
| 101 | 09.04.56 | 06.05.74 | 04.84 | 03.87 | North Wall Point Yard |
| 102 | 04.08.56 | 03.10.74 | 04.84 | 03.87 | North Wall Point Yard |
| 103 | 13.08.56 | 17.11.77 | 04.84 | - | Carrick-On-Suir (P) |
| 104 | 30.08.56 | 15.07.74 | 04.84 | 01.87 | North Wall Point Yard |
| 105 | 17.09.56 | 22.11.77 | 04.84 | 03.87 | North Wall Point Yard |
| 106 | 08.11.56 | 07.02.78 | 04.84 | 12.86 | North Wall Point Yard |
| 107 | 25.02.57 | 25.05.77 | 04.84 | 02.87 | North Wall Point Yard |
| 108 | 16.04.57 | 10.01.73 | 04.84 | 01.87 | North Wall Point Yard |
| 109 | 19.06.57 | 20.01.75 | 04.84 | 02.87 | North Wall Point Yard |
| 110 | 13.07.57 | 15.11.77 | 04.84 | 04.87 | North Wall Point Yard |
| 111 | 15.10.57 | 13.05.69 | 04.84 | 04.87 | North Wall Point Yard |
| 112 | 23.12.57 | 27.07.73 | 04.84 | 02.87 | North Wall Point Yard |

Built using equipment ordered for 6 twin-engined locomotives.
103 has been preserved by the Irish Traction Group.

## 113 (B) CLASS  Bo-Bo

**Built:** 1947-51 by CIE at Inchicore Works, Dublin.
**Engine:** Sulzer 6LDA28 of 960 hp (716 kW) at 710 rpm.
**Transmission:** Electric.
**Traction Motors:** Metropolitan Vickers MV157.
**Maximum Tractive Effort:** 46000 lbf (205 kN).
**Continuous Tractive Effort:** 23000 lbf (102 kN) at 16 mph.
**Power At Rail:**
**Weight:** 80 tons.
**Length Over Buffers:** 47 ft 8 in (14.53 m).
**Wheel Diameter:** 3 ft 8 in (1118 mm).
**Maximum Speed:** 55 mph.
**Multiple Working:** Within class (later removed).
**Works Numbers:** Not allocated.
**Notes:** Originally numbered 1100 and 1101, renumbered B113 and B114 in 1957. CIE Class C2A until 1958. The engines in these locomotives were originally rated at 915 hp (683 kW) at 750 rpm, but were up-rated in 1956 to the figures shown above. These locomotives were originally fitted with Spanner Swirlyflow train heating boilers, these being removed upon the introduction of steam heating vans.

| Loco No. | Month to Traffic | Date Stopped | Date Withdrawn | Month Cut | Cut Up/ Store Location |
|---|---|---|---|---|---|
| 113 | 04.50 | 07.01.75 | 18.12.77 | - | Inchicore Works |
| 114 | 10.51 | 30.08.71 | 18.12.77 | 04.95 | Inchicore Works |

113 was out of service from 05.01.72 until 11.10.74 when modifications to the braking system was undertaken and the locomotive reinstated. 114 was similarly treated on 04.12.74 but never returned to traffic.
113 has been retained by Iarnród Éireann as B113 and was cosmetically restored in 1996 for display at the 150th Anniversary celebrations of the opening of Inchicore Works.

# 121 (B) CLASS    Bo-Bo

**Built:** 1960 by General Motors, La Grange, Illinois, USA.
**Engine:** General Motors 8-567CR of 950 hp (709 kW) at 835 rpm (as built).
[1] General Motors 8-B645E of 950 hp (709 kW) at 835 rpm (ex 201 class).
[2] General Motors 8-567CR of 950 hp (709 kW) at 835 rpm (ex 141 class).
Certain locomotives were subsequently fitted with engines recovered from withdrawn 201 (C) class locomotives. In addition, engines have also been exchanged with 141 class locomotives. The details shown are correct at the time of publication.
**General Motors Designation:** GL8.
**Transmission:** Electric.
**Traction Motors:** General Motors D47.
**Maximum Tractive Effort:** 35000 lbf (156 kN).
**Continuous Tractive Effort:** 30400 lbf (135 kN) at 8 mph.
**Power At Rail:** 709 hp (529 kW).
**Weight:** 64 tons.
**Length Over Buffers:** 39 ft 10$\frac{1}{4}$ in (12.15 m).
**Wheel Diameter:** 3 ft 4 in (1016 mm).
**Maximum Speed:** 75 mph.
**Multiple Working:** With any IE / NIR GM built locomotive (except 201 class).
**Works Numbers:** 26271 - 26285 in order.
**Notes:** Originally numbered B121 to B135.

| Loco No. | Fittings | Date to Traffic | Date Stopped | Date Withdrawn | Month Cut | Cut Up/Store Location |
|---|---|---|---|---|---|---|
| 121 | SAMN | 20.02.61 | 29.06.95 | 24.07.02 | 04.03 | Inchicore Works |
| 122 | SAMP | 04.03.61 | .12.01 | 24.07.02 | 11.02 | Inchicore Works |
| 123 [2] | SAMP | 08.04.61 | .08.02 | | | Inchicore Works |
| 124 [2] | SAMP | 29.03.61 | | | | |
| 125 | SAMN | 29.03.61 | 06.03.86 | 24.07.02 | 12.02 | Inchicore Works |
| 126 [1] | SAMP | 20.02.61 | .07.95 | 24.07.02 | 03.03 | Inchicore Works |
| 127 [1] | SAMP | 14.03.61 | 26.07.02 | 27.02.03 | 05.03 | Inchicore Works |
| 128 | SAMP | 20.02.61 | 08.01.03 | 27.02.03 | 05.03 | Inchicore Works |
| 129 [2] | SAMP | 20.03.61 | 17.02.03 | 27.02.03 | 04.03 | Inchicore Works |
| 130 | SAMP | 20.02.61 | .06.01 | 24.07.02 | 03.03 | Inchicore Works |
| 131 [2] | SAMP | 20.02.61 | 18.12.01 | 27.02.03 | 03.03 | Inchicore Works |
| 132 | SAMP | 05.04.61 | 19.05.94 | 24.07.02 | 12.02 | Inchicore Works |
| 133 [1] | SAMP | 16.03.61 | 08.02.03 | 27.02.03 | 05.03 | Inchicore Works |
| 134 [2] | SAMP | 20.02.61 | | | | |
| 135 [1] | SAMN | 20.02.61 | 28.02.03 | 27.02.03 | 04.03 | Inchicore Works |

121, 125 & 132 were stopped following fire damage on 29.06.95, 06.03.86 and 19.05.94 respectively. They were then cannibalised for spares.
123 was stopped in 08.02 with ground relay faults, but continued in use as Inchicore Works pilot until 08.03.
126 was stopped following serious engine damage in 07.95 and was then cannibalised for spares.
The push/pull equipment on 132 was commissioned, but was subsequently de-commissioned due to excessive engine noise.

# 141 (B) CLASS                          Bo-Bo

**Built:** 1962 by General Motors, La Grange, Illinois, USA.
**Engine:** General Motors 8-567CR of 950 hp (709 kW) at 835 rpm.
[1] General Motors 8-B645E of 950 hp (709 kW) at 835 rpm (ex 201 class).
[2] General Motors 8-567CR of 950 hp (709 kW) at 835 rpm (ex 121 class).
[3] General Motors 8-645E of 950 hp (709 kW) at 835 rpm (ex 181 class).
Certain locomotives were subsequently fitted with engines recovered from withdrawn 201 (C) class locomotives. In addition, engines have also been exchanged with locomotives of classes 121 and 181. The details shown are correct at the time of publication.
**General Motors Designation:** JL8.
**Transmission:** Electric.
**Traction Motors:** General Motors D57.
**Maximum Tractive Effort:** 35000 lbf (156 kN).
**Continuous Tractive Effort:** 30400 lbf (135 kN) at 8 mph.
**Power At Rail:** 709 hp (529 kW).
**Weight:** 67 tons.
**Length Over Buffers:** 44 ft 0$^1$/$_2$ in (13.42 m).
**Wheel Diameter:** 3 ft 4 in (1016 mm).
**Maximum Speed:** 75 mph.
**Multiple Working:** With any IE / NIR GM built locomotive (except 201 class).
**Works Numbers:** 27467 - 27503 in order.
**Notes:** Originally numbered B141 to B177.

| Loco No. | Fittings | Date to Traffic | Date Stopped | Date Withdrawn | Month Cut | Cut Up/Store Location |
|---|---|---|---|---|---|---|
| 141 | SAM | 13.12.62 | | | | |
| 142 [1] | SAM | 03.12.62 | | | | |
| 143 | SAM | 20.06.63 | | | | |
| 144 | SAM | 14.01.63 | | | | |
| 145 [1] | SAM | 10.01.63 | | | | |
| 146 | SAM | 14.12.62 | | | | |
| 147 | SAM | 14.12.62 | | | | |
| 148 [3] | SAM | 08.12.62 | | | | |
| 149 [1] | SAM | 14.12.62 | | | | |
| 150 | SAM | 03.12.62 | 31.05.03 | 24.09.04 | | Inchicore Works |
| 151 [1] | SAM | 08.12.62 | | | | |
| 152 | SAM | 03.12.62 | | | | |
| 153 | SAM | 13.12.62 | | | | |
| 154 [2] | SAM | 11.12.62 | | | | |
| 155 | SAM | 03.12.62 | | | | |
| 156 [1] | SAM | 03.12.62 | | | | |
| 157 [1] | SAM | 05.12.62 | 26.07.03 | 24.09.04 | | Inchicore Works |
| 158 | SAM | 03.12.62 | 22.03.99 | 24.07.02 | 03.03 | Inchicore Works |
| 159 | SAM | 13.12.62 | | | | |
| 160 | SAM | 08.12.62 | | | | |
| 161 | SAM | 06.12.62 | .05.96 | 24.07.02 | 11.02 | Inchicore Works |
| 162 | SAM | 05.12.62 | | | | |
| 163 [1] | SAM | 05.12.62 | | | | |

| 164 [3] | SAM | 05.12.62 | | | | |
|---|---|---|---|---|---|---|
| 165 | SAM | 19.12.62 | | | | |
| 166 [3] | SAM | 14.12.62 | | | | |
| 167 | SAM | 13.12.62 | | | | |
| 168 | SAM | 08.12.62 | | | | |
| 169 [2] | SAM | 28.12.62 | | | | |
| 170 [1] | SAM | 19.12.62 | | | | |
| 171 [2] | SAM | 04.01.63 | | | | |
| 172 [3] | SAM | 28.12.62 | | | | |
| 173 [1] | SAM | 21.12.62 | | | | |
| 174 [2] | SAM | 21.12.62 | 05.10.93 | 24.07.02 | 12.02 | Inchicore Works |
| 175 | SAM | 04.01.63 | | | | |
| 176 [2] | SAM | 21.12.62 | | | | |
| 177 | SAM | 28.12.62 | | | | |

143 is confined to pilot duties and restricted to 40 mph. A note to this effect is painted on each cab side.
158 was withdrawn following collision damage sustained at Limerick on 22.03.99.
161 was originally stopped with a defective cooling fan gearbox 05.96, but was subsequently cannibalised for spares.
174 was stopped 05.10.93 awaiting a body overhaul, but this was never carried out. The locomotive was then cannibalised for spares.

**Former name:**
150   INCHICORE WORKS 150  1846-1996 /  ARDLANNA INSE CHAOÍR 150  1846-1996
(note: named at Inchicore Works open day 15th June 1996, all four nameplates had been stolen / removed by May 1998).

# 181 (B) CLASS                                                                                   Bo-Bo

**Built:** 1966 by General Motors, La Grange, Illinois, USA.
**Engine:** General Motors 8-645E of 1100 hp (821 kW) at 900 rpm.
[1] General Motors 8-B645E of 1100 hp (821 kW) at 900 rpm (ex 201 class).
[2] General Motors 8-567CR of 950 hp (709 kW) at 835 rpm (ex 121 class).
Certain locomotives were subsequently fitted with engines recovered from withdrawn 201 (C) class locomotives. In addition, engines have also been exchanged with 121 class locomotives. The details shown are correct at the time of publication.
**General Motors Designation:** JL18.
**Transmission:** Electric.
**Traction Motors:** General Motors D77.
**Maximum Tractive Effort:** 37500 lbf (167 kN).
**Continuous Tractive Effort:** 26400 lbf (118 kN) at 11 mph.
**Power At Rail:** 810 hp (604 kW).
**Weight:** 67 tons.
**Length Over Buffers:** 44 ft 0½ in (13.42 m).
**Wheel Diameter:** 3 ft 4 in (1016 mm).
**Maximum Speed:** 75 mph.
**Multiple Working:** With any IE / NIR GM built locomotive (except 201 class).
**Works Numbers:** 31248 - 31259 in order.
**Notes:** Originally numbered B181 to B192.

| Loco No. | Fittings | Date to Traffic | Date Stopped | Date Withdrawn | Month Cut | Cut Up/Store Location |
|---|---|---|---|---|---|---|
| 181 | SAM | 03.12.66 | | | | |
| 182 | SAM | 28.11.66 | | | | |
| 183 | SAM | 27.11.66 | | | | |
| 184 [1] | SAM | 29.11.66 | | | | |
| 185 | SAM | 08.12.66 | | | | |
| 186 [2] | SAM | 29.11.66 | | | | |
| 187 | SAM | 28.11.66 | | | | |
| 188 | SAM | 28.11.66 | 08.11.03 | 24.09.04 | | Inchicore Works |
| 189 [1] | SAM | 02.12.66 | | | | |
| 190 [1] | SAM | 03.12.66 | | | | |
| 191 | SAM | 03.12.66 | 20.08.91 | .04.98 | 05.98 | Inchicore Works |
| 192 | SAM | 06.12.66 | | | | |

191 ran away from North Wall on 17.08.91, eventually colliding with a set of buffer stops at Clonsilla before catching fire.

## 201 (C) CLASS                                                                                    Bo-Bo

**Built:** 1956-57 by Metropolitan Vickers at Dukinfield Works, Manchester.
**Original Engine:** Crossley ESTV8 of 550 hp (410 kW) at 1000 rpm.
233 and 234 were re-engined with Maybach MD650 engines of 980hp (731 kW) at 1200 rpm on 17.05.66 and 13.12.65 respectively, and retained these until rebuilt.
**Rebuilt:** 1969-80 by CIE at Inchicore Works, Dublin.
**Replacement Engine:** General Motors 8-B645E of 1100 hp (821 kW) at 900 rpm.
**Transmission:** Electric.
**Traction Motors:** Metropolitan Vickers MV137CW.
**Maximum Tractive Effort:** 34440 lbf (153 kN).
**Continuous Tractive Effort:**
**Power At Rail:** 842 hp (629 kW).
**Weight:** 61.5 tons.
**Length Over Buffers:** 42 ft (12.80 m).
**Wheel Diameter:** 3 ft 2 in (965 mm).
**Maximum Speed:** 80 mph.
**Multiple Working:** 233 and 234 (when fitted with Maybach MD650 engines), with 121, 141 and 181 class locomotives.
**Works Numbers:** 947-980 in order. All works plates show built 1956.
**Notes:** Originally numbered C201 to C234, renumbered B201 to B234 when re-engined and later 201 to 234.

| Loco No. | Fittings | Date to Traffic | Date Rebuilt | Date Stopped | Date Withdrawn | Month Cut | Cut Up/Preservation Location |
|---|---|---|---|---|---|---|---|
| 201 | N | 04.03.57 | 15.06.71 | 15.08.73 | 05.11.77 | .73 | Inchicore Works |
| 202 | N | 04.03.57 | 21.04.72 | 16.07.83 | 05.10.84 | 08.90 | V.Berry, Leicester |
| 203 | N | 28.03.57 | 06.04.72 | 22.08.78 | 13.04.84 | 09.92 | Inchicore Works |
| 204 | N | 28.03.57 | 20.04.71 | 20.11.81 | 13.04.84 | 08.92 | Inchicore Works |
| 205 | SN | 03.04.57 | 18.09.72 | 28.06.85 | 25.09.86 | 07.90 | V.Berry, Leicester |
| 206 | SN | 12.04.57 | 08.09.69 | 16.08.84 | 25.09.86 | 07.92 | Inchicore Works |
| 207 | N | 03.04.57 | 24.03.72 | 19.11.79 | 13.04.84 | 09.92 | Inchicore Works |
| 208 | SN | 17.06.57 | 08.07.72 | 30.07.85 | 25.09.86 | 09.90 | V.Berry, Leicester |

| 209 | SN | 20.05.57 | 19.05.72 | 06.10.84 | 25.09.86 | 11.93 | Inchicore Works |
| 210 | SN | 16.09.57 | 25.04.71 | 30.11.83 | 18.09.85 | 10.92 | Inchicore Works |
| 211 | SN | 20.05.57 | 02.06.72 | 15.06.85 | 25.09.86 | 11.90 | V.Berry, Leicester |
| 212 | SN | 06.07.57 | 05.05.72 | 23.05.86 | 25.09.86 | 06.90 | V.Berry, Leicester |
| 213 | SN | 11.06.57 | 08.02.72 | 29.11.86 | 24.11.86 | 09.92 | Inchicore Works |
| 214 | N | 15.06.57 | 21.07.72 | 08.03.84 | 18.09.85 | 07.90 | V.Berry, Leicester |
| 215 | SN | 06.06.57 | 16.07.71 | 18.01.85 | 25.09.86 | 06.90 | V.Berry, Leicester |
| 216 | N | 11.07.57 | 16.11.71 | 04.07.85 | 01.04.86 | - | Sold to NIR (no.104) |
| 217 | SN | 13.06.57 | 14.12.71 | 07.11.83 | 18.09.85 | 10.92 | Inchicore Works |
| 218 | N | 21.06.57 | 21.07.72 | 29.11.86 | 24.11.86 | - | Sold to NIR (no.105) |
| 219 | N | 01.07.57 | 06.10.72 | 26.06.85 | 25.09.86 | 09.90 | V.Berry, Leicester |
| 220 | SN | 24.06.57 | 20.12.72 | 01.02.85 | 25.09.86 | 10.90 | V.Berry, Leicester |
| 221 | SN | 12.08.57 | 14.02.72 | 12.08.86 | 25.09.86 | 09.90 | V.Berry, Leicester |
| 222 | SN | 13.07.57 | 10.03.70 | 30.07.86 | 25.09.86 | 06.90 | V.Berry, Leicester |
| 223 | SN | 15.07.57 | 17.07.72 | 03.06.86 | 25.09.86 | 10.92 | Inchicore Works |
| 224 | SN | 10.07.57 | 10.09.71 | 12.11.84 | 01.04.86 | 02.96 | Ballymena |
| 225 | SN | 23.07.57 | 27.01.72 | 15.06.86 | 25.09.86 | 06.90 | V.Berry, Leicester |
| 226 | SN | 21.08.57 | 10.06.72 | 05.05.84 | 25.09.86 | - | Carrick-On-Suir (P) |
| 227 | SN | 31.08.57 | 08.10.71 | 14.12.85 | 01.04.86 | - | Sold to NIR (no.106) |
| 228 | N | 05.10.57 | 22.09.72 | 24.07.86 | 01.04.86 | - | Sold to NIR (no.107) |
| 229 | SN | 12.10.57 | 08.03.72 | 23.03.84 | 25.09.86 | 07.92 | Inchicore Works |
| 230 | SN | 18.11.57 | 18.03.71 | 14.12.85 | 01.04.86 | - | Sold to NIR (no.108) |
| 231 | SN | 01.01.58 | 24.02.72 | 09.07.83 | 18.09.85 | - | Inchicore Works (P) |
| 232 | SN | 22.01.58 | 16.04.71 | 29.11.86 | 24.11.86 | 03.91 | V.Berry, Leicester |
| 233 | SN | 22.01.58 | 29.08.80 | 08.03.85 | 25.09.86 | 08.90 | V.Berry, Leicester |
| 234 | SN | 22.01.58 | 02.07.79 | 04.09.85 | 01.04.86 | - | Sold to NIR (no.109) |

216, 224, 227, 228, 230 and 234 were originally sent to NIR on a leasing arrangement, but were subsequently purchased by NIR on 1st April 1986. However, 228 was still used by CIE until its despatch to Belfast on 24th July 1986. Due to 224 being found to have a bent frame after delivery, 218 was subsequently obtained as a replacement.
201 suffered bomb damage at Meigh down home signal on 15.08.73 whilst working the 22:15 Dundalk to Londonderry freight.
207 was withdrawn following a collision at Dalkey on 16.11.79.
213, 218 and 232 all ran in service for a few days after the official withdrawal date.
213 was subsequently used as Inchicore Works pilot until February 1986.
226 and 231 (as C231) have been preserved by the Irish Traction Group.
227 was purchased from NIR (as no. 106) for preservation as a static exhibit at Cahirciveen, Co. Kerry. It is presently numbered C202.

## 201 CLASS                                                      Co-Co

**Built:** 1994-95 by General Motors Locomotive Group, London, Ontario, Canada.
**Engine:** General Motors 12-710G3B of 3200 hp at 900 rpm.
**General Motors Designation:** JT42HCW.
**Transmission:** Electric.  **Traction Motors:** General Motors D43.
**Maximum Tractive Effort:**  **Continuous Tractive Effort:**
**Power At Rail:**
**Weight:** 112 tons.
**Length Over Buffers:** 68 ft 9 in (20.949 m).
**Wheel Diameter:** 3 ft 4 in (1016 mm).

**Maximum Speed:** 100 mph.
**Train Heating:** Electric (HEP).
**Multiple Working:** Within class. However, the use of this facility is prohibited.
**Works Numbers:** 928303-1 to 928303-10 (201 - 205, 210 - 214) in order.
938400-1 to 938400-20 (215 - 234) in order.
938500-1 to 938500-2 (206 - 207) in order.

| Loco No. | Fittings | Date to Traffic | Name in Gaelic | Name in English |
|---|---|---|---|---|
| 201 | SAMH | 29.07.94 | ABHAINN NA SIONNAINE | RIVER SHANNON |
| 202 | SAMH | 15.08.94 | ABHAINN NA LAOI | RIVER LEE |
| 203 | SAMH | 09.09.94 | ABHAINN NA COIRIBE | RIVER CORRIB |
| 204 | SAMH | 10.10.94 | ABHAINN NA BEARÚ | RIVER BARROW |
| 205 | SAMH | 29.09.94 | ABHAINN NA FEOIRE | RIVER NORE |
| 206 | SAMHP | 05.05.95 | ABHAINN NA LIFE | *(RIVER LIFFEY)* |
| 207 | SAMHP | 14.04.95 | ABHAINN NA BÓINNE | RIVER BOYNE |
| 210 | SAMH | 10.12.94 | ABHAINN NA HÉIRNE | RIVER ERNE |
| 211 | SAMH | 05.10.94 | ABHAINN NA SUCA | RIVER SUCK |
| 212 | SAMH | 21.10.94 | ABHAINN NA SLAINE | RIVER SLANEY |
| 213 | SAMH | 24.10.94 | ABHAINN NA MUAIDHE | RIVER MOY |
| 214 | SAMH | 17.10.94 | ABHAINN NA BROSANI | RIVER BROSNA |
| 215 | SAMHP | 11.03.95 | AN ABHAINN MHÓR | RIVER AVONMORE |
| 216 | SAMHP | 08.03.95 | ABHAINN NA DOTHRA | RIVER DODDER |
| 217 | SAMHP | 02.03.95 | ABHAINN NA FLEÍSCE | RIVER FLESK |
| 218 | SAMHP | 08.03.95 | ABHAINN NA GARBHÓIGE | RIVER GARAVOGUE |
| 219 | SAMHP | 02.03.95 | *(ABHAINN NA TOLCHANN)* | RIVER TOLKA |
| 220 | SAMHP | 04.03.95 | AN ABHAINN DHUBH | RIVER BLACKWATER |
| 221 | SAMHP | 16.03.95 | ABHAINN NA FÉILGE | RIVER FEALGE |
| 222 | SAMHP | 25.02.95 | *(ABHAINN NA DARGAILE)* | RIVER DARGLE |
| 223 | SAMHP | 04.03.95 | ABHAINN NA HAINNIRE | RIVER ANNER |
| 224 | SAMHP | 25.02.95 | ABHAINN NA FÉILE | *(RIVER FEALE)* |
| 225 | SAMHP | 21.04.95 | ABHAINN NA DAOILE | RIVER DEEL |
| 226 | SAMHP | 30.03.95 | ABHAINN NA SIÚIRE | *(RIVER SUIR)* |
| 227 | SAMHP | 14.04.95 | *(ABHAINN NA LEAMHNA)* | RIVER LAUNE |
| 228 | SAMHP | 22.04.95 | AN ABHAINN BHUÍ | *(RIVER OWENEA)* |
| 229 | SAMHP | 28.04.95 | ABHAINN NA MAINGE | RIVER MAINE |
| 230 | SAMHP | 24.04.95 | ABHAINN NA BANDAN | *(RIVER BANDON)* |
| 231 | SAMHP | 02.05.95 | ABHAINN NA MÁIGHE | *(RIVER MAIGUE)* |
| 232 | SAMHP | 09.05.95 | *(ABHAINN NA CHOMARAIGH)* | RIVER CUMMERAGH |
| 233 | SAMHP | 11.05.95 | ABHAINN NA CHLÁIR | RIVER CLARE |
| 234 | SAMHP | 30.05.95 | *(ABHAINN NA HEATHARLAÍ)* | RIVER AHERLOW |

Locomotive No. 201 was flown in an Antonov 124-100 cargo plane from London Ontario, Canada, to Dublin, arriving at Dublin Airport on 09.06.94. This locomotive worked a fertiliser train on 14.06.94 and an Executive Special on 24.06.94 following its naming at Inchicore Works, but did not officially enter traffic until 29.07.94 as it was still classified as being "on test" at that time.
Names shown *(in italics)* were allocated but never fitted.
226 also carries a commemorative plaque "Thurles 150", which was fitted 04.98.
Due to weight restrictions these locomotives are banned from operating over certain routes and restricted over others. Full details are shown in Section 5.

## 301 (D) CLASS 0-6-0

**Built:** 1946-48 by CIE at Inchicore Works, Dublin.
**Engine:** Mirrlees TLDT6 of 487 hp (363 kW) at 710 rpm.
**Transmission:** Electric.
**Traction Motors:** Two Brush traction motors.
**Maximum Tractive Effort:** 24000 lbf (107 kN).
**Continuous Tractive Effort:**
**Power At Rail:**
**Weight:** 52.95 tons.
**Length Over Buffers:** 29 ft (8.84 m).
**Wheel Diameter:** 4 ft (1219 mm).
**Maximum Speed:** 25 mph.
**Works Numbers:** Not allocated.
**Notes:** These locomotives were originally numbered 1000 to 1004 respectively and were renumbered D301 to D305 in 1957. CIE class J1A until 1958.

| Loco No. | Month to Traffic | Date Stopped | Date Withdrawn | Month Cut | Cut Up Location |
|---|---|---|---|---|---|
| 301 | 12.47 | 22.06.60 | 17.10.76 | 03.77 | Inchicore Works |
| 302 | 02.48 | 13.06.60 | 17.10.76 | 03.77 | Inchicore Works |
| 303 | 04.48 | 09.02.70 | 17.10.76 | 03.77 | Inchicore Works |
| 304 | 06.48 | 26.05.72 | 17.10.76 | 03.77 | Inchicore Works |
| 305 | 09.48 | 13.06.66 | 17.10.76 | 03.77 | Inchicore Works |

## 401 (E) CLASS C

**Built:** 1956-58 by CIE at Inchicore Works, Dublin.
**Engine:** Maybach MD220 of 420 hp (313 kW) at 1600 rpm.
**Transmission:** Hydraulic.
**Transmission Type:** Mekydro KL64 Torque Converter.
**Maximum Tractive Effort:** 21728 lbf (97 kN).
**Continuous Tractive Effort:**
**Power At Rail:** 356 hp (266 kW).
**Weight:** 38.8 tons.
**Length Over Buffers:** 29 ft 4¼ in (8.95 m).
**Wheel Diameter:** 3 ft 2 in (965 mm).
**Maximum Speed:** 25 mph.
**Works Numbers:** Not allocated.
**Notes:** Numbered E401 to E419.

| Loco No. | Fittings | Date to Traffic | Date Stopped | Month Withdrawn | Month Cut | Cut Up Location |
|---|---|---|---|---|---|---|
| 401 | X | 10.07.57 | 06.08.65 | 12.10.77 | 12.77 | Inchicore Works |
| 402 | X | 22.10.57 | 10.09.75 | 25.02.77 | 04.89 | Mullingar Scrapyard |
| 403 |   | 11.11.57 | 18.10.76 | 25.02.77 | 04.89 | Mullingar Scrapyard |
| 404 |   | 03.01.58 | 16.03.77 | 01.06.83 | .84 | Inchicore Works |
| 405 |   | 15.11.57 | 07.10.77 | 25.02.77 | .84 | Inchicore Works |

| | | | | | | | |
|---|---|---|---|---|---|---|---|
| 406 | X | 18.11.57 | 10.03.76 | 25.02.77 | 11.77 | | Inchicore Works |
| 407 | X | 18.11.57 | 31.05.76 | 01.06.83 | 08.83 | | Mullingar Scrapyard |
| 408 | | 23.11.57 | 11.09.78 | 14.07.83 | 05.89 | | Mullingar Scrapyard |
| 409 | | 12.12.57 | 14.09.78 | 14.07.83 | 11.87 | | Mullingar Scrapyard |
| 410 | X | 09.01.58 | 09.04.79 | 14.07.83 | 11.87 | | Mullingar Scrapyard |
| 411 | X | 25.01.58 | 07.09.67 | 12.10.77 | 11.77 | | Inchicore Works |
| 412 | | 27.01.58 | 30.12.77 | 14.07.83 | .84 | | Inchicore Works |
| 413 | X | 12.02.58 | 20.04.75 | 25.02.77 | 01.78 | | Inchicore Works |
| 414 | | 03.02.58 | 12.02.77 | 01.06.83 | .84 | | Inchicore Works |
| 415 | X | 21.02.58 | 20.01.67 | 12.10.77 | 01.79 | | Inchicore Works |
| 416 | X | 22.02.58 | 02.01.76 | 01.06.83 | .84 | | Inchicore Works |
| 417 | X | 25.03.58 | 05.07.67 | 12.10.77 | 01.78 | | Inchicore Works |
| 418 | X | 20.04.58 | 19.10.64 | 01.06.83 | .84 | | Inchicore Works |
| 419 | X | 21.03.58 | 13.09.74 | 01.06.83 | .84 | | Inchicore Works |

405 ran in service for some months after the official withdrawal date.

## 421 (E) CLASS                                                                    C

**Built:** 1962-63 by CIE at Inchicore Works, Dublin.
**Engine:** Maybach MD220 of 420 hp (313 kW) at 1600 rpm.
**Transmission:** Hydraulic.
**Transmission Type:** Mekydro KL64U Torque Converter.
**Maximum Tractive Effort:** 23940 lbf (107 kN).
**Continuous Tractive Effort:**
**Power At Rail:** 356 hp (266 kW).
**Weight:** 42.8 tons.
**Length Over Buffers:** 31 ft 4¼ in (9.56 m).
**Wheel Diameter:** 3 ft 2 in (965 mm).
**Maximum Speed:** 25 mph.
**Multiple Working:** Within class only.
**Works Numbers:** Not allocated.
**Notes:** Numbered E421 to E434.

| Loco No. | Fittings | Date to Traffic | Date Stopped | Month Withdrawn | Month Cut | Cut Up/Preservation Location |
|---|---|---|---|---|---|---|
| 421 | M | 14.12.62 | 12.12.83 | 17.07.83 | - | Downpatrick (P) |
| 422 | M | 28.09.62 | 08.02.83 | 17.07.83 | 10.87 | Mullingar Scrapyard |
| 423 | M | 01.10.62 | 06.06.83 | 14.07.83 | .84 | Inchicore Works |
| 424 | M | 28.09.62 | 09.07.79 | 14.07.83 | 10.84 | Mullingar Scrapyard |
| 425 | M | 01.10.62 | 25.11.83 | 14.07.83 | 07.92 | Inchicore Works |
| 426 | M | 09.10.62 | 09.03.82 | 14.07.83 | .84 | Inchicore Works |
| 427 | M | 22.10.62 | 17.11.81 | 14.07.83 | .84 | Inchicore Works |
| 428 | M | 26.11.62 | 21.04.82 | 14.07.83 | - | Inchicore Works (P) |
| 429 | M | 12.12.62 | 22.09.83 | 14.07.83 | 06.92 | Inchicore Works |
| 430 | M | 08.01.63 | 01.06.83 | 14.07.83 | 05.85 | Attymon Junction |
| 431 | M | 25.01.63 | 08.12.80 | 14.07.83 | 12.88 | Inchicore Works |
| 432 | M | 22.01.63 | 15.02.83 | 14.07.83 | - | Downpatrick (P) |
| 433 | M | 13.04.63 | 24.03.83 | 14.07.83 | 12.88 | Inchicore Works |
| 434 | M | 15.02.63 | 19.02.83 | 14.07.83 | 10.87 | Mullingar Scrapyard |

421, 425 & 429 ran in service for some months after the official withdrawal date.
421 & 432 have been preserved by the Downpatrick Steam Railway, Co. Down.
428 has been preserved by Westrail.
430 was originally purchased by Westrail, but was subsequently broken up for spares for 428.

## 501 (F) CLASS 0-4-0 + 0-4-0

**Built:** 1954 by Walker Brothers, Wigan.
**Engine:** Two Gardner of 224 hp (167 kW) each.
**Transmission:** Mechanical.
**Transmission Type:** Hardy and Spicer.
**Maximum Tractive Effort:** 10300 lbf (46 kN).
**Continuous Tractive Effort:**
**Power At Rail:**
**Weight:** 23 tons.
**Length Over Couplings:** 26 ft 9 in (8.15 m).
**Wheel Diameter:** 2 ft 3 in (686 mm).
**Maximum Speed:** 25 mph plus an overdrive facility for 32 mph on passenger trains.
**Works Numbers:** D31-D33 in order.
**Gauge:** 3 ft 0 in.
**Notes:** These locomotives were delivered numbered C31-C33, but were renumbered in order to F501-F503 before entering traffic. They were constructed for use on the West Clare Railway (narrow gauge) and were withdrawn when the railway closed.

| Loco No. | Date to Traffic | Date Stopped | Date Withdrawn | Month Cut | Cut Up Location |
|---|---|---|---|---|---|
| 501 | 24.10.55 | 31.01.61 | 31.01.61 | .68 | Inchicore Works |
| 502 | 24.10.55 | 31.01.61 | 31.01.61 | .68 | Inchicore Works |
| 503 | 24.10.55 | 31.01.61 | 31.01.61 | .68 | Inchicore Works |

## 601 (G) CLASS B

**Built:** 1956 by Motorenfabrik Deutz at Köln, West Germany.
**Engine:** Deutz A8L 614 of 130 hp (97 kW).
**Transmission:** Hydraulic.
**Transmission Type:** Voith L33yUb Chain Drive.
**Maximum Tractive Effort:**
**Continuous Tractive Effort:**
**Power At Rail:**
**Weight:** 18 tons.
**Length Over Buffers:** 20 ft 8 in (6.3 m).
**Wheel Diameter:** 3 ft 1$^1$/$_2$ in (953 mm).
**Maximum Speed:** 20 mph.
**Works Numbers:** See below.
**Notes:** Numbered G601 to G603.

| Loco No. | Works No. | Date to Traffic | Date Stopped | Date Withdrawn | Month Cut | Cut up/preservation Location |
|---|---|---|---|---|---|---|
| 601 | 56119 | 01.06.56 | 22.07.72 | 27.04.78 | - | Carrick-On-Suir (P) |
| 602 | 56118 | 02.01.57 | 05.05.65 | 27.04.78 | 07.81 | Inchicore Works |
| 603 | 56120 | 11.03.57 | 07.10.69 | 27.04.78 | 07.81 | Inchicore Works |

601 was originally preserved by the Irish Narrow Gauge Trust. It was purchased by the Irish Traction Group in September 1994.

# 611 (G) CLASS                                                                          B

**Built:** 1961-62 by Motorenfabrik Deutz at Köln, West Germany.
**Engine:** Deutz A8L 714 of 160 hp (119 kW).
**Transmission:** Hydraulic.
**Transmission Type:** Voith L33yUb Chain Drive.
**Maximum Tractive Effort:**
**Continuous Tractive Effort:**
**Power At Rail:**
**Weight:** 22 tons.
**Length Over Buffers:** 21 ft 2 in (6.45 m).
**Wheel Diameter:** 3 ft 1½ in (953 mm).
**Maximum Speed:** 26.4 mph.
**Works Numbers:** See below.
**Notes:** Numbered G611 to G617.

| Loco No. | Works No. | Date to Traffic | Date Stopped | Date Withdrawn | Month Cut | Cut up/Preservation Location |
|---|---|---|---|---|---|---|
| 611 | 57225 | 01.06.62 | 22.07.77 | 29.09.77 | - | Downpatrick (P) |
| 612 | 57224 | 25.05.62 | 19.07.71 | 25.02.77 | 07.81 | Inchicore Works |
| 613 | 57226 | 05.06.62 | 17.01.77 | 29.07.77 | - | Downpatrick (P) |
| 614 | 57228 | 08.06.62 | 12.12.67 | 25.02.77 | 07.81 | Inchicore Works |
| 615 | 57223 | 05.06.62 | 11.01.77 | 29.09.77 | 05.89 | Thurles Sugar Factory |
| 616 | 57227 | 04.06.62 | 02.05.77 | 29.07.77 | - | Carrick-On-Suir (P) |
| 617 | 57229 | 24.05.62 | 09.12.76 | 14.11.77 | - | Downpatrick (P) |

611, 613, 615, 616 and 617 were sold to Comhlucht Siuicre Éireann (Irish Sugar Company) on 29.09.77 (except 617 on 14.11.77) for use on their premises at Carlow (616), Thurles (611, 615 & 617) and Tuam (613).
611 was later returned to Limerick and "adopted" by CIE for shunting the wagon works. Originally preserved by the Irish Narrow Gauge Trust, the locomotive was later purchased by the Irish Traction Group in 1994. It was loaned to the Downpatrick Steam Railway from 08.07.96.
613 was originally purchased by Westrail, but is now privately owned at the Downpatrick Steam Railway, Co. Down.
615 was heavily cannibalised for 616 & 617, and was finally broken up during 1989 by the Great Southern Railway Preservation Society.
616 later moved to the CSE premises at Thurles and was then preserved along with 617 by the Great Southern Railway Preservation Society for use on the Tralee - Fenit line. Both locomotives were sold to the Deutz Operators Group in November 1990. In August 1993 the locomotives were moved to Carrick-On-Suir and ownership transferred to the Irish Traction Group.
617 was loaned to the Downpatrick Steam Railway from 27.08.95.

# 801 (K) CLASS 0-8-0

**Built:** 1954 by Maschinenbau Kiel (MAK), Kiel, West Germany, for GNR (B).
**Engine:** MAK of 800 hp (597 kW).
**Transmission:** Hydraulic.
**Transmission Type:** Voith torque converter.
**Maximum Tractive Effort:** 25100 lbf (112 kN).
**Continuous Tractive Effort:** 5760 lbf (26 kN) at 16 mph.
**Power At Rail:**
**Weight:** 56.75 tons.
**Length Over Buffers:** 37 ft 2 in (11.33 m).
**Wheel Diameter:** 4 ft 1¼ in (1250 mm).
**Maximum Speed:** 50 mph.
**Works Numbers:** 800028.
**Note:** Originally numbered 800 by GNR (B). Renumbered K800 by CIE in 1958, and then K801.

| Loco No. | Month to Traffic | Date Stopped | Date Reinstated | Date Stopped | Date Withdrawn | Month Cut Up | Cut Up Location |
|---|---|---|---|---|---|---|---|
| 801 | 12.54 | 07.09.67 | 01.10.74 | 01.11.74 | 17.10.76 | c.02.99 | Galway Metals |

This locomotive was used to power a car crushing plant at Galway Scrap Metals. After a few months of use in 1977 the power unit seized. The remains of the locomotive remained partly dismantled until cut up circa 02.99.

## DIESEL MULTIPLE UNITS

All railcars vehicles are now maintained at the new railcar depot at Drogheda, which opened in 2003. However, some out-based sets may also be serviced at Cork, Limerick or Inchicore as required, returning to Drogheda for exams.

# 2600 CLASS 2 CAR UNITS

**Built:** 1993 by Tokyu Car Corporation, Yokohama, Japan.
**Engine:** Cummins NTA855 of 350 hp at 2100rpm.
**Auxiliary Engine:** Cummins, coupled to a Nishihatsu generator set producing 40 kW / 380 volts.
**Transmission:** Hydraulic.
**Transmission Type:** Niigata three stage gearbox.
**Seats:** 58 + 1 toilet (DC1) or 71 (DC2).
**Weight:** 40.20 tons. **Length:** 20.265 m per car.
**Width:** 9 ft 6in (2.90 m). **Maximum Speed:** 70 mph.
**Normal Formation:** Usual formation will be a DC1 vehicle coupled to a DC2 vehicle. Sets can work in multiple up to eight cars, coupled by means of Dellner automatic couplers. Compatible for use in multiple with 2621, 2700, 2800 and 2900 series vehicles.

| Car No. | Type | Date to Traffic | Date Stopped | Store Location |
|---|---|---|---|---|
| 2601 | DC1 | 16.05.94 | | |
| 2602 | DC2 | 16.05.94 | | |
| 2603 | DC1 | 16.05.94 | | |

| | | | | | |
|---|---|---|---|---|---|
| 2604 | DC2 | 16.05.94 | | | |
| 2605 | DC1 | 16.05.94 | | | |
| 2606 | DC2 | 16.05.94 | | | |
| 2607 | DC1 | 16.05.94 | | | |
| 2608 | DC2 | 16.05.94 | | | |
| 2609 | DC1 | 16.05.94 | 17.06.94 | Inchicore Works | |
| 2610 | DC2 | 16.05.94 | | | |
| 2611 | DC1 | 16.05.94 | | | |
| 2612 | DC2 | 16.05.94 | | | |
| 2613 | DC1 | 16.05.94 | | | |
| 2614 | DC2 | 16.05.94 | | | |
| 2615 | DC1 | 16.05.94 | | | |
| 2616 | DC2 | 16.05.94 | | | |
| 2617 | DC1 | 09.06.94 | | | |

2609 has been cannibalised to provide spares for the rest of the fleet.

## 2621 (FORMERLY 2800) CLASS      2 CAR UNITS

**Built:** 2000 by Tokyu Car Corporation, Yokohama, Japan.
**Engine:** Cummins NTA855-R1 of 350 hp at 2100 rpm (one per car).
**Auxiliary Engine:** Cummins 6B5.9GR of 57.5 kW at 1500 rpm (one per car).
**Transmission:** Hydraulic.
**Transmission Type:** Niigatta.
**Seats:** 36 + 3 tip up + 1 toilet (DC1) or 46 (DC2).
**Weight:** 43.90 tons (DC1) 42.60 tons (DC2).
**Length:** 20.265 m per car.
**Width:** 9 ft 6 in (2.90 m).
**Maximum Speed:** 75 mph.
**Normal Formation:** Usual formation will be a DC1 vehicle coupled to a DC2 vehicle. Sets can work in multiple up to ten cars, coupled by means of Dellner automatic couplers. Compatible for use in multiple with 2600, 2700, 2800 and 2900 series vehicles.

| DC1 | | | DC2 | | Date to Traffic |
|---|---|---|---|---|---|
| 2621 | (2801) | + | 2622 | (2802) | 02.04.01 |
| 2623 | (2803) | + | 2624 | (2804) | 17.04.01 |
| 2625 | (2805) | + | 2626 | (2806) | 03.04.01 |
| 2627 | (2807) | + | 2628 | (2808) | 05.08.01 |
| 2629 | (2809) | + | 2630 | (2810) | 02.04.01 |
| 2631 | (2811) | + | 2632 | (2812) | 17.04.01 |
| 2633 | (2813) | + | 2634 | (2814) | 03.04.01 |
| 2635 | (2815) | + | 2636 | (2816) | 03.04.01 |
| 2637 | (2817) | + | 2638 | (2818) | 02.07.01 |
| 2639 | (2819) | + | 2640 | (2820) | 02.04.01 |

Note: When delivered, these vehicles were numbered in the 28xx series and are still currently running in service carrying these numbers. However, in order to free up a number series for the newer 2800 series railcars currently on order, these vehicles are due to be renumbered into the 262x series during late 2004 / early 2005.

# 2700 CLASS        2 CAR UNITS

**Built:** 1997-8 by GEC Alstom Transporte, Santa Perpetua de Mogoda, Spain.
**Engine:** Cummins NTA855-R1 of 350 hp at 2100 rpm (one per car).
**Auxiliary Engine:** Cummins, coupled to a Nishihatsu generator set.
**Transmission:** Hydraulic.
**Transmission Type:** Niigata DW14G.
**Seats:** 52 + 3 tip up + 1 toilet or * 50 + 1 toilet + cycle rack (M1) or 62 (M2).
**Weight:** 38.70 tons (M1) 37.40 tons (M2).      **Length:** 20.555 m per car.
**Width:** 9 ft 3 in (2.83 m).      **Maximum Speed:** 75 mph.
**Normal Formation:** Usual formation will be a M1 vehicle coupled to a M2 vehicle. Sets can work in multiple up to ten cars, coupled by means of Scharfenberg automatic couplers. One vehicle is a maintenance spare. Compatible for use in multiple with 2600, 2621, 2800 and 2900 series vehicles.

| Car No. | Type | Date to Traffic | Date Stopped | Store Location |
|---|---|---|---|---|
| 2701 | M1 | 19.04.99 | | |
| 2702 | M2 | 19.04.99 | | |
| 2703 | M1 | 19.04.99 | | |
| 2704 | M2 | 19.04.99 | | |
| 2705 | M1 | 04.12.98 | | |
| 2706 | M2 | 04.12.98 | | |
| 2707 | M1 | 04.12.98 | | |
| 2708 | M2 | 04.12.98 | | |
| 2709 | M1 | 13.01.99 | | |
| 2710 | M2 | 13.01.99 | | |
| 2711 | M1 | 04.12.98 | | |
| 2712 | M2 | 04.12.98 | | |
| 2713 | M1 | 17.05.99 | | |
| 2714 | M2 | 17.05.99 | | |
| 2715 | M1 | 20.09.99 | | |
| 2716 | M2 | 20.09.99 | 03.06.00 | Inchicore Works |
| 2717 | M1 | 17.05.99 | | |
| 2718 | M2 | 17.05.99 | | |
| 2719 * | M1 | 10.05.99 | | |
| 2720 | M2 | 10.05.99 | | |
| 2721 * | M1 | 11.07.99 | | |
| 2722 | M2 | 11.07.99 | | |
| 2723 | M1 | 15.08.99 | | |
| 2724 | M2 | 20.10.00 | | |
| 2726 | M2 | 15.08.99 | | |

Note: 2705, 2706, 2707, 2708, 2711 and 2712 were used on passenger services in the Dublin Connolly area on 23.10.98 due to a shortage of rolling stock. They entered regular passenger service on 04.12.98.

# 2700 CLASS                                           SINGLE CAR UNITS

**Built:** 1998 by GEC Alstom Transporte, Santa Perpetua de Mogoda, Spain.
**Engine:** Cummins NTA855-R1 of 350 hp at 2100 rpm (one per car).
**Auxiliary Engine:** Cummins, coupled to a Nishihatsu generator set.
**Transmission:** Hydraulic.
**Transmission Type:** Niigatta DW14G.
**Seats:** 53 + 1 toilet.
**Weight:** 40.20 tons.
**Length:** 21.592 m per car.
**Width:** 9 ft 3 in (2.83 m).
**Maximum Speed:** 75 mph.
**Normal Formation:** Vehicles can operate either singly or in multiple. Vehicles can work in multiple of up to ten cars, coupled by means of Scharfenberg automatic couplers. Compatible for use in multiple with 2600, 2621, 2800 and 2900 series vehicles.

| Car No. | Type | Date to Traffic |
|---------|------|-----------------|
| 2751 | MTC | 18.10.99 |
| 2753 | MTC | 06.10.00 |

# 2800 CLASS                                                4 CAR UNITS

**Built:** On order from CAF
**Engine:**
**Auxiliary Engine:**
**Transmission:** Hydraulic.
**Transmission Type:**
**Seats:**
**Weight:**
**Length:**
**Width:**
**Maximum Speed:**
**Notes:** Expected to be formed into four car sets and used on services from Dublin Connolly to Rosslare and Sligo.

| DM1 |   | MDT |   | MT |   | DM2 | Date to traffic |
|------|---|------|---|------|---|------|-----------------|
| 2801 | + | 2802 | + | 2803 | + | 2804 | |
| 2805 | + | 2806 | + | 2807 | + | 2808 | |
| 2809 | + | 2810 | + | 2811 | + | 2812 | |
| 2813 | + | 2814 | + | 2815 | + | 2816 | |
| 2817 | + | 2818 | + | 2819 | + | 2820 | |
| 2821 | + | 2822 | + | 2823 | + | 2824 | |
| 2825 | + | 2826 | + | 2827 | + | 2828 | |
| 2829 | + | 2830 | + | 2831 | + | 2832 | |
| 2833 | + | 2834 | + | 2835 | + | 2836 | |

# 2900 CLASS            4 CAR UNITS

**Built:** 2001-2003 by CAF S.A. Zaragoza, Spain.
**Engine:** MAN D2876 LUH of 294 kW at 2000 rpm (one per car).
**Auxiliary Engine:** Cummins 6B5.9GR of 54 kW at 1500 rpm (one per car).
**Transmission:** Hydraulic.
**Transmission Type:** Voith Hydrodynamic Turbo-Transmission T211.
**Seats:** 48 (DM1/2), 49 + 1 toilet (MT), 40 + 2 tip up + 1 wheelchair accessible toilet & 2 wheel chair spaces (MDT).
**Weight:** 45 tons.
**Length:** 20.365 m (DM1/2) or 20.265 m (MT/MDT).
**Width:** 9 ft 6 in (2.90 m).
**Maximum Speed:** 75 mph.
**Normal Formation:** Usual formation will be a DM1 + MDT + MT + DM2 vehicle. Sets can work in multiple up to ten cars, coupled by means of Scharfenberg automatic couplers. Compatible for use in multiple with 2600, 2621, 2700 and 2800 series vehicles.

| DM1 | MDT | MT | DM2 | Date to traffic |
|---|---|---|---|---|
| 2901 + | 2902 + | 2903 + | 2904 | 16.10.03 |
| 2905 + | 2906 + | 2907 + | 2908 | 16.10.03 |
| 2909 + | 2910 + | 2911 + | 2912 | 21.07.03 |
| 2913 + | 2914 + | 2915 + | 2916 | 30.06.03 |
| 2917 + | 2918 + | 2919 + | 2920 | 17.09.03 |
| 2921 + | 2922 + | 2923 + | 2924 | 03.10.03 |
| 2925 + | 2926 + | 2927 + | 2928 | 14.12.03 |
| 2929 + | 2930 + | 2931 + | 2932 | 08.12.03 |
| 2933 + | 2934 + | 2935 + | 2936 | 21.07.03 |
| 2937 + | 2938 + | 2939 + | 2940 | 29.08.03 |
| 2941 + | 2942 + | 2943 + | 2944 | 08.12.03 |
| 2945 + | 2946 + | 2947 + | 2948 | 14.12.03 |
| 2949 + | 2950 + | 2951 + | 2952 | 17.11.03 |
| 2953 + | 2954 + | 2955 + | 2956 | 03.12.03 |
| 2957 + | 2958 + | 2959 + | 2960 | 03.12.03 |
| 2961 + | 2962 + | 2963 + | 2964 | 14.12.03 |
| 2965 + | 2966 + | 2967 + | 2968 | 05.01.04 |
| 2969 + | 2970 + | 2971 + | 2972 | 30.01.04 |
| 2973 + | 2974 + | 2975 + | 2976 | 19.02.04 |
| 2977 + | 2978 + | 2979 + | 2980 | ??.04.04 |

# ELECTRIC MULTIPLE UNITS "DART"

Notes: Allocated to Dublin Fairview Depot and operate suburban services between Howth / Malahide and Greystones. All operate on 1500v DC overhead supply system.

## 8101 / 8301 CLASS — 2 CAR "DART" UNITS

**Built:** 1983 by Linke-Hofmann-Busch, Salzgitter, West Germany.
**Brakes:** Rheostatic/Regenerative (1st Service brake). Air/load Dependent (2nd Service brake).
**Seats:** 72 (DMS) or 56 (DTS).
**Wheel Diameter:** 2 ft 9$1/2$ in (840 mm).
**Weight:** 40.34 tons (DMS) + 25.43 tons (DTS).   **Length:** 67 ft 2.7 in (20.490 m).
**Width:** 9 ft 6 in (2.90 m).   **Maximum Speed:** 62 mph.
**Traction Motors:** Four GEC G314BY.
**Multiple Working:** Within class up to four sets.
**Normal Formation:** Usual formation will be a DMS vehicle coupled to a DTS vehicle.
**Works Numbers:** A01-A40 (8101-8140): B01-B40 (8301-8340).

| DMS | | DTS | Date to Traffic | Date Stopped | Month Withdrawn | Month Cut | Cut up Location |
|---|---|---|---|---|---|---|---|
| 8101 | + | 8301 | 23.07.84 | | | | |
| 8102 | + | 8302 | 24.07.84 | | | | |
| 8103 | + | 8303 | 28.07.84 | | | | |
| 8104 | + | 8304 | 23.07.84 | | | | |
| 8105 | + | 8305 | 23.07.84 | | | | |
| 8106 | + | 8306 | 23.07.84 | | | | |
| 8107 | + | 8307 | 23.07.84 | | | | |
| 8108 | + | 8308 | 23.07.84 | | | | |
| 8109 | + | 8309 | 24.07.84 | | | | |
| 8110 | + | 8310 | 23.07.84 | 14.07.01 | 07.01 | 09.01 | Fairview Depot |
| 8111 | + | 8311 | 24.07.84 | | | | |
| 8112 | + | 8312 | 23.07.84 | | | | |
| 8113 | + | 8313 | 23.07.84 | | | | |
| 8114 | + | 8314 | 24.07.84 | | | | |
| 8115 | + | 8315 | 23.07.84 | | | | |
| 8116 | + | 8316 | 24.07.84 | | | | |
| 8117 | + | 8317 | 30.07.84 | | | | |
| 8118 | + | 8318 | 27.07.84 | | | | |
| 8119 | + | 8319 | 27.07.84 | | | | |
| 8120 | + | 8320 | 23.07.84 | | | | |
| 8121 | + | 8321 | 23.07.84 | | | | |
| 8122 | + | 8322 | 23.07.84 | | | | |
| 8123 | + | 8323 | 30.07.84 | | | | |
| 8124 | + | 8324 | 24.07.84 | | | | |
| 8125 | + | 8325 | 23.07.84 | | | | |
| 8126 | + | 8326 | 24.07.84 | | | | |
| 8127 | + | 8327 | 24.07.84 | | | | |
| 8128 | + | 8328 | 24.07.84 | | | | |
| 8129 | + | 8329 | 26.09.84 | | | | |

| | | | | | | |
|---|---|---|---|---|---|---|
| 8130 | + | 8330 | 11.10.84 | | | |
| 8131 | + | 8331 | 21.11.84 | | | |
| 8132 | + | 8332 | 21.11.84 | | | |
| 8133 | + | 8333 | 22.11.84 | | | |
| 8134 | + | 8334 | 22.11.84 | | | |
| 8135 | + | 8335 | 24.11.84 | | | |
| 8136 | + | 8336 | 13.12.84 | 14.07.01 | 07.01 | 09.01 Fairview Depot |
| 8137 | + | 8337 | 13.12.84 | | | |
| 8138 | + | 8338 | 15.07.85 | | | |
| 8139 | + | 8339 | 11.04.85 | | | |
| 8140 | + | 8340 | 11.04.85 | | | |

Notes: Vehicles 8110+8310 and 8136+8336 were destroyed by a fire at Fairview Depot on 14.07.01. The underframes of 8110 and 8136 were transported to Inchicore Works for component recovery and final scrapping.

## 8201 / 8401 CLASS                                      2 CAR "DART" UNITS

**Built:** 1999 by GEC Alstom Transporte, Santa Perpetua de Mogoda, Spain.
**Overall Length:** 20.555 m per car.
**Weight:** 42.465 tonnes (DMS) + 30.675 tons (DTS).
**Transmission:** Electric.
**Traction Motors:**
**Seats:** 40 per car.
**Maximum Speed:** 62 mph.
**Multiple Working:** Within class up to three sets and with 8501/8601 vehicles.
**Normal Formation:** Usual formation will be a DMS vehicle coupled to a DTS vehicle.

| | | Date to |
|---|---|---|
| DMS | DTS | Traffic |
| 8201 + | 8401 | 10.10.00 |
| 8202 + | 8402 | 10.10.00 |
| 8203 + | 8403 | 10.10.00 |
| 8204 + | 8404 | 20.11.00 |
| 8205 + | 8405 | 10.10.00 |

Note: 8202+8402+8205+8405 were used on a demonstration passenger working on 15.09.00.

## 8501 / 8601 CLASS                                      4 CAR "DART" UNITS

**Built:** 2000 by Tokyu Car Corporation, Yokohama, Japan.
**Brakes:** Dynamic brake (rheostatic brake/regenerating brake) and friction brake (Electro-pneumatic direct brake) with bogie base wheel slide protection.
**Bogie:** TS1024(PMS) , TS1025(DTS)
**Seats:** 40 per car
**Wheel Diameter:**
**Weight:** 39.00 tons (PMS) + 32.67 tons (DTS).
**Width:** 9 ft 6 in (2.90 m).
**Length:** 20.000 m (PMS) 20.130 m (DTS).
**Maximum Speed:** 68 mph.

**Transmission:** Electric.
**Traction Motors:**
**Multiple Working:** Within class up to three sets and with 8201/8401 vehicles.
**Normal Formation:** Usual formation will be a DTS + PMS + PMS + DTS.

| DTS | | PMS | | PMS | | DTS | Date to Traffic |
|---|---|---|---|---|---|---|---|
| 8601 | + | 8501 | + | 8502 | + | 8602 | .05.01 |
| 8603 | + | 8503 | + | 8504 | + | 8604 | .05.01 |
| 8605 | + | 8505 | + | 8506 | + | 8606 | 01.05.01 |
| 8607 | + | 8507 | + | 8508 | + | 8608 | .05.01 |

Details as above, except:
**Built:** 2001 by Tokyu Car Corporation, Yokohama, Japan.
**Brakes:** Dynamic brake (rheostatic brake/regenerating brake) and friction brake (Electro-pneumatic direct brake) with axle base wheel slide protection.
**Bogie:** TS1024A(PMS), TS1025A(DTS).
**Weight:** 39.25 tons (PMS), 33.75 tons (DTS).

| DTS | | PMS | | PMS | | DTS | Date to Traffic |
|---|---|---|---|---|---|---|---|
| 8611 | + | 8511 | + | 8512 | + | 8612 | 02.04.02 |
| 8613 | + | 8513 | + | 8514 | + | 8614 | .04.02 |
| 8615 | + | 8515 | + | 8516 | + | 8616 | .04.02 |

Details as above, except:
**Built:** 2003-04 by Tokyu Car Corporation, Yokohama, Japan.
**Bogie:** TS1024B(PMS), TS1025B(DTS).
**Weight:** 39.00 tons (PMS), 32.67 tons (DTS).
**Notes:** Air conditioned throughout.

| DTS | | PMS | | PMS | | DTS | Date to Traffic |
|---|---|---|---|---|---|---|---|
| 8621 | + | 8521 | + | 8522 | + | 8622 | |
| 8623 | + | 8523 | + | 8524 | + | 8624 | |
| 8625 | + | 8525 | + | 8526 | + | 8626 | |
| 8627 | + | 8527 | + | 8528 | + | 8628 | 31.08.04 |
| 8629 | + | 8529 | + | 8530 | + | 8630 | |
| 8631 | + | 8531 | + | 8532 | + | 8632 | |
| 8633 | + | 8533 | + | 8534 | + | 8634 | |
| 8635 | + | 8535 | + | 8536 | + | 8636 | |
| 8637 | + | 8537 | + | 8538 | + | 8638 | |
| 8639 | + | 8539 | + | 8540 | + | 8640 | |

# COACHING STOCK

# NOTES ON COACHING STOCK

Since the publication of the third edition, additions to the Iarnród Éireann coaching stock fleet have included nine of the former BREL "International" coaches, together with fourteen new coaches, built by De-Dietrich in France, for use on the Dublin to Belfast cross border "Enterprise" service.

A further sixty seven vehicles are presently on order from CAF, primarily for use on InterCity services over the Dublin to Cork line. The first of these vehicles are expected to be delivered during 2005. They will be formed into seven rakes of nine vehicles, with one of each type as a maintenance spare. Each rake will be formed as follows: Driving brake generator van + first class + buffet + 6 x standard class, and will work in push/pull mode with 201 class locomotives. Electric train supply will be provided by the driving brake generator van. The numbers of these new vehicles should not be confused with those of the former BR Mark 2 coaches Nos. 4101-4114 and 4401-4402, which were finally withdrawn in 2003. The brake generator vans used with the former BR Mark 2 vehicles, Nos. 4601-4603, are now due to revert to their original numbers in the 3157-3166 series.

The Cravens built coaches operate with a steam generator van in the train formation to provide steam heating. A small diesel generator is also provided in the van to provide power for the train lighting system. Electrically heated and/or air conditioned Mark 2 and Mark 3 vehicles operate with an electric generator van in the train formation, as most Iarnród Éireann locomotives are not fitted with any form of train supply equipment. Only the newer GM 201 class locomotives are fitted with Head End Power (HEP), and this is only used in conjunction with the De-Dietrich cross border stock.
Note: All coaching stock is of open layout.

## CIE/CRAVENS STANDARD (*BUFFET)

**Built:** 1963 (1504-13), 1964 (1514-43) or 1967 (1544-58) by CIE at Inchicore Works, Dublin, from bodyshells and parts supplied by Cravens Ltd., Sheffield.
**Seats:** 64 (* 47).
**Heating System:** Steam.
**Brakes:** Vacuum.
**Bogies:** B4.
**Weight:** 28.7 tons.
**Length:** 62 ft 8 in (19.l0 m).
**Maximum Speed:** 75 mph.
**Note:** b fitted with guard's emergency brake valve.

| | | | | | |
|---|---|---|---|---|---|
| 1504 | 1515 | 1528 | 1539 | 1547 | |
| 1505 | 1516 | 1529 | 1540 | 1548 | |
| 1506 | 1518 | 1530 | 1541 | 1550 | |
| 1507 | 1520 | 1531 | 1542 | 1551 | |
| 1508 * | 1521 | 1532 | 1543 | 1554 | |
| 1510 | 1522 | 1533 | 1544 | 1555 | |
| 1511 | 1523 | 1535 b | 1545 | 1556 | |
| 1513 | 1526 | 1536 b | 1546 | 1558 b | |
| 1514 | | | | | |

1509 *, 1524, 1525, 1529 and 1549 were withdrawn in 1997 (1524 in 1996) after suffering derailment damage at Belview on 11.08.93.
1512, 1534 & 1553 were scrapped at Mullingar after being fire-bombed on the "Enterprise" service on 12.10.78.
1519 was withdrawn following derailment damage near Tralee on 15.11.93.
1527 was withdrawn following accident damage at Cherryville Junction on 21.08.83.
1537 & 1538 were withdrawn after suffering fire damage at Limerick on 26.05.69.
1517, 1552 & 1557 were withdrawn following fire damage on 13.09.03 whilst working empty stock from Dublin to Cork.
1514, 1515, 1517, 1519, 1520 and 1522 were originally wired to operate as un-powered trailers with former CIE AEC 2600 series railcars.

## DUNDALK ENGINEERING / WERKSPOOR
## BRAKE GENERATING STEAM VAN

**Built:** 1969 by Dundalk Engineering Works, Dundalk, from parts supplied by Werkspoor, Utrecht, The Netherlands.
**Seats:** Nil.
**Bogies:** Werkspoor Design.
**Brakes:** Vacuum.
**Length:** 44 ft 3 in (13.49 m).
**Weight:** 32 tons.
**Boilers:** Two Spanner of 1000 lb/hr.
**Maximum Speed:** 75 mph.
**Generator:** Lister HR3 of $32_{1/4}$ bhp at 1500 rpm.

| 3157 | 3158 | 3160 | 3161 | 3164 |
| --- | --- | --- | --- | --- |

3157 and 3160 are marked "restricted use", and are no longer fitted with boilers.
3162, 3163 & 3166 were converted to Brake Generator Vans 4601-03 respectively during 1990-91.
3156 was scrapped at Inchicore Works 02.95.
3159 was scrapped at Inchicore Works 02.04.
3165 was scrapped at Inchicore Works 05.02.

## DUNDALK ENGINEERING / WERKSPOOR / IE
## BRAKE GENERATOR VAN

**Built:** 1969 by Dundalk Engineering Works, Dundalk, from parts supplied by Werkspoor, Utrecht, The Netherlands.
**Rebuilt:** 1990-91 by IE at Inchicore Works, Dublin.
**Seats:** Nil
**Bogies:** Werkspoor design.
**Brakes:** Air and through vacuum piped.
**Length:** 44 ft 3 in (13.49 m).
**Weight:** 32.0 tons.
**Maximum Speed:** 75 mph.
**Width:** 9 ft (2.74 m).
**Engine:** Cummins NTA 855-G3 of 535 hp (400 kW) at 1800 rpm.
**Alternator:** Dale EM/395/DCE of 283.5kW at 1500 rpm.
**Notes:** Originally converted from Steam Generator Vans 3162, 3163 and 3166 respectively, to operate with former Mark 2 vehicles nos. 4101-4114 and 4401-4402. The vehicles are due to revert to their original numbers during 2004 and remain available for use for air brake stock transfers and test trains etc.

3162 (4601, 3162)          3163 (4602, 3163)          3166 (4603, 3166)

## VARIOUS/BREL                    BRAKE GENERATING STEAM VAN

**Built:** 1952-58 by BR Workshops (* Charles Roberts; † Metropolitan Cammell; ‡ Gloucester RC&W).
**Rebuilt:** 1972 by BREL at Derby C & W Works.
**Seats:** Nil.

**Bogies:** B5.
**Brakes:** Vacuum.
**Length:** 63 ft 5 in (19.33 m).
**Weight:** 37.18 tons.
**Boiler:** Spanner of 2000 lb/hr.
**Width:** 9 ft (2.74 m).
**Maximum Speed:** 75 mph.
**Generator:** Lister HR3 of $32^{1/4}$ hp at 1500 rpm.
**Notes:** These vehicles were converted in 1972 from earlier BR Mark 1 Brake Corridor Seconds or Brake Corridor Composites (former BR numbers in parentheses).
p - Also fitted with through air pipe.

| | | | | | | | |
|---|---|---|---|---|---|---|---|
| 3172 | (21138) * | 3180 p | (34378) | 3186 p | (34757) | | |
| 3173 | (21146) * | 3183 p | (34687) | 3187 p | (34012) | | |
| 3177 | (34227) | 3184 | (34566) | 3188 p | (34701) | | |
| 3178 p | (34590)‡ | 3185 | (34093) | 3189 p | (34264) | | |
| 3179 p | (34677) | | | | | | |

3181 (34581) was withdrawn following accident damage at Cherryville Junc on 21.08.83.
3191 (34076) was withdrawn following accident damage at Buttevant 01.08.80.
3171 (21140)*, 3176 (21137)*, 3182 (34685), 3190 (34262) and 3192 (34565) were all withdrawn as surplus to requirements during 1994. All except 3192 were scrapped at Inchicore Works 02.95, 3192 passing into departmental use (without re-numbering).
3174 (21143)* and 3175 (21196) † were withdrawn as surplus to requirements and scrapped at Inchicore Works 05.02 and 09.99 respectively.

## CAF — DRIVING BRAKE GENERATOR VAN

**Built:** 2004-05 by CAF S.A at Beasain, Spain.
**Seats:** nil.
**Heating System:** Air Conditioning.
**Brakes:** Air.
**Bogies:** CAF M88.
**Weight:** 48.27 Tonnes (estimated).
**Length:** 23.81m.
**Width:** 2.85m.
**Maximum Speed:** 100 mph (designed for 125 mph).
**Engines:** 2 x MAN D2848 LE202.
**Alternators:** 2 x LETAG of 330KVA.

| | | | | | |
|---|---|---|---|---|---|
| 4001 | 4003 | 4005 | 4007 | 4008 | |
| 4002 | 4004 | 4006 | | | |

## CAF — FIRST

**Built:** 2004-05 by CAF S.A at Beasain, Spain.
**Seats:** 44 + 1 wheelchair space.
**Heating System:** Air Conditioning.
**Brakes:** Air.

**Bogies:** CAF M8.
**Weight:** 42.77 Tonnes (estimated).
**Length:** 23.66m.
**Width:** 2.85.
**Maximum Speed:** 100 mph (designed for 125 mph).

| 4101 | 4103 | 4105 | 4107 | 4108 |
| 4102 | 4104 | 4106 |      |      |

## CAF                                                         STANDARD

**Built:** 2004-05 by CAF S.A at Beasain, Spain.
**Seats:** 69 + 1 wheelchair space with tip up seat.
**Heating System:** Air Conditioning.
**Brakes:** Air.
**Bogies:** CAF M88.
**Weight:** 42.55 Tonnes (estimated).
**Length:** 23.66m (23.81m with buckeye coupler raised).
**Width:** 2.85m.
**Maximum Speed:** 100 mph (designed for 125 mph).
**Note:** Eight vehicles to be equipped with drop head buckeye coupler and retractable buffers, to give two options for coupling to locomotives.

| 4201 | 4210 | 4219 | 4228 | 4236 |
| 4202 | 4211 | 4220 | 4229 | 4237 |
| 4203 | 4212 | 4221 | 4230 | 4238 |
| 4204 | 4213 | 4222 | 4231 | 4239 |
| 4205 | 4214 | 4223 | 4232 | 4240 |
| 4206 | 4215 | 4224 | 4233 | 4241 |
| 4207 | 4216 | 4225 | 4234 | 4242 |
| 4208 | 4217 | 4226 | 4235 | 4243 |
| 4209 | 4218 | 4227 |      |      |

## CAF                                                 RESTAURANT/BUFFET

**Built:** 2004-05 by CAF S.A at Beasain, Spain.
**Seats:** 28.
**Heating System:** Air Conditioning.
**Brakes:** Air.
**Bogies:** CAF M88.
**Weight:** 44.59 Tonnes (estimated).
**Length:** 23.66m.
**Width:** 2.85m.
**Maximum Speed:** 100 mph (designed for 125 mph).

| 4401 | 4403 | 4405 | 4407 | 4408 |
| 4402 | 4404 | 4406 |      |      |

# BREL/CIE STANDARD

**Built:** 1972 by BREL at Derby C & W Works to Mark 2D design with final minor finishing work by CIE at Inchicore Works, Dublin. First Class style bodyshell.
**Seats:** 56 († 62).
**Heating System:** Air conditioning.
**Brakes:** Vacuum.
**Bogies:** B4.
**Weight:** 32 tons.
**Length:** 66 ft (20.12 m).
**Width:** 9 ft (2.74 m).
**Maximum Speed:** 75 mph.

| 5101 | 5102 | 5103 † | 5105 † | 5106 † |

5104 was withdrawn during 2004 as life expired. At the date of publication it was awaiting final disposal.

# BREL/CIE COMPOSITE (*STANDARD)

**Built:** 1972 by BREL at Derby C & W Works to Mark 2D design with final minor finishing work by CIE at Inchicore Works, Dublin.
**Seats:** 24F/24S († 48S,* 54S).
**Heating System:** Air conditioning.
**Brakes:** Vacuum.
**Bogies:** B4.
**Weight:** 31.96 tons.
**Length:** 66 ft (20.12 m).
**Width:** 9 ft (2.74 m).
**Maximum Speed:** 75 mph.
**Note:** All this batch were originally fitted out as Composites and were thus built with centre doors. However, certain vehicles have subsequently had their seating arrangements altered to suit traffic requirements.

| 5151 * | 5153 * | 5155 * | 5157 * | 5159 † |
| 5152   | 5154 * | 5156 * | 5158 * |        |

# BREL/CIE STANDARD

**Built:** 1972 by BREL at Derby C & W Works to Mark 2D design with final minor finishing work by CIE at Inchicore Works, Dublin.
**Seats:** 64.
**Heating System:** Air conditioning.
**Brakes:** Vacuum.
**Bogies:** B4.
**Weight:** 30.96 tons.
**Length:** 66 ft (20.12 m).
**Width:** 9 ft (2.74 m).
**Maximum Speed:** 75 mph.
**Note:** § revised livery similar to 201 class locomotives.

| | | | | |
|---|---|---|---|---|
| 5201 | 5210 | 5217 | 5224 | 5231 |
| 5202 | 5211 | 5218 | 5225 § | 5232 § |
| 5203 | 5212 | 5219 | 5226 | 5233 § |
| 5205 | 5213 § | 5220 | 5227 | 5234 |
| 5206 | 5214 | 5221 | 5228 | 5235 § |
| 5208 | 5215 | 5222 | 5229 | 5236 |
| 5209 § | 5216 § | 5223 | 5230 | |

5204 and 5207 were withdrawn during 2004 as life expired. At the date of publication they were awaiting final disposal.

## BREL/CIE   RESTAURANT BUFFET STANDARD

**Built:** 1972 by BREL at Derby C & W Works to Mark 2D design with final minor finishing work by CIE at Inchicore Works, Dublin.
**Seats:** 26 + wheelchair space.
**Heating System:** Air conditioning.
**Brakes:** Vacuum.
**Bogies:** B4.
**Weight:** 34.2 tons.
**Length:** 66 ft (20.12 m).
**Width:** 9 ft (2.74 m).
**Maximum Speed:** 75 mph.

| | | | | |
|---|---|---|---|---|
| 5401 | 5403 | 5405 | 5406 | 5407 |
| 5402 | 5404 | | | |

5406 was renumbered from 5408 in 1984.

## BREL/CIE   PRESIDENTIAL COACH

**Built:** 1972 by BREL at Derby C & W Works to Mark 2D design with final minor finishing work by CIE at Inchicore Works, Dublin.
**Rebuilt:** 1977 by CIE at Inchicore Works, Dublin.
**Seats:** Loose chairs as required.
**Heating System:** Air conditioning.
**Brakes:** Vacuum.
**Bogies:** B4.
**Weight:** 34.2 tons.
**Length:** 66 ft (20.12 m).
**Width:** 9 ft (2.74 m).
**Maximum Speed:** 75 mph.
**Note:** This vehicle is used to convey the President of Ireland and other VIPs on special occasions. Renumbered from 5406 in 1984.

5408

## BREL/CIE — RESTAURANT BUFFET STANDARD

**Built:** 1972 by BREL at Derby C & W Works to Mark 2D design with final minor finishing work by CIE at Inchicore Works, Dublin.
**Seats:** 26 + wheelchair space.
**Heating System:** Air conditioning.
**Brakes:** Vacuum.
**Bogies:** B4.
**Weight:** 34.2 tons.
**Length:** 66 ft (20.12 m).
**Width:** 9 ft (2.74 m).
**Maximum Speed:** 75 mph.
**Note:** § revised livery similar to 201 class locomotives.

5410          5411 §

5409 was severely damaged by a fire bomb at Newry on 09.08.85. It was subsequently scrapped at Inchicore Works in October 1993.

## BREL/CIE — BRAKE GENERATOR VAN

**Built:** 1972 by BREL at Derby C & W Works to Mark 2D design with final minor finishing work by CIE at Inchicore Works, Dublin.
**Seats:** Nil.
**Heating System:** Electric through wired.
**Brakes:** Vacuum.
**Bogies:** B4.
**Weight:** 32 tons.
**Length:** 66 ft (20.12 m).
**Width:** 9 ft (2.74 m).
**Maximum Speed:** 75 mph.
**Engines:** Two Detroit 8V-71 N (Model No. 7083-7005) of 234 hp at 1575 rpm.
**Alternators:** Two International Electric of 160 kW.
**Note:** § revised livery similar to 201 class locomotives.

| 5601 § | 5603 | 5605 | 5607 | 5609 |
| 5602   | 5604 | 5606 | 5608 | 5610 |

5611 was withdrawn after suffering fire damage at Hazelhatch on 21.08.79.

## IE — DRIVING BRAKE GENERATOR STANDARD

**Built:** 1988-89 by IE at Inchicore Works, Dublin to BREL Mark 3 design & fitted with automatic plug type doors.
**Seats:** 49 (plus 11 tip up and wheelchair space) † 56 (plus 6 tip up).
**Brakes:** Air
**Heating:** Forced Air.
**Weight:** 41 tons.
**Bogies:** BT22C, * Linke Hoffman Busch.

**Width:** 9 ft (2.74 m).
**Length:** 73 ft 7 in (22.70 m).
**Alternator:** Reliance.
**Maximum Speed:** 70 / 90 mph, * 70 mph.
**Engine:** Cummins NTA855R1 of 310 hp (231 kW) at 1500 rpm.
**Note:** These vehicles can operate as hauled stock at 90 mph or in push/pull mode at 70 mph in conjunction with vehicles 6301-6319 & 6402 and modified 121 and 201 class locomotives. 6101-6103 are presently restricted to 70 mph as hauled stock, but are shortly to be fitted with BT22 bogies recovered from former BR Mark 3 sleeping coaches in order to increase their maximum permitted speed as hauled stock to 90 mph.

| 6101 †* | 6102 †* | 6103 * | 6104 | 6105 |
|---|---|---|---|---|

## BREL/IE                                                    STANDARD/*COMPOSITE

**Built:** 1986 by BREL at Derby C & W Works, England.
**Rebuilt:** 1994-97 by IE at Inchicore Works, Dublin.
**Seats:** 72S (* 24S/30F: + 54S).
**Heating System:** Air conditioning.
**Brakes:** Air.
**Bogies:** ABB T4-7b.
**Weight:**
**Length:** 74 ft (22.57 m).
**Width:** 9 ft (2.74 m).
**Maximum Speed:** 100 mph.
**Note:** Converted from former BREL "International" coaches 99521-22/24-28, rebuilt with swing plug doors. These vehicles can operate with vehicles 6208 and 6401, and are regarded as Mark 3a coaches.

| 6201 * | 6203 | 6205 | 6206 | 6207 |
|---|---|---|---|---|
| 6202 + | 6204 |  |  |  |

## BREL/IE                                                                     STANDARD

**Built:** 1986 by BREL at Derby C & W Works, England.
**Rebuilt:** 1997 by IE at Inchicore Works, Dublin.
**Seats:** 72S.
**Heating System:** Air conditioning.
**Brakes:** Air.
**Bogies:** BT22.
**Weight:**
**Length:** 74 ft (22.57 m).
**Width:** 9 ft (2.74 m).
**Maximum Speed:** 100 mph.
**Note:** Converted from former BREL "International" coach 99529, rebuilt with swing plug doors. This vehicle can operate with vehicles 6201-6207 and 6401, and is regarded as a Mark 3a coach. This vehicle can also operate with standard IE Mark 3 coaches in the series 7101-7615. For a short time after conversion it was numbered 7173. Bogies used on this coach were recovered from withdrawn coach 7111.

6208

## IE                                    INTERMEDIATE STANDARD

**Built:** 1988-89 by IE at Inchicore Works, Dublin to BREL Mark 3 design & fitted with automatic plug type doors.
**Seats:** 76.
**Heating System:** Forced Air.
**Brakes:** Air.
**Bogies:** BT22.
**Weight:** 34 tons.
**Length:** 74 ft (22.57 m).
**Width:** 9 ft (2.74 m).
**Maximum Speed:** 70 / 90 mph.
**Note:** These vehicles can operate as hauled stock at 90 mph or in push/pull mode at 70 mph in conjunction with vehicles 6101-6105 & 6402 and modified 121 and 201 class locomotives.

| | | | | | |
|---|---|---|---|---|---|
| 6301 | 6305 | 6309 | 6313 | 6317 | |
| 6302 | 6306 | 6310 | 6314 | 6318 | |
| 6303 | 6307 | 6311 | 6315 | 6319 | |
| 6304 | 6308 | 6312 | 6316 | | |

## BREL/IE                                    BUFFET STANDARD

**Built:** 1986 by BREL at Derby C & W Works.
**Rebuilt:** 1994-97 by IE at Inchicore Works, Dublin.
**Seats:** 24.
**Heating System:** Air conditioning.
**Brakes:** Air.
**Bogies:** ABB T4-7b.
**Weight:**
**Length:** 74 ft (22.57 m).
**Width:** 9 ft (2.74 m).
**Maximum Speed:** 100 mph.
**Note:** Converted from former BREL "International" coach 99523, rebuilt with swing plug doors. This vehicle can operate with vehicles 6201-6208, and is regarded as a Mark 3a coach.

6401

## BREL/INTERFLEET/IE     INTERMEDIATE BUFFET STANDARD

**Built:** 1980 by BREL at Derby C & W Works to BR Mark 3 design.
**Rebuilt:** 2001 By Interfleet Technology, Derby, England.
**Seats:** 45 + 3 tip up.
**Heating System:** Air conditioning.
**Brakes:** Air.
**Bogies:** BT22.
**Weight:** 34 tons.
**Length:** 74 ft (22.57 m).
**Width:** 9 ft (2.74 m).
**Maximum Speed:** 70 / 90 mph.

**Note:** This vehicle was formerly BR TRFK E40513, later rebuilt as an executive saloon. It was originally built for use within HST sets. After several years out of use it was purchased by IE and rebuilt by Interfleet Technology. This vehicle can operate as hauled stock at 90 mph or in push/pull mode at 70 mph in conjunction with vehicles 6101-6105 and 6301-6319 and modified 121 and 201 class locomotives.

6402

## BR/CIE/IE     STANDARD / §‡ FIRST / † COMPOSITE

**Built:** (7101-44) 1984-86 by BREL at Derby C & W Works, with minor finishing work completed by CIE at Inchicore Works, Dublin. (7145-7160) 1986-87 by CIE/IE at Inchicore Works, Dublin. All to BREL Mark 3 design & fitted with automatic plug-type doors.
**Seats:** 72S (§ 64F; † 36F/36S; ‡ 48F, 2+1 seating)    **Heating System:** Air Conditioning.
**Brakes:** Air.    **Bogies:** BT22.
**Weight:** 35 tons.    **Length:** 74 ft (22.57 m).
**Width:** 9 ft (2.74 m).    **Maximum Speed:** 100 mph.

| 7101 | 7114 | 7126 | 7138 | 7150 |
|------|------|------|------|------|
| 7102 | 7115 | 7127 | 7139 | 7151 |
| 7103 | 7116 | 7128 | 7140 | 7152 |
| 7104 ‡ | 7117 | 7129 | 7141 | 7153 |
| 7105 | 7118 | 7130 | 7142 | 7154 |
| 7106 | 7119 | 7131 | 7143 | 7155 |
| 7107 † | 7120 | 7132 | 7144 | 7156 ‡ |
| 7108 | 7121 | 7133 ‡ | 7145 | 7157 § |
| 7109 | 7122 | 7134 | 7146 | 7158 |
| 7110 | 7123 | 7135 | 7147 | 7159 |
| 7112 | 7124 | 7136 | 7148 | 7160 |
| 7113 | 7125 | 7137 | 7149 | |

7111 was destroyed by fire at Inchicore Works on 25.02.97 and scrapped there 06.98.

## CIE/IE     EXECUTIVE COACH

**Built:** 1987 by CIE/IE at Inchicore Works, Dublin, to BREL Mark 3 design & fitted with automatic plug type doors.
**Seats:** 64F, § loose chairs as required.    **Heating System:** Air Conditioning.
**Brakes:** Air.    **Bogies:** BT22.
**Weight:** 35 tons.    **Length:** 74 ft (22.57 m).
**Width:** 9 ft (2.74m).    **Maximum Speed:** 100 mph.
**Note:** § fitted with cocktail bar.

7161 §    7162

## CIE/IE     STANDARD

**Built:** 1987 by CIE/IE at Inchicore Works, Dublin, to BREL Mark 3 design & fitted with automatic plug type doors.
**Seats:** 72.    **Heating System:** Air Conditioning.
**Brakes:** Air.    **Bogies:** BT22.
**Weight:** 35 tons.    **Length:** 74 ft (22.57m).

**Width:** 9 ft (2.74m). **Maximum Speed:** 100 mph.

7163  7164

## CIE/IE   COMPOSITE

**Built:** 1987-88 by CIE/IE at Inchicore Works, Dublin, to BREL Mark 3 design & fitted with automatic plug type doors.
**Seats:** 36S/32F
**Brakes:** Air.
**Weight:** 35 tons.
**Width:** 9 ft (2.74 m).
**Heating System:** Air Conditioning.
**Bogies:** BT22.
**Length:** 74 ft (22.57 m).
**Maximum Speed:** 100 mph.

| 7165 | 7167 | 7169 | 7171 | 7172 |
| 7166 | 7168 | 7170 | | |

## BR/CIE/IE   RESTAURANT BUFFET STANDARD

**Built:** (7401-5) 1984-86 by BREL at Derby C & W Works, with minor finishing work by CIE at Inchicore Works, Dublin. (7406-13)1986-88 by CIE/IE at Inchicore Works, Dublin. All to BREL Mark 3 design & fitted with automatic plug-type doors.
**Seats:** 29 (*30).
**Brakes:** Air.
**Weight:** 37.2 tons.
**Width:** 9 ft (2.74 m).
**Heating System:** Air Conditioning.
**Bogies:** BT22B.
**Length:** 74 ft (22.57 m).
**Maximum Speed:** 100 mph.

| 7401 | 7404 | 7407 | 7410 | 7412 |
| 7402 | 7405 | 7408 | 7411 | 7413 * |
| 7403 | 7406 | 7409 | | |

## BR/CIE/IE   BRAKE GENERATOR VAN

**Built:** (7601-7) 1984-86 by BREL at Derby C & W Works, with minor finishing work by CIE at Inchicore Works, Dublin. (7608-15) 1986-88 by CIE/IE at Inchicore Works, Dublin. All to BREL Mark 3 design.
**Seats:** Nil.
**Brakes:** Air.
**Weight:** 35.8 tons.
**Width:** 9 ft (2.74 m).
**Heating System:** Electric through wired.
**Bogies:** BT22C.
**Length:** 74 ft (22.57 m).
**Maximum Speed:** 100 mph.
**Engines:** Two Detroit 8V-71N (Model No. 7083-7201) of 234 hp (174 kW) at 1575 rpm (* Two Cummins of 295 hp (220 kW).
**Alternators:** Two Newton Derby of 168 kW.
**Note:** All of these vehicles are currently in the process of being modified and fitted with the following equipment:
**Engine:** Cummins LTA 10G3.
**Alternator:** Newage Stamford HD4D of 202 kW at 1500 rpm.

| 7601 | 7604 | 7607 | 7610* | 7613* |
| 7602 | 7605 | 7608* | 7611* | 7614* |
| 7603 | 7606 | 7609* | 7612* | 7615* |

# TRACK MACHINES & ENGINEERS STOCK

The following vehicles are in use by the Civil Engineers Department or form part of the Operating Engineers' stock. Official information was not available for this section and information is thus based on observations.

| Fleet No. | Builder's Number | Builder & Year Built | Type | Function |
|---|---|---|---|---|
| 700 | 26 | Plasser & Theurer, 1974 | EM50 | Recording Car. |
| 703 | 586 | Plasser & Theurer, 1994 | USB4000 | Regulator. |
| 704 |  | Plasser & Theurer, 1994 | USB4000 | Regulator. |
| 705 |  | Plasser & Theurer, 19 | USP3000C | Regulator. |
| 706 | 215 | Plasser & Theurer, 1974 | USP3000C | Regulator. |
| 707 | 281 | Plasser & Theurer, 1976 | USP3000C | Regulator. |
| 708 | 329 | Plasser & Theurer, 1980 | SSP108 | Regulator. |
| 710 | 8918 | Wickham, 1962 | 40 Mk 11 | Inspection Car. |
| 711 | 8917 | Wickham, 1962 | 40 Mk 11 | Inspection Car. |
| 713 | 8916 | Wickham, 1962 | 40 Mk 11 | Inspection Car. |
| 714 | 8920 | Wickham, 1962 | 40 Mk 11 | Inspection Car. |
| 715 |  | ??, 1977 | ? | Tie Inserter. |
| 721 | 507/1 | Hugh Phillips, 1993 | - | Inspection Car. |
| 722 | 0214 | Matisa, 1994 | VM100ST | Inspection Car. |
| 723 | 0215 | Matisa, 1994 | VM100ST | Inspection Car. |
| 726 |  | Plasser & Theurer, 1969 | - | Hedge Cutter. |
| 728 | 1.140 | Plasser & Theurer, 1974 | - | Sandite. |
| 729 | 1.301 | Plasser & Theurer, 1976 | 07-16B | Tamper. |
| 730 | 1.377 | Plasser & Theurer, 1976 | 07-16B | Tamper. |
| 731 | 1.379 | Plasser & Theurer, 1976 | 07-16B | Tamper. |
| 732 | 1.380 | Plasser & Theurer, 1976 | 07-16B | Tamper. |
| 733 | 1.381 | Plasser & Theurer, 1976 | 07-16B | Tamper. |
| 734 | 1.772 | Plasser & Theurer, 1980 | 07-16G | Tamper. |
| 735 | 4980030 | Canron Rail, 1980 | B321 | Tamper. |
| 736 | 4980041 | Canron Rail, 1981 | B321 | Tamper. |
| 737 | 6190131 | Canron Rail, 1991 | E258-HPWL | Tamper. |
| 738 |  | Plasser & Theurer, 1992 | 08-16 | Tamper. |
| 739 |  | Plasser & Theurer, 1992 | 08-16 | Tamper. |
| 740 | 2.517 | Plasser & Theurer, 1991 | 09-16CAT-5/IR | Tamper. |
| 741 | 2.658 | Plasser & Theurer, 1994 | 09-16CAT | Tamper. |
| 742 | 2.894 | Plasser & Theurer, 1999 | 08-16/4x4C | Tamper. |
| 743 | 2.914 | Plasser & Theurer, 1999 | 08-16/4x4C | Tamper. |
| 750 | 506 | Plasser & Theurer, 1976 | 07-275DN | P&C Tamper. |
| 770 |  | Geismar, 1977 | PD350 | 2 x Relaying Gantries. |
| 772 | F77192/3 | Geismar, 1979 | PTH350 | 2 x Relaying Gantries. |
| 774 | F92370/1 | Geismar, 1979 | PTH350 | 2 x Relaying Gantries. |
| 780 | 164 | Plasser & Theurer, 1979 | RM76UHR | Ballast Cleaner. |
| 800 | 255895 | Fairmont, 1990 | RGH-8 | Rail Grinder. |

710 is currently stored at Enniscorthy Goods Store after sustaining collision damage.
721 is named "Jess".
726 was converted from a previous machine, identity unknown.
728 was converted from 07-16B Tamper

736 was originally a single cab machine, but had a second cab fitted during 1994.
741 is an 09 series Tamper, with a Dynamic Track Stabiliser mounted on a trailer.
770, 772 and 774 are pairs of single line Relaying Gantries and are conveyed to and from sites on flat wagons. Each is made up of two gantries and a spacer beam.
780 is jointly owned by Iarnród Éireann and Translink NI Railways.

## DEPARTMENTAL STOCK

The following former coaching stock vehicles are in use as Engineers' vehicles. As no official information was available for this section, the information is based on observations and therefore it is possible some omissions may have occurred.

| Fleet Number | Former Number | Function |
| --- | --- | --- |
| 628A | ? | Weedspray coach. |
| 638A | 2771 | Dormitory for weedspray coach. |
| 639A | ? | Dormitory coach. |
| 652A | ? | Overhead Line Maintenance pantograph coach. |
| 654A | Note 1 | Flat wagon. |
| 655A | Note 1 | Flat wagon. |
| 656A | Note 1 | Flat wagon. |
| 657A | Note 1 | Flat wagon. |
| 658A | Note 1 | Flat wagon. |
| 659A | ? | Overhead Line Maintenance flat wagon. |

Note 1: Five Park Royal coaches Nos. 1385, 1394, 1395, 1399 and 1407 were converted to flat wagons 654A-658A at Inchicore Works in November 1992. However the order of conversion is not known.

## SECTION 2 - TRANSLINK NI RAILWAYS STOCK LIST

### BRIEF HISTORY

Until nationalisation on 1st January 1948, railway services wholly in Northern Ireland were operated by two main constituent companies, The NCC and The B&CDR. The new nationalised concern was known as the UTA. In 1958 the lines of the previously independent GNR(B) in Northern Ireland were absorbed when this company was divided between the UTA and CIE. The railways of the UTA passed to NIR with effect from 1st April 1968 when the former concern was dissolved. In 1996, Ulster Bus and NIR were combined into one operating company, known as Translink. The railway division trades under the banner "Translink NI Railways". A handful of diesel shunting locomotives previously owned by the UTA, some of which survived into NIR ownership, are shown in Appendix 1.

### LOCOMOTIVE CLASSIFICATION

NIR diesel locomotives were originally identified by a two letter code by the operating department. This former classification system has now been discontinued. The former codes are shown in brackets in the class headings.

## 1996 RENUMBERING SCHEME

When Translink was formed in 1996, it was decided to re-number all railway vehicles by adding 8000 to the original number. For example, 80 class power car 81 became 8081, locomotive 102 became 8102 etc. At the time of writing very few vehicles remain to be re-numbered. Any stock not re-numbered at the time of writing (August 2004), or withdrawn/scrapped prior to re-numbering, is shown in the text by its original number. Track machines are soon to be re-numbered in the 7000 series.

# LOCOMOTIVES

## 1 CLASS (DH)                                                          0-6-0

**Built:** 1969 by English Electric at Vulcan Foundry, Newton Le Willows.
**Engine:** Dorman 12QTV of 620 hp (463 kW) at 1800 rpm.
**Transmission:** Hydraulic.
**Transmission Type:** EE Twin Disc DBSG138-2 Torque Converter coupled to a Wiseman 15RLGB Final Drive.
**Maximum Tractive Effort:** 25000 lbf (111 kN).
**Continuous Tractive Effort:**
**Power At Rail:**
**Weight:** 42.5 tons.
**Length Over Buffers:** 28 ft 4 in (8.64 m).
**Wheel Diameter:** 3 ft 6 in (1067 mm).
**Maximum Speed:** 29 mph.
**Works Numbers:** D1266-D1268 / EE3954-EE3956 in order.
**Note:** Original design speed was 42 mph in direct drive, but limited to third stage on torque converter (29 mph) soon after delivery.

| Loco No. | Date to Traffic | Date Stopped | Date Withdrawn | Preservation Location |
|---|---|---|---|---|
| 1 | 31.07.69 | . .86 | .05.89 | Carrick-On-Suir (P) |
| 2 | 27.09.69 | 09.09.89 | 09.09.89 | Carrick-On-Suir (P) |
| 3 | 04.10.69 | . .88 | .05.89 | Carrick-On-Suir (P) |

All three locomotives are preserved by the Irish Traction Group as static exhibits. The engines and transmissions from these locomotives were sold to a marine engine company for scrap prior to the sale of the bodyshells to the ITG.
No.2 was originally withdrawn in May 1989, but was specially reinstated and repainted for a farewell railtour on 10.09.89. However, the locomotive then suffered a major engine failure on 09.09.89 which resulted in its final withdrawal.

## 101 CLASS (DL)                                                        Bo-Bo

**Built:** 1970 by BREL at Doncaster, as sub-contractors for the Hunslet Engine Company, Leeds.
**Engine:** English Electric 8CSVT of 1350hp (1007 kW) at 850 rpm.
**Transmission:** Electric.
**Traction Motors:** English Electric 253AZ.
**Maximum Tractive Effort:** 42000 lbf (187 kN).
**Continuous Tractive Effort:** 25200 lbf (112 kN) at 15 mph.
**Power At Rail:**

**Weight:** 68 tons.
**Length Over Buffers:** 45 ft 2 in (13.77 m).
**Wheel Diameter:** 3 ft 4 in (1016 mm).
**Maximum Speed:** 80 mph.
**Multiple Working:** Within class only.
**Works Numbers:** Hunslet 7197-7199 in order.

| Loco No. | Date to Fittings | Date to Traffic | Former Name | Date Stopped | Month Cut up | Store/Cut up Location |
|---|---|---|---|---|---|---|
| 101 | OAER | 04.07.70 | EAGLE | 23.07.93 | - | RPSI Whitehead |
| 8102 | OAER | 04.07.70 | FALCON | 24.04.02 | - | RPSI Whitehead |
| 103 | OAER | 04.07.70 | MERLIN | 11.10.89 | 06.97 | Ballymena |

101 is stored at the RPSI's premises at Whitehead, minus engine and traction motors.
8102 was out of use from 09.12.98 to 24.02.02 but was then briefly reinstated for one day before being stored again.
8102 is expected to be put on long term loan to the Ulster Folk and Transport Museum at Cultra, but at the time of publication was in store at the RPSI's premises at Whitehead.

# 104 CLASS (MV)  Bo-Bo

**Built:** 1956-57 by Metropolitan Vickers at Dukinfield Works.
**Original Engine:** Crossley ESTV8 of 550 hp (410 kW).
**Rebuilt:** 1970-79 by CIE at Inchicore Works, Dublin.
**Replacement Engine:** General Motors 8-B645E of 1100 hp (821 kW) at 900 rpm.
**Transmission:** Electric.
**Traction Motors:** Metropolitan Vickers MV137CW.
**Maximum Tractive Effort:** 34440 lbf (153 kN).
**Continuous Tractive Effort:**
**Power At Rail:** 842 hp (629 kW).
**Weight:** 61.5 tons.
**Length Over Buffers:** 42 ft (12.80 m).
**Wheel Diameter:** 3 ft 2 in (965 mm).
**Maximum Speed:** 80 mph.
**Multiple Working:** Within class only (in NIR service only).
**Train Brake:** Vacuum.
**Train Heating:** Not fitted.
**Works Numbers:** 962, 964, 973, 974, 976, 980 in order. All works plates showed built 1956.
**Note:** For further details see CIE 201 (C) Class.

| Loco No. | Date to Fittings | Date to Traffic | Former CIE No. | Date Stopped | Date Withdrawn | Month Scrapped | Disposal Location |
|---|---|---|---|---|---|---|---|
| 104 | NR | 23.02.86 | 216 | .09.94 | .08.95 | 09.97 | Belfast Docks |
| 105 | NR | 27.04.91 | 218 | 06.11.93 | .08.95 | 09.97 | Belfast Docks |
| 106 | NR | 23.06.86 | 227 | 18.03.95 | .08.95 | - | Cahirciveen (P) |
| 107 | NR | 10.09.86 | 228 | .06.87 | .03.93 | 01.96 | Ballymena |
| 108 | NR | 03.12.87 | 230 | .12.94 | .08.95 | 09.97 | Belfast Docks |
| 109 | NR | 25.03.86 | 234 | .08.87 | 03.93 | 03.93 | York Road |

It was originally intended that 224 would become 105, but this loco was rejected by NIR upon delivery to York Road Works, Belfast as it had a bent frame. This locomotive was eventually scrapped at Ballymena 01.96.
CAWS fittings on locomotives 224/7/30/4 were removed by CIE before sale.
106 is preserved as a static exhibit at Cahirciveen Heritage Centre, Co Kerry, and is incorrectly numbered C202.
The bodyshells of 104, 105 and 108 were removed from Fortwilliam Sidings, Belfast, to Recycle Engineering, Belfast Docks, on 14.08.97.

# 111 CLASS (GM)                                                  Co-Co

**Built:** 1980-84 by General Motors, La Grange, Illinois, USA
**Engine:** General Motors 12-645E3B of 2475 hp (1845 kW) at 900 rpm.
**General Motors Designation:** JT22CW.
**Transmission:** Electric.
**Traction Motors:** General Motors D77B.
**Maximum Tractive Effort:** 55100 lbf (245 kN).
**Continuous Tractive Effort:** 46850 lbf (209 kN) at 15.1 mph.
**Power At Rail:** 1823 hp (1360 kW).
**Weight:** 99 tons.
**Length Over Buffers:** 57 ft (17.37 m).
**Wheel Diameter:** 3 ft 4 in (1016 mm).
**Maximum Speed:** 90 mph.
**Works Numbers:** 798072/1, 798072/2, 838084 in order.
**Multiple Working:** With any NIR / IE GM built locomotive (except 201 class). However, the use of this facility is now prohibited.

| Loco No. | Fittings | Date to Traffic | Name |
|---|---|---|---|
| 111 | SAMRE | 03.02.81 | GREAT NORTHERN |
| 112 | SAMRE | 03.02.81 | NORTHERN COUNTIES |
| 8113 | SAMR | 07.08.84 | BELFAST & Co DOWN |

The electric train supply equipment fitted to 111 and 112 is isolated.
At the time of writing No. 112 was on long term loan to Iarnród Éireann.
113 worked a passenger train on 12.07.84, but officially entered traffic on the date shown above.

# 201 CLASS                                                       Co-Co

**Built:** 1994 by General Motors Locomotive Group, London, Ontario, Canada.
**Engine:** General Motors 12-710G3B of 3200 hp (2388 kW) at 900 rpm.
**General Motors Designation:** JT42HCW.
**Transmission:** Electric.
**Traction Motors:** General Motors D43.
**Maximum Tractive Effort:**
**Continuous Tractive Effort:**
**Power At Rail:**
**Weight:** 112.0 tons.
**Length Over Buffers:** 68 ft 9 in (20.949 m).
**Wheel Diameter:** 3 ft 4 in (1016 mm).
**Maximum Speed:** 100 mph.

**Works Numbers:** 938435-1 & 938435-2
**Multiple Working:** Within class. However, the use of this facility is prohibited.
**Note:** Nameplates for 209 have been cast, but were never fitted.

| Loco No. | Fittings | Date to Traffic | Name |
|---|---|---|---|
| 8208 | SAMRH | 17.05.95 | RIVER LAGAN |
| 209 | SAMRH | 08.06.95 | *(RIVER FOYLE)* |

## DIESEL ELECTRIC MULTIPLE UNITS

# 3000 CLASS                                     3 CAR UNITS

**Built:** 2003-2004 by CAF S.A. Zaragoza, Spain.
**Engine:** MAN D2876 LUH of 294 kW at 2000 rpm (one per car).
**Auxiliary Engine:** Cummins 6B5.9GR of 54 kW at 1500 rpm (one per car).
**Transmission:** Hydraulic.
**Transmission Type:** Voith Hydrodynamic Turbo-Transmission T211.
**Seats:** 48 + 10 tip up, 1 disabled toilet, 2 wheelchair spaces (DM1), 78 (M), 58 + 6 tip up,1 toilet (DM2).
**Weight:** 48.97 tons (DM1), 45.10 (M), 48.80 (DM2).    **Length:** 23.74 m (DM1/2) or 23.14 m (M).
**Width:** 2.75 m.                                       **Maximum Speed:** 90 mph.
**Normal Formation:** DM1 + M + DM2 .

| Set Number | DM1 |   | M |   | DM2 | Date to traffic |
|---|---|---|---|---|---|---|
| 3001 | 3301 | + | 3501 | + | 3401 | |
| 3002 | 3302 | + | 3502 | + | 3402 | |
| 3003 | 3303 | + | 3503 | + | 3403 | |
| 3004 | 3304 | + | 3504 | + | 3404 | |
| 3005 | 3305 | + | 3505 | + | 3405 | |
| 3006 | 3306 | + | 3506 | + | 3406 | |
| 3007 | 3307 | + | 3507 | + | 3407 | |
| 3008 | 3308 | + | 3508 | + | 3408 | |
| 3009 | 3309 | + | 3509 | + | 3409 | |
| 3010 | 3310 | + | 3510 | + | 3410 | |
| 3011 | 3311 | + | 3511 | + | 3411 | |
| 3012 | 3312 | + | 3512 | + | 3412 | |
| 3013 | 3313 | + | 3513 | + | 3413 | |
| 3014 | 3314 | + | 3514 | + | 3414 | |
| 3015 | 3315 | + | 3515 | + | 3415 | |
| 3016 | 3316 | + | 3516 | + | 3416 | |
| 3017 | 3317 | + | 3517 | + | 3417 | |
| 3018 | 3318 | + | 3518 | + | 3418 | |
| 3019 | 3319 | + | 3519 | + | 3419 | |
| 3020 | 3320 | + | 3520 | + | 3420 | |
| 3021 | 3321 | + | 3521 | + | 3421 | |
| 3022 | 3322 | + | 3522 | + | 3422 | |
| 3023 | 3323 | + | 3523 | + | 3423 | |

Note: Vehicles are in the course of delivery at the time of publication (September 2004).
Sets 3001 - 3006 are fitted with CAWS equipment to work over Iarnród Éireann tracks.

# "80"80 CLASS                                    2 or 3 CAR UNITS

## DRIVING MOTOR BRAKE STANDARD
**Built:** 1974-78 BREL at Derby C & W Works.
**Engine:** English Electric 4SRKT turbo-charged of 560 hp (418 kW) at 850 rpm.
**Traction Motors:** Two EE 538 of 220 hp (164 kW) mounted on the power car bogie remote from the engine.
**Seats:** 42 (*45, +33)                          **Length:** 65 ft 8 in (20.02 m).
**Width:** 9 ft (2.74 m)                          **Weight:** 62 tons.
**Bogies:** B6.                                   **Maximum Speed:** 70 mph.

| Vehicle No. | Date to Traffic | Date Stopped | Month Withdrawn | Month Cut | Cut Up/Store Location |
|---|---|---|---|---|---|
| 67   | 22.12.77 | 04.06.02 | 06.02 |       | Adelaide Yard. |
| 8068 | 18.02.78 |          |       |       |                |
| 8069 | 24.01.78 |          |       |       |                |
| 8081 | 26.11.74 | 18.03.04 | 08.04 |       | Belfast York Road. |
| 8082 | 03.12.74 |          |       |       |                |
| 8083 | 07.01.75 |          |       |       |                |
| 8084 | 24.01.75 | 18.12.02 | 03.04 |       | Adelaide Yard. |
| 8085 | 12.02.75 |          |       |       |                |
| 8086 | 28.02.75 |          |       |       |                |
| 8087 | 25.03.75 | 28.11.03 | 08.04 |       | Belfast York Road. |
| 88 * | 14.04.75 | 25.03.83 | 03.83 | 10.88 | McConnell Metals, Belfast. |
| 8089 | 05.10.74 |          |       |       |                |
| 8090 | 03.02.78 |          |       |       |                |
| 8091 | 21.02.78 |          |       |       |                |
| 8092 | 27.02.78 | 20.02.04 |       |       | Belfast York Road. |
| 8093 | 14.04.78 |          |       |       |                |
| 8094 | 19.04.78 |          |       |       |                |
| 8095 | 14.04.78 | 04.11.00 | 11.00 | 12.01 | Belfast Docks. |
| 8096 + | 15.05.78 |        |       |       |                |
| 8097 | 16.06.78 |          |       |       |                |
| 8098 + | 05.07.78 |        |       |       |                |
| 8099 | 06.07.78 |          |       |       |                |

## Names
| | | | |
|---|---|---|---|
| 8081 | THE BOYS BRIGADE | 8097 | GLENSHESK |
| 8086 | GLENDUN          | 8098 | (GLENOE)  |
| 8094 | GLENARIFF        | 8099 | SIR MYLES HUMPHREYS |
| 8096 | GLENSHANE        |      |           |

67 was withdrawn following derailment damage at Downhill on 04.06.02.
8084 was withdrawn following fire damage on 18.12.02.
88 was withdrawn following a collision at Hilden on 25.03.83.
8095 was withdrawn following fire damage at Kellystown on 04.11.00.

## DRIVING TRAILER STANDARD
**Built:** 1974-78 by BREL at Derby C & W Works.
**Seats:** 81 (*80).
**Length:** 66 ft (20.12 m).
**Width:** 9 ft (2.74 m)
**Weight:** 28 tons.
**Bogies:** B4.
**Maximum Speed:** 70 mph.

| Vehicle No. | Date to Traffic | Date Stopped | Month Withdrawn | Month Cut | Cut Up / Store Location |
|---|---|---|---|---|---|
| 731 | 03.12.74 | 21.03.82 | 03.82 | ? | Magheramorne. |
| 8732 | 26.11.74 | 18.02.04 | 03.04 | | Adelaide Yard. |
| 8733 | 05.10.74 | | | | |
| 8734 | 28.02.75 | | | | |
| 8735 * | 07.01.75 | | | | |
| 8736 | 24.01.75 | 01.03.04 | | | Belfast York Road. |
| 737 | 12.02.75 | 06.07.97 | 07.97 | 10.97 | Fortwilliam. |
| 8738 | 14.04.75 | | | | |
| 8739 | 25.03.75 | .10.01 | 03.04 | | Adelaide Yard. |
| 8740 | 22.12.77 | 04.06.02 | 06.02 | 03.04 | Nutts Corner. |
| 741 | 03.02.78 | 19.09.79 | 09.79 | 06.80 | Magheramorne. |
| 8742 | 24.01.78 | | | | |
| 8743 | 18.02.78 | | | | |
| 8744 | 27.02.78 | | | | |
| 8745 | 21.02.78 | | | | |
| 746 | 14.04.78 | 30.05.90 | 05.90 | 10.93 | Belfast York Road. |
| 8747 | 14.04.78 | | | | |
| 748 | 19.04.78 | 15.05.79 | 05.79 | 06.80 | Magheramorne. |
| 8749 | 15.05.78 | | | | |
| 750 | 15.05.78 | 15.07.88 | 07.88 | 10.93 | Magheramorne. |
| 751 | 16.06.78 | 06.07.97 | 07.97 | 10.97 | Fortwilliam. |

731 was withdrawn following a fire bomb incident at Coleraine on 21.03.82.
737 and 751 were withdrawn following an arson attack at Bell's Row, Lurgan, on 06.07.97.
740 was withdrawn following derailment damage at Downhill on 04.06.02.
741 was withdrawn following a bomb incident at Balmoral on 19.09.79.
746 was withdrawn following a fire at Derriaghy on 30.05.90.
748 was withdrawn following a fire at Crumlin on 25.05.79.
750 was withdrawn following a fire at Coleraine on 15.07.88.

## DRIVING TRAILER STANDARD
**Built:** 1969-70 by BREL at Derby C & W Works to Mark 2C design.
**Seats:** 75.
**Length:** 66 ft (20.12 m).
**Width:** 9 ft (2.74 m).
**Weight:** 32.5 tons.
**Bogies:** B4.
**Maximum Speed:** 70 mph.
**Note:** These vehicles were originally BR TSO's 5516 & 5498 respectively.

| Vehicle No. | Date to Traffic | Date Stopped | Month Withdrawn | Month Cut | Cut Up / Store Location |
|---|---|---|---|---|---|
| 8752 | . .81 | | | | |
| 8753 | .05.84 | | | | |

### DRIVING TRAILER STANDARD
**Built:** 1969 by BREL at Derby C & W Works to Mark 2B design.
**Seats:** 75.
**Length:** 66 ft (20.12 m).
**Width:** 9 ft (2.74 m).
**Weight:** 32 tons.
**Bogies:** B4.
**Maximum Speed:** 70 mph.
**Note:** This vehicle was originally DBSO 811 and was a driving trailer brake standard, the brake area being converted to a seating area 03.01.

| Vehicle No. | Date to Traffic | Date Stopped | Month Withdrawn | Month Cut | Cut Up / Store Location |
|---|---|---|---|---|---|
| 8754 | .07.88 | | | | |

### DRIVING TRAILER BRAKE STANDARD
**Built:** 1969 by BREL at Derby C & W Works to Mark 2B design.
**Rebuilt:** Railcare Glasgow Works 1999.
**Seats:** 72 + 3 tip up.
**Length:** 66 ft (20.12 m).
**Width:** 9 ft (2.74 m).
**Weight:** 32 tons.
**Bogies:** B4.
**Maximum Speed:** 70 mph.
**Note:** 8755 was formerly coach 932, previously numbered 825.
8756 was formerly coach 933, previously numbered 929. This coach was originally BR TSO 5577, being purchased by NIR in 1981.

| Vehicle No. | Date to Traffic | Date Stopped | Month Withdrawn | Month Cut | Cut Up / Store Location |
|---|---|---|---|---|---|
| 8755 | 18.06.99 | | | | |
| 8756 | 06.07.99 | | | | |

### TRAILER STANDARD
**Built:** 1969-74 by BREL at Derby C & W Works. + **Rebuilt:** Railcare Glasgow Works 1999.
**Seats:** 87 (* 74, + 76).
**Length:** 66 ft (20.12 m)
**Width:** 9 ft (2.74 m).
**Weight:** 28 tons.
**Bogies:** B4.
**Maximum Speed:** 70 mph.
**Note:** 8774 was formerly BR Mark 2C TSO 5521.
8776, 778, 8779 & 8780 were formerly coaches 824, 826, 827 & 828 respectively.
8775 and 8777 were formerly hauled coaches 930 and 931. These two coaches were originally BR TSO's 5573 and 5531 respectively, being purchased by NIR in 1981.

| Vehicle No. | Date to Traffic | Date Stopped | Month Withdrawn | Month Cut | Cut Up / Store Location |
|---|---|---|---|---|---|
| 8761 | 26.11.74 | | | | |
| 8762 | 03.12.74 | | | | |
| 8763 | 05.10.74 | | | | |
| 8764 | 07.01.75 | 14.06.03 | 06.03 | | Belfast York Road. |
| 8765 | 18.07.77 | | | | |
| 8766 | 08.08.77 | | | | |
| 8767 | 01.08.77 | 04.06.02 | 06.02 | 03.04 | Nutts Corner. |
| 8768 | 24.01.78 | | | | |
| 8769 | 23.11.77 | | | | |
| 770 | 22.12.77 | 19.09.79 | 09.79 | 06.80 | Magheramorne. |
| 8771 | 11.11.77 | | | | |
| 772 | 18.02.78 | 06.07.97 | 07.97 | 10.97 | Fortwilliam. |
| 8773 | 21.02.78 | | | | |
| 8774 * | . .82 | | | | |
| 8775 + | 09.04.99 | | | | |
| 8776 * | 12.06.84 | | | | |
| 8777 + | 26.04.99 | | | | |
| 778 | 12.01.84 | 06.07.97 | 07.97 | 10.97 | Fortwilliam. |
| 8779 * | 11.07.84 | | | | |
| 8780 * | 23.03.84 | | | | |

767 was withdrawn following derailment damage at Downhill on 04.06.02.
770 was withdrawn following a bomb incident at Balmoral on 19.09.79.
772 was withdrawn following an arson attack at Bell's Row, Lurgan, on 06.07.97.
778 was withdrawn following an arson attack at Bell's Row, Lurgan, on 06.07.97.

## "8"450 CASTLE CLASS                                   3 CAR UNITS

**Note:** The power equipment used on these units was salvaged from the former 70 class units, and from 80 class vehicle 88.

Built on former BR Mark 1 carriage underframes: 3763, 3795, 3911, 4088, 4090, 4092, 4400, 4500, 4504, 4511, 4516, 4523, 4608, 4625, 4646, 4648, 4655, 4657, 4661, 4707, 4710, 4863, 4877, 4878, 4882, 4892 & 4897 (order of conversion unknown).

### DRIVING MOTOR BRAKE STANDARD
**Built:** 1985-87 by BREL at Derby C & W Works.
**Engine:** English Electric 4SRKT turbo-charged of 550hp (410 kW) at 850 rpm.
**Traction Motors:** Two EE 538 of 220 hp (164 kW) mounted on the power car bogie remote from the engine.
**Seats:** 38 (+ 13 tip-up).
**Length:** 65 ft 8 in (20.02 m).
**Width:** 9 ft (2.74 m).
**Weight:** 62 tons.
**Bogies:** BR Mk.6.
**Maximum Speed:** 70 mph.

| Vehicle No. | Date to Traffic |
|---|---|
| 8451 | 28.10.85 |
| 8452 + | 09.11.85 |
| 8453 | .12.85 |
| 8454 + | 06.03.86 |
| 8455 | .05.86 |
| 8456 + | .07.86 |
| 8457 + | .11.86 |
| 8458 + | 21.01.87 |
| 8459 | 05.06.87 |

**Names**

| | | | |
|---|---|---|---|
| 8451 | (BELFAST CASTLE) | | |
| 8452 | OLDERFLEET CASTLE | 8456 | GOSFORD CASTLE |
| 8453 | MOIRY CASTLE | 8457 | BANGOR CASTLE |
| 8454 | CARRICKFERGUS CASTLE | 8458 | ANTRIM CASTLE |
| 8455 | GALGORM CASTLE | 8459 | KILLYLEAGH CASTLE |

**DRIVING TRAILER STANDARD**
**Built:** 1985-87 by BREL at Derby C & W Works.
**Seats:** 68 ( + 15 tip-up).
**Length:** 65 ft 8 in (20.02 m).
**Width:** 9 ft (2.74 m).
**Weight:** 32.4 tons.
**Bogies:** B4.
**Maximum Speed:** 70mph.

| Vehicle No. | Date to Traffic |
|---|---|
| 8781 | 28.10.85 |
| 8782 + | 09.11.85 |
| 8783 | .12.85 |
| 8784 + | 06.03.86 |
| 8785 | .05.86 |
| 8786 + | .07.86 |
| 8787 + | .11.86 |
| 8788 + | 21.01.87 |
| 8789 | 05.06.87 |

**TRAILER STANDARD**
**Built:** 1985-87 by BREL at Derby C & W Works.
**Seats:** 78 ( + 15 tip-up).
**Length:** 66 ft (20.12 m).
**Width:** 9 ft (2.74 m ).
**Weight:** 30.4 tons.
**Bogies:** B4.
**Max Speed:** 70 mph.

| Vehicle No. | Date to Traffic |
|---|---|
| 8791 | 28.10.85 |
| 8792 + | 09.11.85 |
| 8793 | .12.85 |
| 8794 + | 06.03.86 |
| 8795 | .05.86 |
| 8796 + | .07.86 |
| 8797 + | .11.86 |
| 8798 + | 21.01.87 |
| 8799 | 05.06.87 |

# LEYLAND RAILBUS

**Built:** 1981 by BREL at Derby C & W Works.
**Engine:** Leyland 690 of 200 hp (149 kW).
**Transmission:** Mechanical. SOC type SE4 epicyclic gearbox and cardan shafts to SCG type RF28 final drive.
**Seats:** 52S. **Length:** 50 ft 2¼ in (15.30 m)
**Width:** 8 ft (2.44 m). **Weight:** 19.40 tons.
**Maximum Speed:** 75 mph.
**Note:** This manufacturers prototype was used as a demonstrator on British Rail before being sold to NIR and was formerly BR RDB977020.

| Allocated No. | Date to Traffic | Date Stopped | Store Location |
|---|---|---|---|
| RB3 | 08.08.82 | 17.12.92 | Downpatrick |

This vehicle was displayed at the Ulster Folk and Transport Museum, Cultra, arriving there on 21.09.93 and departing on 01.10.00. From 31.03.01 it has been on long term loan to the Downpatrick Steam Railway. Allocated number RB3, but this is not carried.

# COACHING STOCK

# NOTES ON COACHING STOCK

Until 1996, NIR coaching stock had been purchased from BREL either new or second hand since 1969 when a major coaching stock renewal programme was approved. This included the introduction of a locomotive hauled "Enterprise Express" train between Belfast and Dublin, powered by one of the three new locomotives built by BREL at Doncaster Works, as subcontractors for The Hunslet Engine Company, Leeds. An initial order of eight Mark 2 vehicles, followed later by a further order of five Mark 2 vehicles, was utilised for this service, all being bought new from BREL. In 1981, following the arrival of the 111 Class locomotives, a further order of twelve Mark 2 vehicles was made, all being second hand ex. British Rail Western Region. This has since been supplemented by the arrival of eight more Mark 2 vehicles, but some of the original order were subsequently converted to "80"80 class multiple unit vehicles. In 1996, fourteen new coaches from De-Dietrich, France, were delivered for use on the cross border "Enterprise" service with the new GM built 201 class locomotives (see next section). During 2001, eight former "Gatwick Express" coaches were acquired by Translink NI Railways to replace the remaining Mark 2 coaches, which had by then all been withdrawn.

## BREL                                      BRAKE GENERATOR VAN

**Built:** 1969 by BREL at Derby C & W Works to Mark 2B design. Converted to standard class generator van upon sale to NIR.
**Brakes:** Air.                                **Bogies:** B4/B5.
**Weight:** 36 tons.                            **Length:** 66 ft (20.12 m).
**Width:** 9 ft (2.74 m).                       **Maximum Speed:** 70 mph.
**Engine:** Detroit 8V-71 N TD2 (Model No. 7083-7005) of 234 hp (175 kW) at 1575 rpm.
**Alternator:** Markon B range, series 2.
**Note:** This vehicle was formerly BR BFK 14104, being purchased by NIR in 1981. It was converted to open plan seating in 1988. Seating was removed late 2001 and the vehicle converted to work with the former "Gatwick Express" coaches 8941-8948.

8911

## BREL                                                 STANDARD

**Built:** 1973-74 by BREL at Derby C & W Works to Mark 2F design.
**Rebuilt:** Railcare Glasgow Works 2001.       **Seats:** 56 (*52 + wheel chair space).
**Heating System:** Air conditioned.            **Brakes:** Air.
**Bogies:** B4.                                 **Weight:** 32 tons.
**Length:** 66 ft (20.12 m).                    **Width:** 9 ft (2.74 m).
**Maximum Speed:** 70 mph.
**Notes:** Former BR carriages, converted in 1983-84 for use on London Victoria to Gatwick Airport services and renumbered as class 488/3 EMU vehicles.

| | | | |
|---|---|---|---|
| 8941 * | (72634, 6089) | 8945 | (72626, 6017) |
| 8942 | (72637, 6098) | 8946 | (72627, 5974) |
| 8943 | (72605, 6082) | 8947 | (72646, 6078) |
| 8944 | (72609, 6080) | 8948 * | (72647, 6081) |

Vehicles are permanently coupled in pairs as follows:

8941 + 8942, 8943 + 8944, 8945 + 8948, 8946 + 8947.

## TRACK MACHINES AND ENGINEERS VEHICLES

The following vehicles are in use by the Civil Engineers Department. All are based in Belfast, and can be found anywhere on the Translink NI Railway's system.

| Fleet No. | Works No. | Builder & Year Built | Type | Function |
|---|---|---|---|---|
| HC1 | 323 | P&T, 1971 | AL203 | Hedge Cutter (oou) |
| 7005 | 1.345 | P&T, 1976 | MU07-16 | Tamper & Liner |
| 7007 | 1.452 | P&T,1978 | MU07-16 | Tamper & Liner (oou) |
| - | 315 | P&T,1978 | USP30000 | Ballast Regulator |
| (780) | 164 | P&T,1979 | RM76UHR | Ballast Cleaner |

| | | | | | |
|---|---|---|---|---|---|
| - | F83282 | Donelli,1983 | | | PD350 Relaying Gantry |
| - | 83018 | Donelli,1983 | | | Sleeper Space Beam |
| - | F83283 | Donelli,1983 | | | PD350 Relaying Gantry |
| - | 402783 | Donelli,1983 | PRD6 | | Sleeper Positioner & Rail Threader |
| - | 46 | P&T, 1986 | K355APT | | Rail Welder |
| - | 1165 | Donelli,1988 | | | Hopper Trailer |
| - | 558 | Donelli,1988 | VMT850GR | | Formation Repair Machine |
| - | 1166 | Donelli,1988 | | | Tipping Trailer |
| - | ? | Donelli, 2001 | | | Water Tank Trailer |
| 7008 | 2.673 | P&T,1994 | MU08-165P4 | | Tamper & Liner |
| 7009 | 3076/03 | P&T, 2003 | 08-16/4x4C80RT | | Tamper |
| 7010 | ? | P&T, 2003 | USP5000RT | | Ballast Regulator |

Notes: P&T = Plasser & Theurer.
7009 was formerly Network Rail registered as DR73926 (number still carried).
HC1 is a modified AL203 liner/consolidator, converted by NIR using equipment by Turner.
780 is jointly owned by NIR and IE. 780 is the allocated IE number.

## ROAD / RAIL VEHICLES

| Fleet Number | Works Number | Builder & Year Built | Road Type | Description | Registration Number |
|---|---|---|---|---|---|
| - | 132S20603 | Atlas, 1979 | 1302D | Road/Rail Excavator | TOI 882 |
| - | 132S22224 | Atlas, 1982 | 1302E | Road/Rail Excavator | YOI 8544 |
| - | 136S38697 | Atlas, 1992 | 1304K | Road/Rail Excavator | YXI 4404 |
| - | 136S38743 | Atlas, 1993 | 1304K | Road/Rail Excavator | YXI 4405 |
| KGT1 | | Giesmar, ? | | | ? |
| KGT2 | 4412 | Giesmar, 1998 | | | ? |

## SECTION 3 - JOINTLY OWNED CROSS BORDER STOCK

## COACHING STOCK

The following vehicles are jointly owned by IE (odd numbered vehicles) and Translink NI Railways (even numbered vehicles) to operate cross border services between Belfast and Dublin.

## DE-DIETRICH                                    DRIVING BRAKE FIRST

**Built:** 1996 by De-Dietrich, Reichshoffen, France.
**Seats:** 30F (2+1)                             **Heating System:** Air Conditioning.
**Brakes:** Air.                                 **Bogies:** De-Dietrich
**Weight:** 39.70 tonnes.                        **Length:** 23.00 m.
**Width:**                                       **Maximum Speed:** 100 mph.

9001            9002            9003            9004

## DE-DIETRICH — FIRST

**Built:** 1996 by De-Dietrich, Reichshoffen, France.
**Seats:** 47F (2+1)
**Brakes:** Air.
**Weight:** 37.74 tonnes.
**Width:**

**Heating System:** Air Conditioning.
**Bogies:** De-Dietrich
**Length:** 23.00 m.
**Maximum Speed:** 100 mph.

| 9101 | 9102 | 9103 | 9104 |
|---|---|---|---|

## DE-DIETRICH — STANDARD

**Built:** 1996 by De-Dietrich, Reichshoffen, France.
**Seats:** 71S (* 68 + wheelchair space)
**Brakes:** Air.
**Weight:** 37.54 tonnes.
**Width:**

**Heating System:** Air Conditioning.
**Bogies:** De-Dietrich
**Length:** 23.00 m.
**Maximum Speed:** 100 mph.

| 9201 | 9205 | 9208 | 9211 | 9214 * |
|---|---|---|---|---|
| 9202 | 9206 | 9209 | 9212 | 9215 * |
| 9203 | 9207 | 9210 | 9213 * | 9216 * |
| 9204 | | | | |

## DE-DIETRICH — RESTAURANT STANDARD

**Built:** 1996 by De-Dietrich, Reichshoffen, France.
**Seats:** 6 bar stools
**Brakes:** Air.
**Weight:** 38.00 tonnes.
**Width:**

**Heating System:** Air Conditioning.
**Bogies:** De-Dietrich
**Length:** 23.00 m.
**Maximum Speed:** 100 mph.

| 9401 | 9402 | 9403 | 9404 |
|---|---|---|---|

## SECTION 4 - "LUAS" DUBLIN TRAM SYSTEM

This section contains details of the new tram system presently under construction in and around the Dublin area. Two isolated sections have so far been built to the European standard gauge of 1435mm and electrified at 750V DC overhead. The Red Line (line A) runs from Tallaght to Dublin Connolly, whilst the Green Line (line B) runs from Sandyford to St. Stephen's Green. The Green Line for the most part runs on the alignment of the former Harcourt Street to Shanganagh Junction line. The Red Line is due to open on 28th September 2004. The Green Line opened on 30th June 2004.

The system has been built by the Railway Procurement Agency (see www.rpa.ie) and is operated by Connex. Alstom Ireland Ltd, who are responsible for maintenance of the tram vehicles at Sandyford Depot (Green Line) and Red Cow Depot (Red Line).

Red Line Stock

## 3000 CLASS                                         CITADIS 301 LRV

**Built:** 2002 by Alstom, La Rochelle, France.
**Brakes:**                                       **Seats:** 56 + 198 standing.
**Wheel Diameter:**                       **Weight:** 35.40 tons.
**Length:** 30.00 m                     **Width:** 2.40 m.
**Maximum Speed:** 70 km/h.
**Traction Motors:** Four of 140 kW.

| | | | | |
|---|---|---|---|---|
| 3001 | 3007 | 3012 | 3017 | 3022 |
| 3002 | 3008 | 3013 | 3018 | 3023 |
| 3003 | 3009 | 3014 | 3019 | 3024 |
| 3004 | 3010 | 3015 | 3020 | 3025 |
| 3005 | 3011 | 3016 | 3021 | 3026 |
| 3006 | | | | |

Green Line Stock

## 4000 CLASS                                    CITADIS TGA 401 LRV

**Built:** 2003 by Alstom, La Rochelle, France or Alstom, Barcelona (extension section).
**Brakes:**                                       **Seats:** 80 + 276 standing.
**Wheel Diameter:**                       **Weight:** 50.00 tons.
**Length:** 40.00 m.                    **Width:** 2.40 m.
**Maximum Speed:** 70 km/h.
**Traction Motors:** Four of 140 kW and two of 120 kW on centre section.

| | | | | |
|---|---|---|---|---|
| 4001 | 4004 | 4007 | 4010 | 4013 |
| 4002 | 4005 | 4008 | 4011 | 4014 |
| 4003 | 4006 | 4009 | 4012 | |

## UNILOK LOCOMOTIVES                             D124 TYPE

**Built:** 2003 by
**Engine:**
**Transmission:**
**Transmission Type:**
**Weight:**
**Length Over Buffers:**
**Maximum Speed:**
**Works Numbers:**

-    Sandyford Depot
-    Red Cow Depot

## Distance Tables

**Red Line**

| Location | Distance (km) |
|---|---|
| end of line | 0.00 |
| Tallaght | 0.10 |
| Hospital | 0.70 |
| Cookstown | 1.30 |
| Belgard | 2.40 |
| Kingswood | 3.30 |
| Red Cow | 5.50 |
| Kylemore | 7.30 |
| Bluebell | 8.00 |
| Blackhorse | 8.80 |
| Drimnagh | 9.40 |
| Goldenbridge | 9.80 |
| Suir Road | 10.20 |
| Rialto | 10.90 |
| Fatima | 11.30 |
| James's | 11.80 |
| Heuston | 12.40 |
| Museum | 12.90 |
| Smithfield | 13.50 |
| Four Courts | 13.80 |
| Jervis | 14.40 |
| O'Connell | 14.90 |
| Busarus | 15.40 |
| Connolly | 15.60 |

**Green Line**

| Location | Distance (km) |
|---|---|
| St Stephen's Green | 0.00 |
| Harcourt | 0.56 |
| Charlemont | 0.86 |
| Ranelagh | 1.36 |
| Beechwood | 1.98 |
| Cowper | 2.48 |
| Milltown | 3.22 |
| Windy Arbour | 4.13 |
| Dundrum | 5.26 |
| Balally | 6.22 |
| Kilmacud | 7.31 |
| Stillorgan | 8.32 |
| Sandyford | 8.74 |
| Depot Gates | 8.83 |
| end of line | 9.00 |

# SECTION 5 - DISTANCE TABLES & SIGNALBOX DETAILS

This section contains details of distances along all IE and Translink NI Railways routes used for both passenger and freight. Details of permanent speed restrictions, and their locations, are also given, as well as signalbox and method of operation. The information is arranged in tabular form as follows:

**Heading** - Gives details of the Method of Operation of the line. The following abbreviations are used:

| | |
|---|---|
| AB | Absolute Block (using Harper's Instruments). |
| EKT | Electric Key Token (Tyers). |
| ETS | Electric Train Staff (Railway Signal Co.). |
| ETT | Electric Train Tablet (Tyers). |
| TCB | Track Circuit Block. |

Sidings are generally operated by telephone.

**1st Column** - Place. Open passenger stations are shown in CAPITALS. Stations shown as ** are due to be re-opened.
Signalboxes and Interlockings are indicated by abbreviations after the name as follows:

BP               Block Post.
GB             Gate Box. Non-block post signalbox controlling an adjacent level crossing.
SF              Shunting Frame. Non-block post signalbox controlling sidings.
SI               Signal Interlocking. Relay or Solid State Interlocking controlled by a remote signalbox (Dublin Connolly in the case of IE).

An E prefix indicates a signalbox only open under emergency or irregular operating conditions. Details of signalboxes are also given (where known) in italic type. This takes the form (Design of Signal box/Year Built/No. of Levers). Details of GB and SF are only given where the cabins were previously "traditional style" block posts.

The following abbreviations are used concerning signalbox designs:

BNCR      Belfast & Northern Counties Railway.
DSER      Dublin & South Eastern Railway.
DWWR    Dublin, Wicklow & Wexford Railway.
GNR(I)      Great Northern Railway (Ireland).
GSR        Great Southern Railway.
GSWR     Great Southern & Western Railway.
MGWR    Midland Great Western Railway.
McK&H    McKenzie & Holland (Signalling contractors).
RSCo       Railway Signal Company (Signalling contractors).
S&F         Saxby & Farmer (Signalling contractors).
VDU        Indicates control by computer style keyboard, tracker ball and VDU screen(s).

**2nd Column -** Milepost distance shown in miles and chains.

**3rd Column -** Distance along the route from the station shown at the head of the table (shown in miles).

**4th Column -** Details of locations of permanent speed restrictions. U relates to the Up direction only and D relates to the down direction only. X denotes over crossover. Locations are given in relation to the milepost mileage's as shown in the 1st column. Where a distance is shown, for example as 78:50, this would indicate 78 miles and 50 chains.

**5th Column -** Cross references with other tables are given at stations and junctions where appropriate.

### NOTES
1. Signalling information is given as at 31st May 2004.
2. No information is given on open ground frames, or Translink NI Railways emergency crossover ground frames.
3. 201 class locomotives are restricted in operation over certain lines, and in their maximum permitted speed over other lines (or sections of line). Notes relating to these restrictions appear at the head of each table where applicable.

# INDEX TO TABLES

Table 1        Dublin Heuston to Cobh.
Table 2        Kyle Crossing to Milltown Crossing.
Table 3        Kildare to Waterford.
Table 3A     Lavistown North Junction to Lavistown South Junction.
Table 4        Limerick to Rosslare Harbour Pier.

| | |
|---|---|
| Table 5 | Keane's Points to Limerick Junction. |
| Table 6 | Ballybrophy to Limerick. |
| Table 7 | Mallow to Tralee. |
| Table 8 | Portarlington to Galway. |
| Table 9 | Dublin Connolly to Sligo. |
| Table 10 | Dublin Connolly to Liffey Junction. |
| Table 11 | Athlone to Westport. |
| Table 12 | Manulla Junction to Ballina. |
| Table 13 | Mullingar to Athlone Midland. |
| Table 14 | Dublin Connolly to Rosslare Harbour Pier. |
| Table 15 | Dublin Connolly to Bangor. |
| Table 16 | Howth Junction to Howth. |
| Table 17 | Lisburn to Antrim. |
| Table 18 | Coleraine to Portrush. |
| Table 19 | Belfast Great Victoria Street to Larne Harbour. |
| Table 19A | Central Junction to Belfast Great Victoria Street. |
| Table 20 | Belfast Yorkgate to Londonderry. |
| Table 21 | Limerick Check to Castlemungret. |
| Table 22 | Limerick to Athenry. |
| Table 23 | Glounthaune to Midleton. |
| Table 24 | Islandbridge Junction to Alexandra Road. |
| Table 25 | Athy to Tegral Sidings. |
| Table 26 | Portlaoise to Conniberry. |
| Table 27 | Sligo to Sligo Quay. |
| Table 28 | Drogheda to Tara Mines. |
| Table 29 | Church Road Junction to East Wall Junction. |
| Table 30 | Newcomen Junction to North Wall Midland Yard. |

# TABLE 1  DUBLIN HEUSTON - COBH

Double track throughout.
**Line Maximum Speed:** 100 mph Dublin Heuston to Cork.
50 mph Cork to Cobh 2600/2700 Class railcars, 40 mph all other traffic.
**Method of Operation:** TCB - Dublin Heuston to Limerick Junction North
Control Levers - Limerick Junction North to Limerick Junction South.
TCB - Limerick Junction South.
AB - Cork to Cobh.

| | | | | |
|---|---|---|---|---|
| DUBLIN HEUSTON | 0:00 | 0.00 | 20 | D 0-$^1/_2$ |
| | | | 10 | U $^1/_2$-0 |
| | | | 40 | D $^1/_2$-$^3/_4$ |
| Islandbridge Junction | 0:53 | 0.66 | | | Table 24 |
| Heuston SER (BP) | | | 60 | D $^3/_4$-1$^3/_4$ |
| (Interlocking building/2002/VDU) | | | 25 | U 1$^1/_4$-$^1/_2$ |
| Inchicore | 1:60 | 1.75 | 90 | D 1$^3/_4$-27$^1/_2$ |
| | | | 40 | U 1$^1/_2$-1$^1/_4$ |
| | | | 60 | U 3-1$^1/_2$ |
| CHERRY ORCHARD & PARKWEST | 3:09 | 3.12 | | |

62

| | | | | | |
|---|---|---|---|---|---|
| CLONDALKIN | 4:32 | 4.40 | | | |
| Lucan South | 6:33 | 6.34 | | | |
| HAZELHATCH & CELBRIDGE (SI) | 10:00 | 10.00 | | | |
| Straffan | 13:10 | 13.13 | | | |
| SALLINS & NAAS (SI) | 17:72 | 17.90 | | | |
| DROICHEAD NUA (SI) | 25:38 | 25.47 | | | |
| CURRAGH | 27:40 | 27.50 | 90 | U $27_{1/2}$-3 | |
| | | | 70 | $27_{1/2}$-29 | |
| KILDARE (SI) | 30:00 | 30.00 | 90 | 29-$32_{1/2}$ | |
| Cherryville Junction (SI) | 32:35 | 32.43 | | | Table 3 |
| MONASTEREVAN | 36:54 | 36.68 | 90 | D $40_{1/4}$-$40_{3/4}$ | |
| | | | 60 | D $40_{3/4}$-$41_{1/4}$ | |
| PORTARLINGTON (SI) | 41:50 | 41.63 | 30 | Through Station | |
| Portarlington Junction | 41:55 | 41.69 | 90 | D $41_{3/4}$-$42_{3/4}$ | Table 8 |
| | | | 60 | U $42_{3/4}$-$42_{1/4}$ | |
| | | | 90 | U $43_{1/4}$-$42_{3/4}$ | |
| | | | 90 | $50_{3/4}$-$66_{1/2}$ | |
| PORTLAOISE (SI) | 50:72 | 50.90 | | | Table 26 |
| Mountrath & Castletown | 59:40 | 59.50 | | | |
| BALLYBROPHY (SI) | 66:52 | 66.65 | 70 | Through Station | Table 6 |
| | | | 90 | D $66_{3/4}$-$72_{1/4}$ | |
| | | | 90 | U $72_{1/4}$-67 | |
| | | | 70 | $72_{1/4}$-$72_{3/4}$ | |
| Lisduff (SI) | 72:34 | 72.41 | 90 | $72_{3/4}$-$87_{1/4}$ | |
| TEMPLEMORE | 78:60 | 78.75 | | | |
| THURLES (SI) | 86:35 | 86.44 | | | |
| Thurles Sugar Factory (closed) | 87:20 | 87.25 | 70 | $87_{1/4}$-$87_{3/4}$ | |
| | | | 80 | $87_{3/4}$-$89_{3/4}$ | |
| | | | 90 | D $89_{3/4}$-$102_{1/2}$ | |
| Goold's Cross | 94:78 | 94.98 | | | |
| Dundrum | 99:30 | 99.38 | 90 | U $103_{3/4}$-$89_{3/4}$ | |
| | | | 80 | D $102_{1/2}$-$103_{3/4}$ | |
| | | | 90 | D $103_{3/4}$-106 | |
| | | | 80 | U 105-$103_{3/4}$ | |
| | | | 90 | U $106_{1/4}$-105 | |
| | | | 60 | D 106-$106_{1/4}$ | |
| Kyle Crossing | 106:23 | 106.29 | 40 | $106_{1/4}$-$106_{1/2}$ | Table 2 |
| Limerick Junction North (BP & SI) | | | | | |
| (CIE Rebuild/c.1967/54 + EC Panel) | | | | | |
| LIMERICK JUNCTION | 107:00 | 107.00 | 15 | Platform Roads | Table 5 |
| Limerick Junction South (BP) | | | 25 | Through Yard | |
| (GSWR/ ?/45) | | | 60 | D $107_{1/4}$-$108_{1/4}$ | |
| | | | 40 | U $107_{1/2}$-$107_{1/4}$ | |
| | | | 60 | U $108_{1/4}$-$107_{1/2}$ | |
| | | | 90 | $108_{1/4}$-110 | |
| | | | 80 | D 112:10-$113_{1/2}$ | |
| Emly | 113:40 | 113.50 | 80 | U $114_{3/4}$-$113_{1/2}$ | |
| Knocklong | 117:04 | 117.05 | | | |
| Killmallock | 124:09 | 124.11 | 80 | D 129-$131_{1/4}$ | |
| CHARLEVILLE | 129:16 | 129.20 | 80 | U $131_{1/4}$-129 | |

| | | | | | |
|---|---|---|---|---|---|
| | | | | 90 | D 131¼-138½ |
| | | | | 90 | U 133¼-131¼ |
| | | | | 85 | U 134¼-133¼ |
| Buttevant (GB) | | 137:16 | 137.20 | 80 | D 138½-140¾ |
| (CIE/1958/1) | | | | 90 | U 138½-134¼ |
| | | | | 90 | D 140¾-143¼ |
| | | | | 80 | U 140¼-138½ |
| | | | | 90 | D 143¼-144¾ |
| | | | | 90 | U 144-140¼ |
| MALLOW (EBP & SI) | | 144:37 | 144.46 | 80 | U 145¼-144 |
| (RSCo-GSWR/c.1889/EC Panel) | | | | 80 | D 144¾-147 |
| Killarney Junction | | 145:18 | 145.23 | 40 | Through Junction Table 7 |
| | | | | 90 | D 147-150¾ |
| Mourne Abbey | | 148:18 | 148.23 | 90 | U 150¾-145¼ |
| | | | | 70 | D 150¾-154 |
| | | | | 70 | U 153¾-150¾ |
| | | | | 90 | D 154-161½ |
| Rathduff | | 154:24 | 154.30 | | |
| BLARNEY ** | | 159:28 | 159.35 | 65 | D 161½-162 |
| Rathpeacon (SI) | | 161:31 | 161.39 | 60 | D 162-163½ |
| | | | | 90 | U 162-153¾ |
| KILBARRY ** | | 163:16 | 163.20 | 50 | D 163½-164¼ |
| | | | | 70 | U 164¼-162 |
| | | | | 30 | 164¼-165:20 |
| CORK (BP) | | 165:20 | 165.25 | 15 | Through Station |
| (GSWR Hip Roof/c.1932/38 + Panel) | | | | 30 | U 166-165¾ |
| Tivoli | | 166:45 | 166.56 | | |
| DUNKETTLE ** | | 168:14 | 168.18 | | |
| LITTLE ISLAND (BP) | | 169:60 | 169.75 | | |
| (GSWR Hip Roof/c.1924/3 + Panel) | | | | | |
| GLOUNTHAUNE (BP) | | 171:04 | 171.06 | | |
| (in station buildings/c.1931/20) | | | | | |
| Cobh Junction | | 171:07 | 171.10 | 25 | 172-172¼ Table 23 |
| | | | | 10 | 172-172¼ (201 class) |
| FOTA | | 172:41 | 172.51 | 25 | 172:50-172¾ |
| | | | | 10 | 172:50-172¾ (201 class) |
| CARRIGALOE | | 174:25 | 174.31 | | |
| RUSHBROOKE | | 175:57 | 175.71 | 30 | D 176¼-176½ |
| COBH (BP) | | 176:61 | 176.77 | 15 | D Approaching Station |
| (CIE/1959/30 + Panel) | | | | | |

# TABLE 2 KYLE CROSSING - MILLTOWN CROSSING

Single line Kyle Crossing to Milltown Crossing.
**Line Maximum Speed:** 20 mph Kyle Crossing to Milltown Crossing
**Method of Operation:** TCB - Kyle Crossing to Milltown Crossing.

| | | | | | |
|---|---|---|---|---|---|
| Kyle Crossing | 106:23 | 0.00 | 20 | Through Curve | Table 1 |
| Milltown Crossing | 106:70 | 0.59 | | | |
| (Mileage from Limerick) | 21:33 | 0.59 | | | Table 4 |

# TABLE 3 KILDARE - WATERFORD

Single line Cherryville Junction to Waterford West.
**Line Maximum Speed:** 90 mph Kildare to Cherryville Junction.
80 mph Cherryville Junction to Waterford.
**Method of Operation:** TCB - Kildare to Waterford West (axle counters Cherryville Junction to Lavistown North Junction and Lavistown South Junction to Waterford West).
AB - Waterford West to Waterford.

| | | | | | |
|---|---|---|---|---|---|
| KILDARE (SI) | 30:00 | 0.00 | | | |
| Cherryville Junction (SI) | 32:36 | 2.44 | 20 | Through Junction | Table 1 |
| | | | 35 | U 33-32$_{1/2}$ | |
| | | | 55 | U 34-33 | |
| | | | 55 | D 32$_{1/2}$-34 | |
| Kildadangan | 36:46 | 6.58 | | | |
| Kilberry | 40:70 | 10.88 | 60 | D 43$^{3/4}$-44$^{1/4}$ | |
| | | | 40 | D 44$^{1/4}$-44$^{3/4}$ | |
| ATHY | 44:64 | 14.80 | 25 | Through Station | Table 25 |
| | | | 40 | U 45$_{1/2}$-45 | |
| | | | 60 | U 46-45$_{1/2}$ | |
| Mageney | 51:00 | 21.00 | 60 | D 54:50-55:10 | |
| | | | 40 | D 55:10-55:50 | |
| CARLOW | 55:68 | 25.85 | 20 | Through Station | |
| | | | 30 | U 56$_{1/2}$-56 | |
| | | | 50 | U 57-56$_{1/2}$ | |
| | | | 70 | 57-58$_{1/2}$ | |
| Milford | 60:09 | 30.11 | 75 | U 65$^{3/4}$-65$^{1/4}$ | |
| | | | 55 | D 65$^{1/4}$-65$^{3/4}$ | |
| MUINE BHEAG | 66:00 | 36.00 | 30 | Through Station | |
| | | | 55 | U 66$^{3/4}$-66$^{1/4}$ | |
| | | | 70 | D 68$^{3/4}$-69:10 | |
| | | | 70 | U 69$^{1/4}$-69 | |
| | | | 70 | D 73-74$^{1/4}$ | |
| Gowran | 74:18 | 44.23 | 70 | U 74$_{1/2}$-73$^{1/4}$ | |
| | | | 70 | D 77$_{1/2}$-78:30 | |
| Lavistown North Junction | 77:73 | 47.91 | 50 | 78:30-78:50 | Table 3A |
| | | | 70 | U 78:30-77:50 | |
| Lavistown West Junction | 78:38 | 48.48 | 70 | U 79-78:50 | |

| | | | | | |
|---|---|---|---|---|---|
| | | | 55 | D 79$^{3}$/$_{4}$-80:10 | |
| | | | 30 | D 80:10-80$^{3}$/$_{4}$ | |
| KILKENNY | 80:66 | 50.83 | 10 | D 80$^{3}$/$_{4}$-80:70 | |
| (Mileage from Portlaoise) | 28:26 | 50.83 | 10 | U 28$^{1}$/$_{2}$-28$^{1}$/$_{4}$ | |
| | | | 30 | U 29-28$^{1}$/$_{2}$ | |
| | | | 55 | U 29$^{1}$/$_{2}$-29 | |
| | | | 70 | D 30$^{1}$/$_{4}$-30$^{1}$/$_{2}$ | |
| Lavistown West Junction | 30:58 | 53.14 | 50 | 30$^{1}$/$_{2}$-30$^{3}$/$_{4}$ | |
| | | | 70 | 30$^{3}$/$_{4}$-31 | |
| Lavistown South Junction | 31:09 | 53.53 | 70 | D 32$^{3}$/$_{4}$-33$^{3}$/$_{4}$ | Table 3A |
| | | | 70 | U 34-32:70 | |
| Bennetsbridge | 34:25 | 56.81 | 60 | D 38$^{1}$/$_{2}$-38$^{3}$/$_{4}$ | |
| THOMASTOWN | 39:03 | 61.54 | 40 | Through Station | |
| | | | 50 | 39-39:30 | |
| | | | 70 | 39:30-40$^{3}$/$_{4}$ | |
| | | | 65 | 40$^{3}$/$_{4}$-41$^{1}$/$_{2}$ | |
| | | | 70 | 41$^{1}$/$_{2}$-44$^{3}$/$_{4}$ | |
| Ballyhale loop | 43:37 | 65.96 | 70 | 47$^{1}$/$_{4}$-54 | |
| Mullinavat | 51:49 | 74.11 | 40 | D 54-54:10 | |
| | | | 60 | U 54:10-54 | |
| | | | 70 | D 54:10-55 | |
| Kilmacow | 54:51 | 77.14 | 70 | U 54:70-54:10 | |
| | | | 50 | D 55-55:10 | |
| | | | 40 | U 55-54:70 | |
| | | | 70 | D 55:10-57 | |
| | | | 70 | U 56-55 | |
| | | | 60 | U 56:10-56 | |
| | | | 70 | U 57-56:10 | |
| Waterford West (BP) | 58:37 | 80.96 | 45 | 57-58 | |
| | | | 30 | 58-58$^{1}$/$_{2}$ | |
| (Mileage from Mallow) | 75:05 | 80.96 | 20 | 75-75:50 | Table 4 |
| (GSWR Hip Roof/1923/48) | | | | | |
| WATERFORD (Central BP) | 75:56 | 81.59 | | | |
| (GSWR Hip Roof/1923/64) | | | | | |

# TABLE 3A LAVISTOWN NORTH JUNCTION TO LAVISTOWN SOUTH JUNCTION

Single line throughout.
**Line Maximum Speed:** 25 mph Lavistown North Junction to Lavistown South Junction.
**Method of Operation:** TCB - Lavistown North Junction to Lavistown South Junction.

| | | | | | |
|---|---|---|---|---|---|
| Lavistown North Junction | 77:73 | 0.00 | 25 | Through Curve | Table 3 |
| Mileage change | 0:00 | 0.00 | | | |
| Lavistown South Junction | 0:49 | 0.62 | | | |
| Mileage from Portlaoise | 31:09 | 0.62 | | | Table 3 |

# TABLE 4  LIMERICK - ROSSLARE HARBOUR PIER

Single line Killonan Junction to Waterford West Junction and Waterford station to Rosslare.
**Line Maximum Speed:** 60 mph Limerick to Killonan Junction.
70 mph Killonan Junction to Keane's Points.
40 mph Keane's Points to Waterford West.
20 mph Waterford West to Abbey Junction.
40 mph Abbey Junction to Rosslare Strand.
70 mph Rosslare Strand to Rosslare Harbour.
**Method of Operation:** TCB - Limerick to Limerick Junction North.
ETS - Limerick Junction North to Waterford West.
AB - Waterford West to Waterford Central.
ETS - Waterford Central to Ballygeary.
201 class only permitted in an emergency (no reduction in speed), Keane's Points to Waterford West. Only in an emergency on passenger trains between Waterford and Rosslare. May operate normally between Waterford and Wellingtonbridge on freight trains, but at a maximum of 30 mph.

| | | | | | |
|---|---|---|---|---|---|
| LIMERICK (BP) | 0:00 | 0.00 | 15 | 0-$^{3}/_{4}$ | |
| (CIE Rebuild/1974/Panel) | | | 25 | U 1-$^{3}/_{4}$ | |
| Limerick Check (BP) | 0:49 | 0.56 | | | Table 21 |
| (GSWR Gable Roof/1910/50) | | | | | |
| Ennis Junction | 0:70 | 0.85 | | | Table 22 |
| Killonan Junction (BP) | 4:18 | 4.23 | 40 | Through Junction | Table 6 |
| (RSCo/ ?/3 + Panel) | | | | | |
| Boher | 7:50 | 7.63 | | | |
| Dromkeen | 11:46 | 11.58 | | | |
| Pallas | 13:76 | 13.95 | | | |
| Oola | 18:35 | 18.88 | | | |
| Milltown Crossing | 21:33 | 21.41 | | | Table 2 |
| Keane's Points | 21:56 | 21.70 | | | Table 5 |
| TIPPERARY (BP) | 24:63 | 24.79 | | | |
| (RSCo/1892/21) | | | | | |
| Bansha | 29:49 | 29.61 | | | |
| CAHIR | 38:26 | 38.33 | | | |
| CLONMEL (BP) | 49:20 | 49.25 | | | |
| (GSWR Hip Roof/c.1923/34) | | | | | |
| Kilsheelan (GB) | 55:25 | 55.31 | | | |
| (GSWR Hip Roof/c.1923/7) | | | | | |
| CARRICK-ON-SUIR (BP) | 63:06 | 63.08 | | | |
| (GSWR Hip Roof/c.1924/15) | | | | | |
| Fiddown and Portlaw | 67:28 | 67.35 | | | |
| Grange (GB) | 70:03 | 70.04 | 35 | 71$^{1}/_{2}$-72$^{1}/_{2}$ | |
| (GSWR Hip Roof/c.1923/3) | | | | | |
| Dunkitt | 75:44 | 75.55 | 30 | Over Viaduct | |
| Waterford West (BP) | 76:50 | 76.63 | | | |
| (Mileage from Mallow) | 75:05 | 76.63 | | | Table 3 |
| (GSWR Hip Roof/1923/48) | | | | | |
| WATERFORD (Central BP) | 75:56 | 77.27 | 20 | 75$^{3}/_{4}$-76$^{1}/_{4}$ | |

| | | | | | |
|---|---|---|---|---|---|
| (GSWR Hip Roof/1923/64) | | | | | |
| Abbey Junction (GB) | 76:20 | 77.82 | 10 | Through Junction | |
| (GSWR Hip Roof/1923/6) | | | | | |
| Belview | 79:58 | 81.30 | 20 | D 80:70-81:30 | |
| Barrow Bridge | 81:40 | 83.07 | 5 | Over Barrow Bridge | |
| (Bridge Control Box) | | | 20 | U $82_{1/2}$-82 | |
| (Overhead/1906/9) | | | | | |
| CAMPILE | 84:48 | 86.17 | 35 | D $87$-$87_{1/4}$ | |
| BALLYCULLANE | 89:20 | 90.82 | | | |
| WELLINGTONBRIDGE (BP) | 93:27 | 94.91 | 35 | D $94_{3/4}$-95 | |
| (GSWR Hip Roof/1923/20) | | | 30 | $95_{1/4}$-$97_{1/4}$ | |
| Duncormick | 98:02 | 99.59 | | | |
| BRIDGETOWN | 103:16 | 104.76 | 30 | $104_{1/4}$-$105_{1/2}$ | |
| Killinick | 107:54 | 109.24 | | | |
| ROSSLARE STRAND (BP) | 110:66 | 112.39 | 65 | Through Station | Table 14 |
| (RSCo-GSWR/1910/26) | | | 65 | $110_{3/4}$-$111_{1/4}$ | |
| | | | 60 | $112_{3/4}$-113 | |
| | | | 40 | 113-$113_{3/4}$ | |
| Kilrane | 113:04 | 114.61 | 15 | $113_{3/4}$-114 | |
| ROSSLARE EUROPORT | 113:76 | 115.51 | 5 | 114-$114_{1/4}$ | |
| (Ballygeary BP) | | | | | |
| (Container/1997/Outside GF/6) | | | | | |
| Rosslare Harbour Pier | 114:20 | 115.81 | | | |

# TABLE 5  KEANE'S POINTS - LIMERICK JUNCTION

Single line throughout.
**Line Maximum Speed:**   20 mph Keane's Points to Limerick Junction.
**Method of Operation:**   TCB - Keane's Points to Limerick Junction.

| | | | | |
|---|---|---|---|---|
| Keane's Points | 21:56 | 0.00 | 20 Through Curve | Table 4 |
| LIMERICK JUNCTION | 22:09 | 0.21 | | |
| (Mileage from Dublin Heuston) | 107:00 | 0.21 | | Table 1 |

# TABLE 6  BALLYBROPHY - LIMERICK

Single line Ballybrophy to Killonan Junction.
**Line Maximum Speed:**   40 mph Ballybrophy to Killonan Junction.
                          60 mph Killonan Junction to Limerick.
**Method of Operation:**  ETS - Ballybrophy to Killonan Junction.
                          TCB - Killonan Junction to Limerick.
201 class only permitted in an emergency (no reduction in speed).

| | | | | |
|---|---|---|---|---|
| BALLYBROPHY (SI) | 66:52 | 0.00 | | Table 1 |
| (Mileage Change) | 0:00 | 0.00 | | |
| ROSCREA (BP) | 10:04 | 10.05 | | |
| (RSCo-GSWR/ ?/24) | | | | |
| CLOUGHJORDAN | 20:00 | 20.00 | | |
| NENAGH (SF) | 29:33 | 29.41 | | |

(GSWR Hip Roof/c.1923/3)
Silvermines Junction              35:19     35.24
Shallee                           36:02     36.03
BIRDHILL (BP)                     42:36     42.45     25     46-52³/₄
(GSWR Hip Roof/c.1923/24 + Panel)
CASTLECONNELL                     47:05     47.06
Lisnagry                          48:58     48.73
Annecotty                         50:44     50.55
Killonan Junction (BP)            52:46     52.58     40     Through Junction
(Mileage from Limerick)           4:18      52.58                                   Table 4
(RSCo/ ?/3 + Panel)
Ennis Junction                    0:70      55.96     25     U 1-³/₄                Table 22
Limerick Check (BP)               0:49      56.25     15     ¹/₄-0                  Table 21
(GSWR Gable Roof/1910/50)
LIMERICK (BP)                     0:00      56.81
(CIE Rebuild/1974/Panel)

# TABLE 7  MALLOW - TRALEE

Single line Killarney Junction to Tralee.
**Line Maximum Speed:**    70 mph.
**Method of Operation:**   TCB - Mallow to Banteer (axle counters from Beet Factory to Banteer).
                           ETS - Banteer to Tralee.

MALLOW (EBP & SI)                 144:37    0.00
(RSCo-GSWR/c.1889/EC Panel)
Killarney Junction                145:18    0.76      40     Through Junction       Table 1
(Mileage Change)                  0:00      0.76      60     ¹/₂-3¹/₄
Beet Factory Siding               1:24      2.06
Lombardstown                      5:50      6.26      45     D 10¹/₄-10¹/₂
BANTEER (BP)                      10:54     11.67     25     D Through Station
(GSWR Hip Roof/c.1923/30)                             45     U 11¹/₂-11
Rathcool                          14:60     15.70     45     D 18¹/₄-18¹/₂
MILLSTREET (BP)                   19:00     19.76     25     Through Station
(GSWR Hip/1920's/18)                                  40     U 19¹/₂-19¹/₄
                                                      60     U 19³/₄-19¹/₂
                                                      60     D 19¹/₄-19³/₄
                                                      45     D 25-25¹/₄
RATHMORE (BP)                     25:37     26.23     25     Through Station
(CIE/ ?/24)                                           45     U 25³/₄-25¹/₂
                                                      60     29-38
Headford Junction                 32:52     33.60     50     38-39:10
                                                      30     39:10-39:30
Killarney Check / Tralee Junction 39:55     40.31     15     Through Junction
KILLARNEY (BP)                    39:69     40.62     15     Approaching Station
(S&F/1880's/36)                                       25     U 40-39³/₄
                                                      40     D 39³/₄-40¹/₄
                                                      40     U 40-40¹/₄
                                                      60     40-47¹/₄
Ballybrack                        46:56     47.65     50     47¹/₄-50¹/₄

| FARRANFORE (BP) | 50:44 | 51.31 | 25 | Through Station |
| (RSCo/1885/36) | | | 40 | U 51-50$^{3/4}$ |
| | | | 60 | D 50$^{3/4}$-60$^{3/4}$ |
| Gortatlea | 54:28 | 55.11 | 60 | U 60$^{3/4}$-51 |
| | | | 40 | D 60$^{3/4}$-61 |
| | | | 25 | D 61-61$^{1/4}$ |
| TRALEE (BP) | 61:45 | 62.33 | 15 | Approaching Station. |
| (GSR/1935/50) | | | | |

## TABLE 8  PORTARLINGTON - GALWAY

Single line Portarlington Junction to Galway.
**Line Maximum Speed:** 80 mph.
**Method of Operation:** TCB - Portarlington to Galway (axle counters Ballinasloe to Galway).

| PORTARLINGTON (SI) | 41:50 | 0.00 | 30 | Through Station | |
| Portarlington Junction | 41:55 | 0.06 | 10 | Through Junction | Table 1 |
| | | | 30 | 41$^{3/4}$-42 | |
| | | | 50 | U 42-42$^{1/2}$ | |
| Bord na Móna Bridge | 45:50 | 4.00 | | | |
| Geashill (SI) | 50:24 | 8.67 | 70 | Through Station | |
| | | | 60 | D 57$^{1/4}$-57$^{1/2}$ | |
| TULLAMORE (SI) | 57:71 | 16.26 | 40 | Through Station | |
| | | | 70 | 58-58:30 | |
| CLARA (SI) | 64:64 | 23.15 | 40 | Through Station | |
| Ballycumber | 68:18 | 26.58 | 70 | 70:50-71$^{1/2}$ | |
| Clonydonnin (SI - EBP) | 72:64 | 31.17 | 50 | D 80-80$^{1/2}$ | |
| (CIE/1974/EC Panel) | | | | | |
| ATHLONE | 80:37 | 38.83 | 20 | Through Station | |
| Athlone East Junction | 80:64 | 39.30 | | | Tables 11,13 |
| (Mileage from Broadstone) | 77:65 | 39.30 | 20 | Over Shannon Bridge | |
| Athlone Midland (SI) | 78:05 | 39.55 | | | |
| Athlone West Junction | 78:24 | 39.78 | 35 | U 78$^{1/2}$-78$^{1/4}$ | Table 11 |
| | | | 50 | U 78$^{3/4}$-78$^{1/2}$ | |
| Carrowduff | 84:67 | 46.32 | 70 | 84:30-85$^{3/4}$ | |
| | | | 50 | D 91-91$^{1/4}$ | |
| | | | 30 | 91$^{1/4}$-91$^{1/2}$ | |
| BALLINASLOE | 91:53 | 53.15 | 70 | D Through Station | |
| | | | 50 | U Through Station | |
| | | | 40 | Through Loop | |
| WOODLAWN | 101:38 | 62.95 | 70 | Through Station | |
| | | | 40 | Through Loop | |
| ATTYMON | 107:15 | 68.67 | | | |
| ATHENRY | 113:41 | 74.99 | 40 | Through Loop | Table 22 |
| | | | 70 | 119:30-125$^{1/2}$ | |
| ORANMORE ** | 121:32 | 82.89 | 50 | 125$^{1/2}$-126 | |
| | | | 30 | U 126$^{1/2}$-126 | |
| | | | 30 | D 126-126$^{1/4}$ | |
| GALWAY | 126:53 | 88.14 | 15 | D Approaching Station | |

# TABLE 9  DUBLIN CONNOLLY - SLIGO

Double line Dublin Connolly to Maynooth. Single line Maynooth to Sligo.
**Line Maximum Speed:**   70 mph. Dublin Connolly to Maynooth.
                          75 mph Maynooth to Sligo.
**Method of Operation:**  TCB - Dublin Connolly to Maynooth.
                          ETS - Maynooth to Sligo.
201 class may operate normally between Dublin Connolly and Longford, but only are permitted in an emergency between Longford and Sligo (no reduction in speed).

| | | | | | |
|---|---|---|---|---|---|
| DUBLIN CONNOLLY (BP) | 0:00 | 0.00 | 20 | 0-0:44 | Tables 10,14,15 |
| (CIE/1976/VDU) | | | | | |
| Ossary Road Junction | 0:24 | 0.30 | | | |
| North Strand Junction | 0:44 | 0.55 | | | |
| (Mileage from Islandbridge Junction) | 4:18 | 0.55 | | | Table 24 |
| DRUMCONDRA | 3:24 | 1.47 | | | |
| Glasnevin | 3:00 | 2.40 | | | |
| Glasnevin Junction | 2:55 | 2.09 | | | Table 24 |
| (Mileage from Liffey Junction) | 0:58 | 2.09 | | | Table 10 |
| Liffey Junction | 0:00 | 2.81 | 30 | Through Junction | |
| (Mileage from Broadstone) | 1:33 | 2.81 | | | |
| BROOMBRIDGE | 1:53 | 3.06 | | | |
| Reilly's Crossing (GB) | 2:00 | 3.40 | | | |
| (Container/1991/Switches) | | | | | |
| ASHTOWN | 3:08 | 4.50 | 60 | $3-3^{3}/_{4}$ | |
| Blanchardstown | 4:43 | 5.94 | 60 | $4^{1}/_{4}-4^{1}/_{2}$ | |
| CASTLEKNOCK | 4:60 | 6.15 | | | |
| COOLMINE | 5:60 | 7.15 | 60 | $5^{1}/_{4}-6$ | |
| CLONSILLA (GB) | 7:08 | 8.50 | 60 | $7^{1}/_{4}-7^{3}/_{4}$ | |
| (MGWR/c.1924/32) | | | | | |
| Lucan (North) | 8:72 | 10.03 | 50 | $8^{3}/_{4}-9^{1}/_{4}$ | |
| LEIXLIP CONFEY | 10:00 | 11.40 | 60 | 10-10:50 | |
| | | | 50 | 10:50-11:10 | |
| LEIXLIP LOUISA BRIDGE | 11:20 | 12.15 | 40 | 11:10-12:30 | |
| | | | 40 | D $14^{1}/_{4}-14^{1}/_{2}$ | |
| MAYNOOTH (BP) | 14:72 | 16.30 | 20 | D Through Station | |
| (In station building/2000/VDU) | | | 60 | $15-15^{1}/_{2}$ | |
| | | | 60 | $18^{1}/_{2}-18^{3}/_{4}$ | |
| KILCOCK | 18:49 | 20.01 | 70 | $18^{3}/_{4}-19^{3}/_{4}$ | |
| Kilcock (former station) | 19:12 | 20.55 | | | |
| Fern's Lock | 20:75 | 22.34 | 70 | $23^{1}/_{2}-25$ | |
| | | | 70 | $26-27^{1}/_{2}$ | |
| ENFIELD (BP) | 26:40 | 27.90 | 70 | $29^{1}/_{4}-31^{1}/_{4}$ | |
| (CIE/c.1950/32) | | | | | |
| Moyvalley | 30:28 | 31.75 | 70 | $32^{1}/_{2}-34^{3}/_{4}$ | |
| Hill of Down | 35:55 | 37.09 | | | |
| Killucan (BP) | 41:60 | 43.15 | 70 | 41:10-41:70 | |
| (MGWR-RSCo/1889/24) | | | 50 | D $49^{1}/_{2}-49^{3}/_{4}$ | |

| | | | | | |
|---|---|---|---|---|---|
| | | | 35 | D 49¾-50 | |
| MULLINGAR (BP) | 50:17 | 51.61 | 20 | Through Station | Table 13 |
| (MGWR/1920/65) | | | 35 | U 50:50-50:30 | |
| | | | 50 | U 51-50:50 | |
| Multyfarnham (GB) | 57:63 | 59.19 | | | |
| (MGWR/1923/30) | | | | | |
| Inny Junction | 60:69 | 62.26 | | | |
| Street and Rathowen | 63:18 | 64.63 | | | |
| EDGEWORTHSTOWN (BP) | 67:42 | 68.92 | 50 | D Through Station | |
| (MGWR/1924/22) | | | 25 | U Station Loop | |
| LONGFORD (BP) | 76:22 | 77.67 | | | |
| (RSCo/1893/30) | | | | | |
| Newtownforbes | 80:05 | 81.46 | | | |
| DROMOD (BP) | 87:22 | 88.67 | 50 | D 91½-91:70 | |
| (MGWR/1924/24) | | | | | |
| Shannon Bridge | 92:00 | 93.40 | 25 | Over Bridge | |
| Drumsna | 93:00 | 94.40 | 50 | U 92½-92:10 | |
| | | | 50 | D 97-97:30 | |
| | | | 35 | D 97:30-97¾ | |
| CARRICK ON SHANNON | 97:62 | 99.17 | 20 | Through Station | |
| | | | 35 | U 98¼-97:70 | |
| | | | 50 | U 98:50-98¼ | |
| BOYLE (BP) | 106:28 | 107.75 | 50 | 106-106½ | |
| (RSCo/1894/26) | | | | | |
| Kilfree Junction | 112:40 | 113.90 | | | |
| BALLYMOTE | 120:06 | 121.47 | | | |
| COLLOONEY | 127:56 | 129.10 | | | |
| Collooney Junction | 128:03 | 129.44 | 60 | 129¼-130¼ | |
| Ballysodare | 129:61 | 131.16 | 50 | 133-133½ | |
| | | | 35 | 133½-134 | |
| SLIGO (BP) | 134:16 | 135.40 | 20 | Approaching Station | Table 27 |
| (MGWR/1923/28) | | | | | |

## TABLE 10 DUBLIN CONNOLLY - LIFFEY JUNCTION

Double line throughout.
**Line Maximum Speed:** 30 mph.
**Method of Operation:** TCB - Controlled by Connolly CTC.

**Note:** at the time of writing this line is closed, and used only as a head shunt from North Wall Yard, as far as temporary buffer stops just west of Croke Park Stadium.

| | | | | | |
|---|---|---|---|---|---|
| DUBLIN CONNOLLY (BP) | 0:00 | 0.00 | | | Tables 9,14,15 |
| (Mileage change) | 2:46 | 0.00 | 10 | 2:46-2:24 | |
| (CIE/1976/VDU) | | | | | |
| Newcomen Junction | 2:24 | 0.28 | 20 | Through Junction | Table 30 |
| Glasnevin Junction | 0:58 | 1.85 | | | Table 9 |
| Liffey Junction | 0:00 | 2.57 | | | |
| (Mileage from Broadstone) | 1:33 | 2.57 | | | |

001 (A) class locomotive No. 002 awaits departure from Dublin Connolly with the 18:30 service to Rosslare Harbour Pier on 17th February 1990.
*David Garnett*

071 class locomotive No. 082 is pictured at Inchicore Depot between duties on 26th June 2003.
*Ken Manto*

Withdrawn Sulzer101 (B) class No.103 stored at Inchicore works in the early 1990's.
*Andrew Marshall*

Prototype Sulzer Locomotive No. B113 on display at the Inchicore 150 open day event on 15th June 1996.
*Andrew Marshall*

121 (B) class locomotive No. B121 Shunt at Mullingar in June 1961. *Colour-Rail IR401*

Locomotive No. 143 has been confined to pilot duties for several years and is pictured at Inchicore Depot on 13th April 2004. *Ken Manto*

201 (C) class locomotive No. C208 at Inchicore Works in May 1967.
*Alan Watts, Colour-Rail NG206*

201 is unloaded from a Russian Antonov 124-100 aircraft at Dublin Airport on 9th June 1994 after having been flown over from Canada.
*Courtesy of Irish Rail*

Preserved Maybach locomotive No. E428, owned by Westrail on display at the Inchicore Open Day 15th June 1996.
*Andrew Marshall*

West Clare locomotive No. F501 at Doonbeg on a freight service in April 1957.
*K. Cooper, Colour-Rail NG206*

Deutz locomotive No. G603 freshly re-painted at Inchicore in June 1961.

*Colour-Rail IR 638*

Preserved Deutz G class locomotives Nos. G611, G617 and G613 await departure from Downpatrick Station on 9th April 2000.

*Andrew Marshall*

MAK Locomotive No. K801 ex-works at Inchicore in June 1959.    *Colour-Rail IR 639*

2600 series railcar set Nos. 2605 + 2606 approaching Cobh with a local train from Cork.
*Paul Roche*

2800 series railcar set Nos. 2816 + 2815 at Inchicore on 7th July 2000 awaiting a test run.
*Andrew Marshall*

DART set Nos. 8403 + 8203 + an unidentified 8601 class set on the 12.55 Malahide to Bray service at Dublin Connolly on 17th August 2004.
*Ken Manto*

Recently delivered DART set Nos. 8624 + 8524 + 8523 + 8623 in store at Greystones
on 17th August 2004, awaiting commissioning to traffic.
*Ken Manto*

Cravens Buffet coach No. 1508 at Inchicore on 1st May 2004.
*Ken Manto*

Redundant "Dutch" Electric Generator Van No. 4603, has been retained as a brake van for air-braked stock transfers, and is seen here at Inchicore.  
*Ken Manto*

Mark 2D coach No. 5216 was painted in a revised livery to match the 201 class locomotives. Nine such coaches have been repainted in this livery.  
*Ken Manto*

Recently repainted, track recording No. 700 (EM50) stands at Inchicore on 15th May 2004.
*Ken Manto*

"Hunslet" Locomotive No. 102 shunts at Coleraine on 8th February 1994. *Martin Baumann*

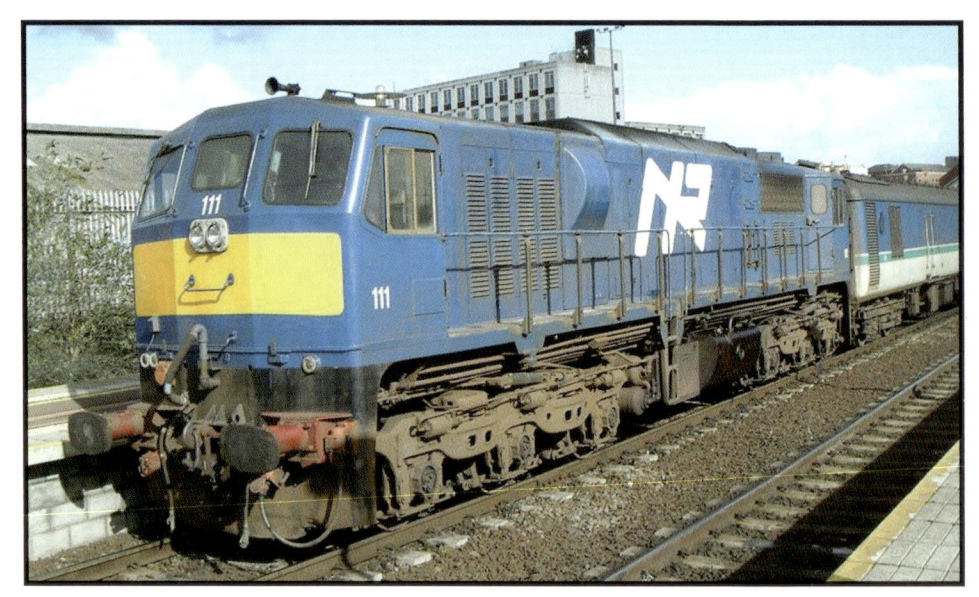

Locomotive No. 111 awaits departure from Belfast Great Victoria Street with the 17.15 service to Newry on 5th March 2004.
*Martin Baumann*

NIR 201 class locomotive No. 208 awaits departure with the 8.20 Dublin Connolly to Belfast Central service on 17th May 1995.
*Martin Baumann*

"80"80 class railcar set Nos. 8090 + 8769 + 8733 leaving Belfast Central with the 12.25 service to Coleraine on 5th March 2004.  *Martin Baumann*

Castle "8" 450 class set Nos. 8455 + 8795 + 8785 at GreenIsland with the 13.05 Belfast Central to Carrickfergus service on 5th March 2004.  *Martin Baumann*

CAF 3001 class set Nos. 3002 + 3003 on a Newry to Belfast test train at Lisburn on 20th August 2004. *Martin Baumann*

De-Dietrich coach No. 9203 on commissioning test at Inchicore. *Andrew Marshall*

An un-identified LUAS CITADIS 301 type tram turns back at Tallaght whilst on test on 13th April 2004.
*Ken Manto*

Recently overhauled RPSI coach No. 180 (ex BR FK 13475) at Belfast Central on 2nd May 2004.
*Ken Manto*

Former B&CDR locomotive No. 28 is pictured at Grosvenor Road in its UTA days during August 1967.
*R.F. Whitford, Colour-Rail IR573*

CIE railbus No. 2508 stands at Inchicore Works in June 1961.
*Colour-Rail IR405*

# TABLE 11  ATHLONE - WESTPORT

Single line throughout.
**Line Maximum Speed:** 70 mph.
**Method of Operation:** TCB - Athlone to Knockcroghery.
ETS - Knockcroghery to Westport.

| | | | | | |
|---|---|---|---|---|---|
| ATHLONE | 80:37 | 0.00 | 20 | Through Station | |
| Athlone East Junction | 80:64 | 0.34 | | | Tables 8, 13 |
| (Mileage from Broadstone) | 77:65 | 0.34 | 20 | Over Shannon Bridge | |
| Athlone Midland (SI) | 78:05 | 0.59 | 35 | U 78$^{1/2}$-78$^{1/4}$ | |
| Athlone West Junction | 78:24 | 0.83 | 20 | 78$^{1/4}$-78:70 | Table 8 |
| | | | 30 | U 79:10-78:70 | |
| | | | 45 | U 79:30-79:10 | |
| Kiltoom | 84:01 | 6.53 | | | |
| Knockcroghery (BP) | 90:00 | 12.53 | 50 | Through Station | |
| (RSCo/1904/VDU) | | | | | |
| Ballymurry | 92:71 | 15.41 | 40 | 95:70-96$^{1/4}$ | |
| ROSCOMMON (BP) | 96:26 | 18.74 | 30 | Through Station | |
| (RSCo/1921/34) | | | 45 | U 97-96$^{3/4}$ | |
| Donomon | 101:73 | 24.44 | | | |
| Ballymoe | 107:74 | 30.14 | | | |
| CASTLEREA (BP) | 112:75 | 35.13 | 45 | U 112$^{1/2}$-112$^{1/4}$ | |
| (RSCo/1901/26) | | | | | |
| Ballinlough | 118:60 | 41.28 | 45 | D 123:30-123:50 | |
| | | | 30 | D 123:50-123:70 | |
| BALLYHAUNIS (BP) | 124:19 | 46.28 | 20 | Through Station | |
| (?/ ?/1 7) | | | 30 | U 124:50-124:30 | |
| | | | 45 | U 124:70-124:50 | |
| | | | 45 | D 134$^{1/4}$-134$^{1/2}$ | |
| | | | 40 | U 134:70-134$^{1/2}$ | |
| | | | 15 | Through X over 134:70 | |
| CLAREMORRIS (BP) | 135:00 | 57.53 | 40 | Through Station | |
| (GSR Hip Roof/1941/66) | | | | | |
| Balla | 142:30 | 64.77 | | | |
| MANULLA JUNCTION (BP) | 145:76 | 68.48 | 45 | D 149:50-149:70 | Table 12 |
| (Portakabin/1988/Panel) | | | | | |
| CASTLEBAR | 150:10 | 72.65 | 30 | Through Station | |
| | | | 45 | U 150:70-150:50 | |
| Islandeady | 155:40 | 78.03 | 50 | D 160-160$^{1/2}$ | |
| | | | 35 | D 160$^{1/2}$-160$^{3/4}$ | |
| WESTPORT (BP) | 161:18 | 83.67 | 20 | D Approaching Station | |
| (RSCo/c.1896/30) | | | | | |

# TABLE 12  MANULLA JUNCTION - BALLINA

Single line throughout.
**Line Maximum Speed:**  60 mph.
**Method of Operation:**  ETS - Manulla Junction to Ballina.

| | | | | | |
|---|---|---|---|---|---|
| MANULLA JUNCTION (BP) | 145:76 | 0.00 | 20 | Through Station | Table 11 |
| (Portakabin/1988/Panel) | | | 20 | U $146_{1/2}$-145:70 | |
| | | | 30 | U $146_{3/4}$-$146_{1/2}$ | |
| Ballyvary | 150:63 | 4.84 | | | |
| River Moy Bridge | 156:00 | 10.05 | | | |
| FOXFORD | 157:14 | 11.23 | 40 | D $165_{3/4}$-166:10 | |
| BALLINA (BP) | 166:47 | 20.57 | 20 | D Approaching Station | |
| (CIE/1977/Panel) | | | | | |
| Crossmolina Siding | 166:60 | 20.80 | | | |

# TABLE 13  MULLINGAR - ATHLONE MIDLAND

Single line throughout.
**Line Maximum Speed:**  30 mph.
**Method of Operation:**  ETS - Mullingar to Moate.
TCB - Moate to Athlone.
201 class only permitted in an emergency.
**Note:** Line unused, but method of operation believed to be that which would be used if a train was run.

| | | | | | |
|---|---|---|---|---|---|
| MULLINGAR (BP) | 50:17 | 0.00 | | | Table 9 |
| (MGWR/1920/65) | | | | | |
| Newbrook | 51:40 | 1.29 | | | |
| Castletown | 58:17 | 8.00 | | | |
| Streamstown | 61:56 | 11.49 | | | |
| Moate | 68:27 | 18.11 | 10 | $72_{3/4}$-$73_{3/4}$ | |
| (RSCo/1890/24) | | | | | |
| Athlone East Junction | 77:65 | 27.60 | | | Tables 8, 11 |
| Athlone Midland (SI) | 78:05 | 27.85 | | | |

# TABLE 14  DUBLIN CONNOLLY - ROSSLARE HARBOUR PIER

Double line Dublin Connolly to Bray, Single line Bray to Rosslare Harbour Pier.
**Line Maximum Speed:**  60 mph Dublin Connolly to Greystones.
70 mph Greystones to Rosslare Europort.
**Method of Operation:**  TCB - Dublin Connolly to Wicklow.
ETS - Wicklow to Rosslare.
201 class may operate normally between Dublin Connolly and Arklow, but only are permitted in an emergency between Arklow and Rosslare Europort (no reduction in speed).

| | | | | | |
|---|---|---|---|---|---|
| DUBLIN CONNOLLY (BP) | 0:00 | 0.00 | 20 | Through Station | Table 9, 10, 15 |
| (Mileage Change) | 1:00 | 0.00 | 30 | 1-0:50 (to Grand Canal Dock) | |
| (CIE/1976/VDU) | | | | | |

| | | | | |
|---|---|---|---|---|
| TARA STREET | 0:20 | 0.75 | | |
| DUBLIN PEARSE (SI) | 0:00 | 1.00 | 20 | Relief main at Station |
| (Mileage Change) | 0:00 | 1.00 | | |
| GRAND CANAL DOCK | 0:75 | 1.94 | 25 | Through Station |
| LANSDOWNE ROAD (EGB) | 1:07 | 2.09 | 40 | U 1:10-0:70 |
| (?/ ?/Switches) | | | | |
| SANDYMOUNT | 1:56 | 2.68 | | |
| SYDNEY PARADE (EGB) | 2:20 | 3.25 | | |
| ( ?/ ?/Switches) | | | | |
| Merrion | 2:52 | 3.65 | | |
| BOOTERSTOWN (SI) | 3:20 | 4.25 | | |
| BLACKROCK | 4:07 | 5.09 | | |
| SEAPOINT | 4:60 | 5.75 | | |
| SALTHILL & MONKSTOWN | 5:26 | 6.33 | 45 | D $5_{1/2}$-$5_{3/4}$ |
| | | | 30 | $5_{3/4}$-6:10 |
| DÚN LAOGHAIRE (SI) | 6:00 | 7.00 | 20 | 6:10-$6_{3/4}$ |
| SANDYCOVE & GLASTHULE | 6:58 | 7.73 | 30 | $6_{3/4}$-$8_{3/4}$ |
| GLENAGEARY | 7:20 | 8.25 | | |
| DALKEY (SI) | 8:05 | 9.06 | 40 | $8_{3/4}$-$9_{3/4}$ |
| KILLINEY | 9:74 | 10.93 | | |
| SHANKILL | 11:00 | 12.00 | | |
| Shanganagh Junction | 11:77 | 12.96 | | |
| (Mileage from Harcourt Street) | 10:42 | 12.96 | | |
| Woodbrook | 11:10 | 13.56 | 40 | D $11_{1/2}$-12 |
| BRAY (EBP & SI) | 12:20 | 14.69 | 25 | 12-13 |
| (GSWR Hip Roof/1927/EC Panel) | | | 50 | 13-$13_{1/2}$ |
| | | | 40 | $13_{1/2}$-$15_{1/2}$ |
| GREYSTONES (BP & SI) | 17:05 | 19.50 | 40 | Through Up Loop |
| (GSWR Hip Roof/1926/VDU) | | | 50 | Through Down Loop |
| KILCOOLE | 19:66 | 22.26 | | |
| Newcastle | 22:38 | 24.91 | 50 | D $27_{1/4}$-$27_{1/2}$ |
| | | | 35 | D $27_{1/2}$-$27_{3/4}$ |
| Wicklow Junction | 27:60 | 30.19 | | |
| WICKLOW (BP) | 28:20 | 30.69 | 20 | Through Station |
| (DWWR/1884/22) | | | 35 | U $28_{1/2}$-$28_{1/4}$ |
| Rathnew | 29:54 | 32.11 | 50 | U $28_{3/4}$-$28_{1/2}$ |
| Glenealy | 33:20 | 35.68 | 65 | D 36:10-37 |
| | | | 65 | U $37_{1/4}$-36:10 |
| | | | 45 | D 37-$37_{1/4}$ |
| RATHDRUM (BP) | 37:24 | 39.74 | 30 | Through Station |
| (DWWR/1888/13) | | | 45 | U $38_{1/4}$-38 |
| | | | 60 | D 38-$41_{1/4}$ |
| | | | 60 | U $41_{1/4}$-$38_{1/4}$ |
| | | | 50 | $41_{1/4}$-$42_{3/4}$ |
| | | | 60 | $42_{3/4}$-$44_{1/4}$ |
| Avoca | 42:66 | 45.26 | 50 | $44_{1/4}$-$45_{1/2}$ |
| Woodenbridge Junction | 44:60 | 47.19 | 60 | $45_{1/2}$-48:30 |
| Shelton Abbey | 46:68 | 49.29 | | |
| ARKLOW (BP) | 49:04 | 51.49 | 40 | Through Station |
| (DWWR/1893/16) | | | 55 | U $49_{1/4}$-49 |

| | | | | | |
|---|---|---|---|---|---|
| Inch | 53:38 | 55.91 | 60 | 57:70-59$^{1/4}$ | |
| GOREY (BP) | 59:33 | 61.85 | 40 | Through Station | |
| (DWWR/1891/18) | | | 55 | U 59$^{3/4}$-59$^{1/2}$ | |
| | | | 60 | 61-63:10 | |
| Camolin | 67:08 | 69.53 | | | |
| Ferns | 69:71 | 72.33 | 60 | 74-76 | |
| | | | 50 | 76-77$^{3/4}$ | |
| ENNISCORTHY (BP) | 77:40 | 79.94 | 30 | Through tunnel | |
| (DSER/1923/18) | | | 40 | 78$^{1/4}$-78$^{1/2}$ | |
| | | | 40 | 80:50-81:50 | |
| Edermine Ferry | 81:03 | 83.47 | 50 | 81:50-82$^{3/4}$ | |
| | | | 40 | 82$^{3/4}$-84$^{3/4}$ | |
| Macmine Junction | 83:30 | 85.81 | 60 | 84$^{3/4}$-86$^{1/2}$ | |
| Killurin | 86:16 | 88.64 | 40 | 86$^{1/2}$-87 | |
| | | | 50 | D 87-92$^{1/4}$ | |
| | | | 50 | U 92$^{1/2}$-87 | |
| | | | 25 | D 92$^{1/4}$-92:54 | |
| WEXFORD (SF) | 92:54 | 95.11 | 5 | 92:54-92$^{3/4}$ | |
| (McK&H/1893/3) | | | 5 | 6$^{1/4}$-5:30 | |
| (Mileage to Rosslare Strand) | 6:20 | 95.44 | 25 | U 5:30-5 | |
| Wexford South | 5:25 | 96.38 | 40 | U 5-4$^{1/2}$ | |
| | | | 40 | D 5:30-4$^{1/2}$ | |
| ROSSLARE STRAND (BP) | 0:00 | 101.69 | 65 | Through Station | Table 4 |
| (Mileage from Mallow) | 110:66 | 101.69 | 65 | 110$^{3/4}$-111$^{1/4}$ | |
| (RSCo-GSWR/1910/26) | | | 60 | 112$^{3/4}$-113 | |
| | | | 40 | 113-113$^{3/4}$ | |
| Kilrane | 113:04 | 103.91 | 15 | 113$^{3/4}$-114 | |
| ROSSLARE EUROPORT | 113:76 | 104:81 | 5 | 114-114$^{1/4}$ | |
| (Ballygeary BP) | | | | | |
| (Container/1997/Outside GF/6 levers) | | | | | |
| Rosslare Harbour Pier | 114:20 | 105.11 | | | |

# TABLE 15   DUBLIN CONNOLLY - BANGOR

Double line throughout (single line over Boyne viaduct).
**Line Maximum Speed:**   90 mph Dublin Connolly to Belfast Central.
  70 mph Belfast Central to Bangor.
**Method of Operation:**   TCB - Dublin Connolly to Bangor.

| | | | | | |
|---|---|---|---|---|---|
| DUBLIN CONNOLLY (BP) | 0:00 | 0.00 | 20 | Through Station | Table 9, 10, 14 |
| (CIE/1976/VDU) | | | 20 | 0-1:10 | |
| | | | 70 | D 1:10-5 | |
| East Wall Junction | 0:57 | 0.71 | | | |
| CLONTARF ROAD | 1:15 | 1.19 | 30 | U 1:30-1:10 | Table 29 |
| Clontarf | 1:51 | 1.64 | 45 | U 1:50-1:30 | |
| KILLESTER (SI) | 2:31 | 2.39 | | | |
| HARMONSTOWN | 3:00 | 3.00 | | | |
| RAHENY | 3:57 | 3.71 | | | |
| KILBARRACK | 4:40 | 4.50 | | | |

| | | | | | |
|---|---|---|---|---|---|
| HOWTH JUNCTION (SI) | 4:64 | 4.80 | 70 | U 5-1:50 | Table 16 |
| PORTMARNOCK | 6:56 | 6.70 | | | |
| MALAHIDE (SI) | 9:00 | 9.00 | 70 | Through Station | |
| DONABATE | 11:35 | 11.44 | | | |
| RUSH & LUSK | 13:74 | 13.93 | | | |
| SKERRIES | 17:77 | 17.96 | | | |
| BALBRIGGAN | 21:60 | 21.75 | | | |
| GORMANSTON | 24:00 | 24.00 | | | |
| MOSNEY | 25:63 | 25.79 | | | |
| LAYTOWN | 27:13 | 27.16 | 70 | D $30^{3/4}$-31:10 | |
| | | | 50 | D $31:10$-$31^{1/2}$ | |
| DROGHEDA (BP + SI) | 31:60 | 31.75 | 30 | Through Station | Table 28 |
| (CIE/1978/Panel + VDU) | | | 25 | U$31:70$-$31^{1/2}$ | |
| Boyne Viaduct | 32:00 | 32.00 | 30 | D Over Viaduct | |
| | | | 50 | U $32^{3/4}$-$32^{1/4}$ | |
| | | | 70 | U $33^{1/4}$-$32^{3/4}$ | |
| Dunleer | 41:56 | 41.70 | | | |
| Dromin Junction | 43:51 | 43.64 | | | |
| Castlebellingham | 47:16 | 47.20 | 70 | D $47^{3/4}$-49:50 | |
| Dundalk South Junction | 53:40 | 53.50 | 70 | U 51-49:10 | |
| DUNDALK (BP) | 54:30 | 54.38 | | | |
| (In station buildings/2002/VDU) | | | | | |
| Mount Pleasant | 57:78 | 57.98 | 85 | $58^{1/2}$-$59^{1/4}$ | |
| Border Post (IE/NIR) | 59:48 | 59.60 | | | |
| Adavoyle | 62:40 | 62.50 | 60 | $64^{3/4}$-$65^{3/4}$ | |
| | | | 75 | $65^{3/4}$-$70^{1/4}$ | |
| NEWRY | 69:20 | 69.25 | 70 | $70^{1/4}$-$76^{1/2}$ | |
| Goraghwood | 71:71 | 71.90 | 45 | $76^{1/2}$-77 | |
| POYNTZPASS | 76:70 | 76.87 | 70 | 77-$79^{1/4}$ | |
| | | | 50 | $79^{1/4}$-$79^{3/4}$ | |
| SCARVA | 79:47 | 79.59 | 85 | $79^{3/4}$-$84^{3/4}$ | |
| Tandragee | 82:00 | 82.00 | 70 | $84^{3/4}$-$86^{3/4}$ | |
| PORTADOWN (BP) | 87:24 | 87.30 | 40 | Through Station | |
| (In station buildings/1970/Panel) | | | 60 | $87^{1/4}$-$87^{3/4}$ | |
| | | | 80 | U $88^{3/4}$-$87^{3/4}$ | |
| LURGAN (GB) | 92:52 | 92.65 | | | |
| (NIR/1981/Switches) | | | | | |
| Lake Street Crossing (GB) | 93:00 | 93.00 | | | |
| (NIR/1981/Switches) | | | | | |
| Bell's Row Crossing (GB) | 93:31 | 93.39 | | | |
| (NIR/1996/switches) | | | | | |
| MOIRA | 98:12 | 98.15 | 70 | 98-106 | |
| Knockmore Junction | 103:35 | 103.44 | | | |
| KNOCKMORE (in up direction only) | 104:08 | 104.10 | | | |
| LISBURN | 105:04 | 105.05 | | | Table 17 |
| HILDEN | 106:01 | 106.01 | 80 | 106-$106^{3/4}$ | |
| LAMBEG | 106:45 | 106.56 | | | |
| DERRIAGHY | 107:40 | 107.50 | | | |
| DUNMURRY (GB) | 108:40 | 108.50 | | | |

(NIR/1981/Switches)

| | | | | | |
|---|---|---|---|---|---|
| FINAGHY | 109:40 | 109.50 | 80 | D 110-110$^{3/4}$ | |
| BALMORAL | 110:24 | 110.30 | 60 | D 110$^{3/4}$-111$^{1/2}$ | |
| ADELAIDE | 111:15 | 111.19 | 50 | 111$^{1/2}$-112 | |
| Central Junction | 111:73 | 111.92 | 25 | 112-112$^{1/4}$ | Table 19A |
| City Junction | 112:13 | 112.16 | 40 | 112$^{1/4}$-113$^{1/2}$ | Table 19 |
| CITY HOSPITAL | 112:20 | 112.25 | | | |
| BOTANIC | 112:40 | 112.50 | | | |
| BELFAST CENTRAL (BP) | 113:39 | 113.49 | 15 | Through Station | |
| (In station buildings/1976/Panel) | | | 15 | 113$^{1/2}$-113$^{3/4}$ | |
| Lagan Junction | 113:71 | 113.89 | 25 | 113$^{3/4}$-114 | Table 19 |
| BRIDGE END | 114:28 | 114.35 | | | |
| Victoria Park | 115:00 | 115.00 | | | |
| SYDENHAM | 115:54 | 115.68 | | | |
| Tillysburn | 116:49 | 116.61 | | | |
| Kinnegar | 117:60 | 117.75 | | | |
| HOLYWOOD | 118:26 | 118.33 | 60 | U 118$^{1/4}$-118 | |
| MARINO | 119:26 | 119.33 | | | |
| CULTRA | 119:78 | 119.97 | | | |
| Craigavad | 120:21 | 120.26 | 60 | 121-121$^{1/4}$ | |
| SEAHILL | 121:44 | 121.55 | | | |
| HELEN'S BAY | 122:73 | 122.91 | | | |
| Crawfordsburn | 123:39 | 123.49 | 60 | 123-123$^{3/4}$ | |
| CARNALEA | 124:34 | 124.42 | | | |
| BANGOR WEST | 125:10 | 125.13 | | | |
| BANGOR | 126:13 | 126.17 | 15 | Approaching Station | |

## TABLE 16  HOWTH JUNCTION - HOWTH

Double line throughout.
**Line Maximum Speed:** 60 mph DART trains, 50 mph all other traffic.
**Method of Operation:** TCB - Howth Junction to Howth.

| | | | | | |
|---|---|---|---|---|---|
| HOWTH JUNCTION (SI) | 4:64 | 0.00 | 20 | Through Junction | Table 15 |
| (Mileage change) | 0:00 | 0.00 | 20 | U $^{1/2}$-0 | |
| | | | 30 | U $^{3/4}$-$^{1/2}$ | |
| BAYSIDE | 1:00 | 1.00 | | | |
| SUTTON | 1:60 | 1.75 | | | |
| | | | 30 | D 3-3$^{1/4}$ | |
| HOWTH (EBP & SI) | 3:34 | 3.43 | 15 | D Approaching Station | |
| (GNR(I)/1892/EC Panel + Levers) | | | | | |

## TABLE 17  LISBURN - ANTRIM

Single line throughout.
**Line Maximum Speed:** 30 mph.
**Method of Operation:** TCB - Lisburn to Antrim.

| | | | | | |
|---|---|---|---|---|---|
| LISBURN | 105:04 | 0.00 | | | Table 15 |
| Knockmore | 104:12 | 0.90 | | | |
| Knockmore Junction | 103:35 | 1.61 | 15 | Through Curve | |
| (Mileage Change) | 0:00 | 1.61 | | | |
| Brookmount | 1:61 | 3.37 | | | |
| Ballinderry (SI) | 5:26 | 6.94 | 20 | $6^{3/4}$-7 | |
| Glenavy | 8:50 | 10.24 | | | |
| Crumlin (SI) | 10:72 | 12.51 | | | |
| Aldergrove | 13:16 | 14.81 | 15 | $18^{1/4}$-$18^{1/2}$ | |
| ANTRIM (EBP) | 18:40 | 20.11 | | | Table 20 |
| (NIR/c.1970/Panel) | | | | | |

## TABLE 18 COLERAINE - PORTRUSH

Single line throughout.
**Line Maximum Speed:** 70 mph.
**Method of Operation:** Normal Operation: One train Working with token under control of Coleraine signalman. On busy days ETT - Coleraine to Portrush.
201 class locomotives not permitted. 071/111 class locomotives not to exceed 50 mph.

| | | | | | |
|---|---|---|---|---|---|
| COLERAINE (BP) | 61:54 | 0.00 | 20 | Over Junction | Table 20 |
| (NCC/c.1923/Panel) | | | | | |
| UNIVERSITY | 62:69 | 1.19 | | | |
| Cromore | 65:00 | 3.32 | | | |
| DHU VARREN | 67:04 | 5.38 | | | |
| PORTRUSH (BP) | 67:53 | 5.99 | 40 | Approaching Station | |
| (NCC/ ?/45) | | | | | |

## TABLE 19 BELFAST GREAT VICTORIA STREET - LARNE HARBOUR

Double line Belfast Yorkgate to Kilroot, Single line Kilroot to Larne Harbour.
**Line Maximum Speed:** 70 mph .
**Method of Operation:** TCB - Belfast Central to Larne Harbour.
201 class may operate normally between Belfast Great Victoria Street and Bleach Green Junction, but are not permitted between Bleach Green Junction and Larne Harbour. 071/111 class locomotives not to exceed 50 mph between Bleach Green Junction and Larne Harbour.

| | | | | | |
|---|---|---|---|---|---|
| BELFAST GREAT VICTORIA STREET | 112:44 | 0.00 | 15 | $112^{1/2}$-112:10 | |
| Westlink Junction | 112:17 | 0.34 | | | Table 19A |
| (Mileage change) | 0:00 | 0.34 | 20 | Through Curve | |
| City Junction | 0:17 | 0.55 | | | |
| (Mileage Change) | 112:13 | 0.55 | 40 | $112^{1/4}$-$113^{1/2}$ | Table 15 |
| CITY HOSPITAL | 112:20 | 0.64 | | | |
| BOTANIC | 112:40 | 0.89 | | | |
| BELFAST CENTRAL (BP) | 113:39 | 1.85 | 15 | Through Station | |
| (In Station buildings/1976/Panel) | | | 15 | $113^{1/2}$-$113^{3/4}$ | |

| | | | | | |
|---|---|---|---|---|---|
| Lagan Junction | 113:71 | 2.25 | 30 | 113³/₄-114 | Table 15 |
| | | | 45 | 114-115 | |
| Queens Quay Junction | 114:11 | 2.50 | | | |
| Donegall Quay Loop | 114:20 | 2.61 | | | |
| BELFAST YORKGATE | 114:54 | 3.04 | | | Table 20 |
| Belfast York Road | 115:00 | 3.37 | 60 | 115-0¹/₂ | |
| (Mileage Change) | 0:00 | 3.37 | | | |
| Greencastle | 2:35 | 5.81 | | | |
| Whitehouse | 3:20 | 6.62 | | | |
| WHITEABBEY | 4:16 | 7.57 | 50 | D 4¹/₂-4³/₄ | |
| Bleach Green Junction | 4:62 | 8.15 | 30 | D 4³/₄-5¹/₂ | Table 20 |
| | | | 50 | U 4³/₄-4¹/₂ | |
| Bleach Green | 4:73 | 8.28 | 20 | U 5¹/₄-4³/₄ | |
| JORDANSTOWN | 5:28 | 8.72 | 50 | D 5¹/₂-7³/₄ | |
| GREENISLAND | 6:56 | 10.07 | 30 | D 7³/₄-8¹/₄ | |
| TROOPERSLANE | 7:72 | 11.27 | 50 | D 8¹/₄-9¹/₂ | |
| Mount | 8:60 | 12.12 | | | |
| CLIPPERSTOWN | 9:20 | 12.62 | 30 | D 9¹/₂-9³/₄ | |
| CARRICKFERGUS | 9:43 | 12.91 | | | |
| Barn | 10:05 | 13.43 | 30 | U 10-5¹/₄ | |
| DOWNSHIRE | 10:38 | 13.85 | | | |
| Eden | 11:08 | 14.47 | | | |
| Kilroot | 11:44 | 14.92 | 30 | D 12¹/₄-12¹/₂ | |
| | | | 50 | 12¹/₂-14¹/₄ | |
| | | | 30 | 14¹/₄-14³/₄ | |
| WHITEHEAD | 14:55 | 18.06 | | | |
| BALLYCARRY | 16:40 | 19.87 | | | |
| Magheramorne Loop | 19:39 | 22.86 | | | |
| MAGHERAMORNE | 19:60 | 23.12 | 30 | Through Curve | |
| GLYNN | 21:48 | 24.97 | 40 | 23-23³/₄ | |
| LARNE TOWN | 23:29 | 26.73 | | | |
| LARNE HARBOUR | 24:00 | 27.37 | 20 | Approaching Station | |

# TABLE 19A CENTRAL JUNCTION - BELFAST GREAT VICTORIA STREET

Double line throughout.
**Line Maximum Speed:** 40 mph.
**Method of Operation:** TCB - Central Junction to Belfast Great Victoria Street.

| | | | | | |
|---|---|---|---|---|---|
| Central Junction | 111:73 | 0.00 | | | Table 15 |
| Westlink Junction | 112:17 | 0.30 | 15 | 112¹/₄-112¹/₂ | Table 19 |
| BELFAST GREAT VICTORIA STREET | 112:44 | 0.64 | | | |

# TABLE 20  BELFAST YORKGATE - LONDONDERRY

Double line - Belfast Yorkgate to Monkstown Junction, Single line Monkstown Junction to Londonderry.
**Line Maximum Speed:**  70 mph Belfast Yorkgate to Monkstown.
  90 mph Monkstown to Antrim.
  70 mph Antrim to Londonderry.
**Method of Operation:**  TCB - Belfast Yorkgate to Coleraine
  ETT - Coleraine to Castlerock.
  EKT - Castlerock to Londonderry.
201 class may operate normally between Belfast Yorkgate and Ballymena, but are not permitted between Ballymena and Londonderry. 071/111 class locomotives not to exceed 50 mph between Ballymena and Londonderry.

| | | | | | |
|---|---|---|---|---|---|
| BELFAST YORKGATE | 114:54 | 0.00 | | | Table 19 |
| Belfast York Road | 115:00 | 0.33 | 60 | 115-0$1/2$ | |
| (Mileage Change) | 0:00 | 0.33 | | | |
| Greencastle | 2:35 | 2.77 | | | |
| Whitehouse | 3:20 | 3.58 | | | |
| WHITEABBEY | 4:16 | 4.53 | | | |
| Bleach Green Junction | 4:62 | 5.11 | | | Table 19 |
| (Change of Mileage) | 7:20 | 5.11 | 50 | $8^{1/2}$-$8^{3/4}$ | |
| Monkstown | 8:55 | 6.55 | | | |
| Monkstown Junction | 8:71 | 6.75 | | | |
| Mossley | 9:49 | 7.47 | | | |
| MOSSLEY WEST | 9:77 | 7.82 | | | |
| Ballyclare Junction | 10:60 | 8.60 | | | |
| Doagh | 13:22 | 11.13 | | | |
| Templepatrick | 16:26 | 14.19 | 30 | Through Loop (90 on main) | |
| Dunadry | 18:35 | 16.30 | | | |
| Muckamore | 19:68 | 17.71 | 70 | $20^{1/2}$-$21^{3/4}$ | |
| ANTRIM (EBP) | 21:62 | 19.64 | | | Table 17 |
| (NIR/c.1970/Panel) | | | | | |
| Cookstown Junction | 24:75 | 22.80 | | | |
| Magherabeg Loop | 27:56 | 25.56 | | | |
| Kellswater | 29:16 | 27.06 | | | |
| BALLYMENA | 33:39 | 31.35 | 40 | Through Curves & Station | |
| | | | 50 | $34^{1/2}$-35 | |
| | | | 40 | D $35^{3/4}$-$36^{1/2}$ | |
| CULLYBACKEY | 36:37 | 34.33 | 40 | U $36^{3/4}$-$35^{3/4}$ | |
| | | | 60 | D 37-$37^{1/2}$ | |
| Glarryford | 41:16 | 39.06 | | | |
| Killagan | 43:32 | 41.26 | | | |
| Dunloy | 46:10 | 43.98 | | | |
| Ballyboyland | 50:33 | 48.27 | | | |
| BALLYMONEY | 53:31 | 51.25 | 30 | Through Station | |
| Macfin | 57:08 | 54.96 | | | |
| COLERAINE (BP) | 61:54 | 59.54 | 40 | Through Station | Table 18 |
| (NCC/c.1923/Panel) | | | 40 | $61^{3/4}$-$62^{3/4}$ | |

| | | | | |
|---|---|---|---|---|
| CASTLEROCK (BP) (NIR/1970/10) | 67:41 | 65.37 | 40 | Through Station |
| Downhill | 68:75 | 66.80 | | |
| Magilligan | 71:70 | 69.74 | | |
| BELLARENA | 74:77 | 72.82 | | |
| Limavady Junction | 79:56 | 77.56 | 50 | Through Curve & Station |
| Ballykelly | 81:51 | 79.50 | | |
| Carrichue | 82:72 | 80.76 | | |
| Eglinton | 87:59 | 85.60 | | |
| Culmore | 90:32 | 88.26 | | |
| Lisahally | 90:69 | 88.72 | 60 | 93-93$^{3/4}$ |
| LONDONDERRY (BP) (In station buildings/1980/Panel) | 95:32 | 93.26 | 40 | Approaching Station |

Note: Mileage at Bleach Green Junction (7:20) has been calculated back from the former Monkstown Junction (8:53) which originally ran from Belfast York Road Station via (a reversal at) Greenisland.

## TABLE 21 LIMERICK CHECK - CASTLEMUNGRET

Single line throughout.
**Line Maximum Speed:** 20 mph.
**Method of Operation:** Worked as a siding controlled by Limerick Check Signalbox.
201 class locomotives only permitted in an emergency (no reduction in speed).

| | | | | |
|---|---|---|---|---|
| Limerick Check (BP) | 0:49 | 0.00 | | Tables 4, 6 |
| (Mileage Change) (GSWR Gable Roof/1910/50) | 0:00 | 0.00 | | |
| Rosbrien Curve | | | 15 | Through Curve |
| Castlemungret | 4:45 | 4.56 | | |

## TABLE 22 LIMERICK - ATHENRY

Single line throughout.
**Line Maximum Speed:** 50 mph Limerick to Ennis.
30 mph Ennis to Athenry.
**Method of Operation:** ETS: Limerick Check to Ennis.
One train working with manual staff Ennis to Athenry.
201 class locomotives only permitted in an emergency (reduction in speed to 20 mph throughout).

| | | | | | |
|---|---|---|---|---|---|
| LIMERICK | 0:00 | 0.00 | | | |
| Limerick Check (BP) (GSWR Gable Roof/1910/50) | 0:49 | 0.56 | | | |
| Ennis Junction | 0:70 | 0.85 | 25 | 3$^{1/4}$-4$^{3/4}$ | Tables 4, 6 |
| Longpavement | 3:70 | 3.85 | | | |
| Cratloe | 9:60 | 9.75 | 40 | 9:50-10$^{1/4}$ | |
| Sixmilebridge | 12:73 | 12.91 | | | |
| Ardsollus and Quin | 19:50 | 19.63 | | | |
| Ballycar | 16:58 | 16.72 | | | |
| Clarecastle | 23:00 | 23.00 | | | |

| | | | | | |
|---|---|---|---|---|---|
| ENNIS (BP) | 24:60 | 24.75 | 25 | Through Station | |
| (RSCo/c.1894/13) | | | | | |
| Upper Fergus Bridge | 25:30 | 25.38 | 20 | Over bridge | |
| | | | 25 | 31-32³/₄ | |
| Crusheen | 32:37 | 32.46 | | | |
| Tubber | 36:64 | 36.80 | | | |
| Gort | 42:25 | 42.31 | | | |
| Ardrahan | 49:06 | 49.08 | 25 | 52-52¹/₂ | |
| | | | 25 | 54:70-56:10 | |
| Craughwell | 55:13 | 55.16 | 25 | 59¹/₄-60¹/₂ | |
| ATHENRY | 60:40 | 60.05 | | | Table 8 |

# TABLE 23 GLOUNTHAUNE - MIDLETON

At the time of writing (August 2004) it has been announced the former line from Glounthaune to Youghal is to be reopened as far as Midleton by 2007. Mileages shown for Carrigtowhill and Midleton are those of the old stations, the replacements may not be in exactly the same locations.

Single line throughout.
**Line Maximum Speed:**
**Method of Operation:**
201 class not permitted.

| | | | |
|---|---|---|---|
| GLOUNTHAUNE (BP) | 171:04 | 0.00 | |
| (in station buildings/c.1932/20) | | | |
| Cobh Junction | 171:07 | 0.04 | Table 1 |
| Change of Mileage | 0:00 | 0.04 | |
| CARRIGTOWHILL ** | 2:60 | 2.79 | |
| MIDLETON ** | 6:18 | 6.27 | |

# TABLE 24 ISLANDBRIDGE JUNCTION - ALEXANDRA ROAD / COASTAL CONTAINER LINE

Double line throughout.
**Line Maximum Speed:** 30 mph.
**Method of Operation:** TCB - Islandbridge Junction to North Strand Junction.
North Wall area worked as sidings.

| | | | | | |
|---|---|---|---|---|---|
| Islandbridge Junction | 0:53 | 0.00 | | | Table 1 |
| (Mileage Change) | 0:00 | 0.00 | 20 | Through Junction | |
| Dublin Heuston (Platform 10) (OOU) | 0:25 | 0.31 | 20 | U Departing Platform | |
| | | | 10 | U Approaching Platform | |
| Cabra | 1:68 | 1.85 | | | |
| Glasnevin Junction | 2:55 | 2.69 | | | Table 9 |
| Glasnevin | 3:00 | 3.00 | | | |
| Drumcondra | 3:50 | 3.63 | | | |
| North Strand Junction | 4:18 | 4.23 | 20 | Through Junction | Table 9 |
| Church Road Junction (SF) | 4:51 | 4.64 | 20 | Through Junction | Table 29 |
| (GSWR Hip Roof/1920's/46) | | | 20 | 4:51-6¹/₄ | |

| Granaries | 5:00 | 5.00 | | |
|---|---|---|---|---|
| Alexandra Road | 6:20 | 6.25 | 5 | Along Tramway |
| Coastal Container Terminal | 6:79 | 6.99 | | |

## TABLE 25  ATHY - TEGRAL SIDING

Single line throughout.
**Line Maximum Speed:**  5 mph.
**Method of Operation:**  Worked as a siding.
201 class locomotives not permitted.

| ATHY | 44:64 | 0.00 | Table 3 |
|---|---|---|---|
| (mileage change) | 0:00 | 0.00 | |
| Tegral Siding | 0:37 | 0.46 | |

## TABLE 26  PORTLAOISE - CONNIBERRY

Single line throughout.
**Line Maximum Speed:**  20 mph.
**Method of Operation:**  Worked as a siding.

| PORTLAOISE (SI) | 50:72 | 0.00 | Table 1 |
|---|---|---|---|
| (Mileage Change) | 0:00 | 0.00 | |
| Conniberry Yard | 0:56 | 0.70 | |

## TABLE 27  SLIGO - SLIGO QUAY

Single line throughout.
**Line Maximum Speed:**  10 mph.
**Method of Operation:**  Worked as a siding controlled by Sligo signalbox.
201 class locomotives not permitted.

| SLIGO (BP) | 134:16 | 0.00 | Table 9 |
|---|---|---|---|
| (Mileage Change) | 0:00 | 0.00 | |
| (MGWR/1923/28) | | | |
| Sligo Quay | 0:20 | 0.25 | |

## TABLE 28  DROGHEDA - TARA MINES

Single line throughout.
**Line Maximum Speed:**  25 mph.
**Method of Operation:**  ETS - Drogheda to Tara Mines.
ETS Instrument at Tara Mines operated by train crew only if required (i.e. two trains between Navan and Tara Mines).

| DROGHEDA (BP) | 31:60 | 0.00 | Table 15 |
|---|---|---|---|
| (Mileage Change) | 0:00 | 0.00 | |
| (CIE/1978/Panel + VDU) | | | |
| Platin Cement Factory | 2:60 | 2.75 | |

| | | | | | |
|---|---|---|---|---|---|
| Duleek | 4:65 | 4.81 | | | |
| Lougher | 8:40 | 8.50 | | | |
| Beauparc | 11:54 | 11.68 | | | |
| Navan (BP) | 16:75 | 16.94 | | | |
| (GNR(I)/c.1892/25) | | | | | |
| Navan Junction | 17:16 | 17.20 | 5 | 17-17:30 | |
| Tara Junction | 17:20 | 17.25 | | | |
| Tara Mines (Hut) | 17:40 | 17.50 | | | |

## TABLE 29 CHURCH ROAD JUNCTION - EAST WALL JUNCTION

Double line throughout.
**Line Maximum Speed:** 20 mph.
**Method of Operation:** Controlled by Connolly CTC.

| | | | | | |
|---|---|---|---|---|---|
| Church Road Junction (SF) | 4:51 | 0.00 | 20 | Through Junction | Table 24 |
| (Mileage Change) | 0:00 | 0.00 | | | |
| (GSWR Hip Roof/1920's/46) | | | | | |
| East Wall Junction | 0:40 | 0.50 | 20 | Through Junction | |
| (Mileage Change) | 0:57 | 0.50 | | | Table 15 |

## TABLE 30 NEWCOMEN JUNCTION - NORTH WALL MIDLAND YARD

Double line throughout.
**Line Maximum Speed:** 30 mph.
**Method of Operation:** Worked as a siding.

| | | | | | |
|---|---|---|---|---|---|
| Newcomen Junction | 2:24 | 0.00 | 20 | Through Junction | Table 10 |
| North Wall Freight Depot (Midland) | 2:71 | 0.59 | | | |

## SECTION 6 - CLOSED RAILWAYS OF IRELAND

Over the years, the rail network in both the Irish Republic and Northern Ireland has contracted sharply, especially during the early part of the 1960's, as more and more services became uneconomic to run. The rash of closures in the early 1960's was mainly due to the recommendations contained in the Beddy Commission Report of 1957 on the rail network, which was furthered under the terms of the 1958 Transport Act which allowed CIE greater commercial freedom. This act repealed some of the old restrictions imposed by previous legislation and allowed CIE to close down certain uneconomic services. This section has been updated and is now thought to contain a full list of all closed railways within Ireland. For additional information in this section we are grateful to Martin Baumann.

| Section | Closed to Passenger | Closed Completely | Railway Company | Mileage |
|---|---|---|---|---|
| Coleraine Waterside - deviation point | 19.11.1860 | .01.1861 | LCR | 0.29 |
| Burt Junc - Farland | .07.1866 | .07.1866 | LLSR | 0.38 |
| Cork Victoria Road - deviation point | 06.02.1873 | 06.02.1873 | CBPR | 1.50 |

| | | | | |
|---|---|---|---|---|
| Parsonstown Junc - Portumna Bridge Quay | 29.11.1878 | 29.11.1878 | GSWR | 12.00 |
| Bushmills - Bushmills Market | freight only | .1890 | GCPBVT | 0.25 * |
| Cork - Grattan Hill Junc | 01.02.1893 | 01.02.1893 | GSWR | 0.48 |
| Charleville North Junc - West Junc | .1906 | .1906 | GSWR | 0.25 |
| Killnick Junc - Felthouse Junc | 01.07.1910 | 28.05.1911 | FRRHC | 2.12 |
| Ballybrack deviation point - Bray Junc | 05.10.1915 | 05.10.1915 | DSER | 2.09 |
| (This closure includes removal of separate lines ex Pearse and Harcourt Street from Shanganagh Junc - Bray Junc) | | | | |
| Fahan Pier - Fahan Pier Junc | 07.01.1920 | 07.01.1920 | LLSR | *0.25 ** |
| Kilrush - Cappagh Pier | .19xx | .192x | GSR | 0.90 * |
| Keady - Castleblaney | 02.04.1923 | 02.04.1923 | GNR | 10.25 |
| Shantalla Junc - Shantalla | freight only | .1923 | GSR | 1.25 |
| Coleraine Harbour - deviation point | 21.03.1924 | 21.03.1924 | NCC | 0.33 |
| Listowel - Ballybunion monorail | 14.10.1924 | 14.10.1924 | L+B | note 1 |
| Portstewart NCC - Portstewart Town | 31.01.1926 | 31.01.1926 | NCC | 1.78 * |
| Cork Summerhill - Tivoli Junc | 01.02.1893 | .1927 | GSR | 0.50 |
| Ballylinan - Wolfhill | freight only | .1929 | GSR | 5.25 |
| Derreenavoggy - Aughabehy | freight only | .1930 | GSR | 2.61 * |
| Limerick Markets - Limerick Factory | freight only | .1930 | GSR | *0.25* |
| Kinsale Junc - Kinsale | 01.09.1931 | 01.09.1931 | GSR | 11.00 |
| Monkstown - Crosshaven | 01.06.1932 | 01.06.1932 | GSR | 7.94 * |
| | | (last trains ran on 31.05.32) | | |
| Monkstown - Cork (Albert Street) | 12.09.1932 | 12.09.1932 | GSR | 8.15 * |
| Dingle Pier Extension | .1930 | .1930 | GSR | 0.75 * |
| Ardglass - Ardglass Harbour | freight only | .1932 | BCDR | 0.26 |
| Castlederg - Victoria Bridge | 30.01.1933 | 30.01.1933 | C+VB | 7.15 * |
| Markethill - Armagh | 01.02.1933 | 01.02.1933 | GNR | 8.75 |
| Ballyclare Paper Mill - Doagh | 01.10.1930 | 01.02.1933 | NCC | 1.50 * |
| Ballina - Killala | 01.10.1931 | 01.07.1934 a | GSR | 8.11 |
| | | (a: first 0.60 retained as siding, now out of use.) | | |
| Cork (Western Rd) - Coachford | 31.12.1934 | 31.12.1934 | GSR | 15.59 * |
| Coachford Junc - Blarney | 31.12.1934 | 31.12.1934 | GSR | 2.38 * |
| Donoughmore Junc - Donoughmore | 31.12.1934 | 31.12.1934 | GSR | 8.36 * |
| Galway (Junc 0.18 before stn)-Clifden | 29.04.1935 | 29.04.1935 | GSR | 48.73 |
| Buncrana - Carndonagh | 02.12.1935 | 02.12.1935 | LLSR | 18.04 * |
| Retreat - Parkmore | freight only | 10.04.1937 | NCC | 2.75 * |
| Parkmore - Rathkenny | 01.10.1930 | 10.04.1937 | NCC | 7.25 * |
| Achill - Westport | 01.10.1937 | 01.10.1937 | GSR | 26.65 |
| Castlegregory - Castlegregory Junc | 17.04.1939 | 17.04.1939 | GSR | 6.00 * |
| Ballyboley Junc - Rathkenny via Ballymena | 01.02.1933 | 02.06.1940 | NCC | 23.75 * |
| Gweedore - Burtonport | 03.06.1940 | 31.07.1940 | LLSR | 10.63 * |
| Limerick Factory- Limerick Bus depot | freight only | .1940 | GSR | *0.25* |
| Maguiresbridge - Tynan | 31.12.1941 | 31.12.1941 | CVR | 37.04 * |
| Birdhill - Killaloe | 17.07.1931 | 24.04.1944 | GSR | 3.25 |
| Killaloe - Killaloe Pier | freight only | 24.04.1944 | GSR | 0.75 |
| Aughrim - Shillelagh | 24.04.1944 | 24.04.1944 | GSR | 12.17 |
| Cork Capwell - Macroom Junc | 02.03.1925 | .1946 | GSR | 0.75 |
| Schull - Skibereen | 27.01.1947 | 27.01.1947 | GSR | 14.33 * |
| Letterkenny - Gweedore | 06.01.1947 | .06.1947 | LLSR | 39.08 * |
| Bessbrook - Newry | 12.01.1948 | 12.01.1948 | B+N | 3.03 * |

| Line | Closed to Passengers | Closed Completely | Operator | Miles |
|---|---|---|---|---|
| Bantry Town - Bantry Pier | .09.1937 | . .1949 | CIE | 0.74 |
| Portrush - Giant's Causeway | 01.10.1949 | 01.10.1949 | GCPBVT | 9.25 * |
| Portrush Harbour - Portrush | freight only | . .1949 b | UTA | 0.75 |

(b: approx. 0.25 mile retained as a siding until 1969.)

| Line | Closed to Passengers | Closed Completely | Operator | Miles |
|---|---|---|---|---|
| Limerick Bus Depot - Market Branch Junc | freight only | . .1950 | CIE | *0.25* |
| Newcastle Junc - Downpatrick South Junc | 15.01.1950 | 15.01.1950 | UTA | 11.19 |
| Downpatrick South Junc - East Junc | 15.01.1950 | 15.01.1950 | UTA | 0.38 |
| Downpatrick East Junc - Downpatrick | 15.01.1950 | 15.01.1950 | UTA | 0.37 |
| Downpatrick East Junc - North Junc | 15.01.1950 | 15.01.1950 | UTA | 0.30 |
| Downpatrick North Junc - South Junc | 15.01.1950 | 15.01.1950 | UTA | 0.38 |
| Downpatrick North Junc - Comber | 15.01.1950 | 15.01.1950 | UTA | 18.19 |
| Ballynahinch Junc - Ballynahinch | 15.01.1950 | 15.01.1950 | UTA | 3.59 |
| Ardglass Junc - Ardglass | 15.01.1950 | 15.01.1950 | UTA | 8.45 |
| Ballymacarrett Junc - Donaghadee | 22.04.1950 | 22.04.1950 | UTA | 21.75 |
| Donaghadee - Donaghadee Harbour | freight only | 22.04.1950 c | UTA | 0.10 |

(c: out of use since 193x.)

| Line | Closed to Passengers | Closed Completely | Operator | Miles |
|---|---|---|---|---|
| Larne Town-Larne Harbour | 01.06.1932 | 03.07.1950 | UTA | 1.00 * |
| Larne Town - Ballyboley Junc | 01.02.1933 | 03.07.1950 | UTA | 6.75 * |
| Ballyboley Junc - Ballyclare Paper Mill | 01.10.1930 | 03.07.1950 | UTA | 4.25 * |
| Ballymoney - Ballycastle | 03.07.1950 | 03.07.1950 | UTA | 16.25 * |
| Ballyclare - Lisnalinchy Racecourse | 01.01.1938 | 03.07.1950 | UTA | 2.06 |
| Lisnalinchy Racecourse - Kingsbog Junc | 03.07.1950 | 03.07.1950 | UTA | 1.50 |
| Dungiven - Limavady | 01.01.1933 | 03.07.1950 | UTA | 10.27 |
| Drapperstown - Drapperstown Junc | 01.10.1930 | 03.07.1950 | UTA | 6.64 |
| Kilrea - Macfin | 28.08.1950 | 28.08.1950 | UTA | 13.49 |
| Dundalk Quay Street - Greenore | 31.12.1951 | 31.12.1951 | DNGR | 12.58 |
| Greenore - Newry King Street Junc | 31.12.1951 | 31.12.1951 | DNGR | 14.26 |
| Dundalk East Junc - Dundalk West Junc | 01.02.1952 | 01.01.1952 | GNR | 0.50 |
| Glenties - Stranorlar | 15.02.1947 | 10.03.1952 | CDRJC | 24.00 * |

(Last freight train operated 19.09.1949 Stranorlar - Cloghan (MP 6.75) and return.)

| Line | Closed to Passengers | Closed Completely | Operator | Miles |
|---|---|---|---|---|
| Woodenbridge Junc - Aughrim | 24.04.1944 | 01.05.1953 | CIE | 4.54 |
| Tralee - Dingle | 17.04.1939 | 27.06.1953 | CIE | 31.21 * |
| Londonderry - Buncrana | 10.08.1953 | 10.08.1953 | LLSR | 12.19 * |
| Letterkenny - Tooban Junc | 10.08.1953 | 10.08.1953 | LLSR | 18.50 * |
| Macroom Junc - Macroom | 01.07.1935 | 10.11.1953 | CIE | 23.55 |
| Mitchelstown - Fermoy | 27.01.1947 | 01.12.1953 | CIE | 12.00 |
| Kilmessan Junc - Athboy | 27.01.1947 | 01.01.1954 | CIE | 12.15 |
| Cashel - Goolds Cross | 27.01.1947 | 01.09.1954 d | CIE | 5.75 |

(d: last train ran on 25.07.1954.)

| Line | Closed to Passengers | Closed Completely | Operator | Miles |
|---|---|---|---|---|
| Londonderry (Victoria Rd) - Strabane | 31.12.1954 | 31.12.1954 | CDRJC | 14.28 * |

(Strabane-Londonderry and return Sunday School special operated on 30.06.1955.)

| Line | Closed to Passengers | Closed Completely | Operator | Miles |
|---|---|---|---|---|
| Craigavon Bridge - Londonderry (CDR) | freight only | 31.12.1954 | LPHC | 0.10 |
| Killeshandra - Crossdowney | 27.01.1947 | 01.03.1955 | CIE | 7.01 |
| Magherafelt - Cookstown | 28.08.1950 | 01.05.1955 | UTA | 11.18 |
| Limavady - Limavady Junc | 03.07.1950 | 02.05.1955 | UTA | 3.25 |
| Dundalk Quay Street - Barrack St | 01.01.1952 | . .1955 | CIE | 0.43 |
| Scarva - Castlewellan | 02.05.1955 | 02.05.1955 | GNR | 25.00 |
| Castlewellan - Newcastle | 02.05.1955 | 02.05.1955 | UTA | 4.00 |
| Markethill - Goraghwood | 01.02.1933 | 02.05.1955 | GNR | 8.50 |
| Shantonagh Junc - Cootehill | 10.03.1947 | 20.06.1955 | GNR | 7.50 |

| Line | Date 1 | Date 2 | Operator | Miles |
|---|---|---|---|---|
| Banbridge - Newforge | 29.04.1956 | 29.04.1956 | GNR | 14.75 |
| Armagh - Keady | 01.01.1932 | 01.10.1957 | GNR | 8.00 |
| Glaslough - Brownstown | 01.10.1957 | 01.10.1957 | GNR | 20.86 |
| Bundoran - Bundoran Junc | 01.10.1957 | 01.10.1957 | GNR | 35.25 |
| Bundoran Junc Curves | 01.10.1957 | 01.10.1957 | GNR | 0.50 |
| Fintona - Fintona Junc | 01.10.1957 | 01.10.1957 | GNR | 0.69 |
| Omagh - Enniskillen | 01.10.1957 | 01.10.1957 | GNR | 25.75 |
| Enniskillen - Clones | 01.10.1957 | 01.10.1957 | GNR | 22.50 |
| Enniskillen - Collooney Junc | 01.10.1957 | 01.10.1957 | SLNCR | 41.50 |
| Collooney Junc - Collooney (GSWR) | freight only | 01.10.1957 e | SLNCR | 0.63 |

(e: only used as siding after 1944.)

| Line | Date 1 | Date 2 | Operator | Miles |
|---|---|---|---|---|
| Collooney Junc - Ballysodare | 01.10.1957 | 01.10.1957 | SLNCR | 2.21 |
| Carrickfergus Harbour Junc - C Harbour | freight only | . .1957 | UTA | 1.14 |
| Monaghan - Glaslough | 14.10.1957 | 02.06.1958 | GNR | 5.75 |
| Shanganagh Junc - Dublin Harcourt St | 01.01.1959 | 01.01.1959 | CIE | 10.81 |
| Sallins - Tullow | 21.01.1947 | 01.04.1959 | CIE | 34.75 |
| Ballyhaise - Belturbet | 14.10.1957 | 01.04.1959 f | CIE | 4.25 |
| Bellturbet - Dromod | 01.04.1959 | 01.04.1959 f | CIE | 33.75 * |
| Ballinamore - Arigna | 01.04.1959 | 01.04.1959 f | CIE | 14.75 * |
| Arigna - Derreenavoggy | freight only | 01.04.1959 f | CIE | 1.61 * |

(f: last trains actually ran on 10.04.1959.)

| Line | Date 1 | Date 2 | Operator | Miles |
|---|---|---|---|---|
| Cookstown Junc - Magherafelt | 28.08.1950 | 05.10.1959 | UTA | 17.70 |
| Magherafelt - Kilrea | 28.08.1950 | 05.10.1959 | UTA | 15.75 |
| Coalisland - Cookstown | 16.01.1956 | 05.10.1959 | UTA | 9.00 |
| Killybegs - Donegal | 01.01.1960 | 01.01.1960 | CDRJC | 19.25 * |
| Donegal - Ballyshannon | 01.01.1960 | 01.01.1960 | CDRJC | 15.50 * |
| Donegal - Stranorlar | 01.01.1960 | 01.01.1960 | CDRJC | 17.75 * |
| Strabane - Letterkenny | 01.01.1960 | 01.01.1960 | CDRJC | 19.75 * |
| Dundalk - Clones | 14.10.1957 | 01.01.1960 | CIE | 39.44 |
| Clones - Monaghan | 14.10.1957 | 01.01.1960 | CIE | 11.75 |
| Clones - Cavan | 14.10.1957 | 01.01.1960 | CIE | 15.50 |
| Cavan - Inny Junc | 27.01.1947 | 01.01.1960 | CIE | 24.73 |
| Carrickmacross - Inniskeen | 10.03.1947 | 01.01.1960 | CIE | 6.50 |
| Claremorris [+0.08] - Ballinrobe | 01.01.1960 | 01.01.1960 | CIE | 12.46 |
| Kenmare - Headford Junc | 01.01.1960 | 01.01.1960 | CIE | 21.94 |
| Stranorlar - Strabane | 01.01.1960 | 06.02.1960 | CDRJC | 13.75 * |
| Farranfore - Valentia Harbour | 01.02.1960 | .08.1960 | CIE | 39.25 |
| Waterford Manor - Tramore | 31.12.1960 | 31.12.1960 | CIE | 7.25 |
| Cork Albert Quay - Drimoleague Junc | 01.04.1961 | 01.04.1961 | CIE | 45.75 |
| Drimoleague Junc - Bantry Town | 01.04.1961 | 01.04.1961 | CIE | 22.00 |
| Drimoleague Junc - Baltimore | 01.04.1961 | 01.04.1961 | CIE | 16.00 |
| Baltimore - Baltimore Pier | freight only | 01.04.1961 | CIE | 0.25 |
| Clonakilty Junc - Ballinascarthy | 01.04.1961 | 01.04.1961 | CIE | 5.25 |
| Ballinascarthy - Clonakilty | 01.04.1961 | 01.04.1961 | CIE | 3.75 |
| Ballinascarthy - Courtmacsherry | 24.02.1947 | 01.04.1961 | CIE | 9.25 |
| West Cork Junction - Bandon low level | . .1894 | 01.04.1961 | CIE | 0.30 |
| Liffey Junc - Dublin Broadstone | 18.01.1937 | 08.04.1961 | CIE | 1.41 |

(Freight ceased 10.07.1944, loco depot open until 08.04.1961.)
(Line traversed by RPSI railtour on 07.10.72.)

| Line | Date 1 | Date 2 | Operator | Miles |
|---|---|---|---|---|
| Ennis - Moyasta Junc | 01.12.1961 | 01.12.1961 | CIE | 42.91 * |

| Line | Date 1 | Date 2 | Operator | Miles |
|---|---|---|---|---|
| Moyasta Junc - Moyasta East Junc | 01.12.1961 | 01.12.1961 | CIE | *0.40* * |
| Moyasta Junction - Moyasta West Junc | 01.12.1961 | 01.12.1961 | CIE | *0.24* * |
| Moyasta West Junc - Kilkee | 01.12.1961 | 01.12.1961 | CIE | 4.75 * |
| Moyasta West Junc - Moyasta East Junc | .1954 | 01.12.1961 | CIE | *0.50* * |
| Moyasta East Junc - Kilrush | 01.12.1961 | 01.12.1961 | CIE | 3.75 * |
| Londonderry GD - Londonderry MQ | 01.01.1888 | 31.08.1962 | LPHC | 1.00 |

(LLSR passenger trains on mixed gauge: GD: Graving Dock, MQ: Middle Quay.)

| Line | Date 1 | Date 2 | Operator | Miles |
|---|---|---|---|---|
| Londonderry MQ - Craigavon Bridge | freight only | 31.08.1962 | LPHC | 0.65 |
| Craigavon Bridge - Londonderry (GN) | freight only | 31.08.1962 | LPHC | 0.10 |
| Craigavon Bridge | freight only | 31.08.1962 | LPHC | 0.20 |
| Craigavon Bridge - Londonderry (NCC) | freight only | 31.08.1962 | LPHC | 0.25 |
| Coniberry Junc - Mountmellick | 27.01.1947 | 01.01.1963 | CIE | 6.86 |
| Roscrea - Birr | 01.01.1963 | 01.01.1963 | CIE | 10.96 |
| C+B Junc - Banagher | 24.02.1947 | 01.01.1963 | CIE | 18.75 |
| Castlecomer Junc - Castlecomer | 26.01.1931 | 01.01.1963 | CIE | 7.50 |
| Castlecomer - Deerpark Colliery | freight only | 01.01.1963 | CIE | 2.00 |
| Coolnamona - Kilkenny | 01.01.1963 | 01.01.1963 | CIE | 25.57 |
| Kilfree Junc - Ballaghadereen | 04.02.1963 | 04.02.1963 | CIE | 9.54 |
| Banteer - Newmarket | 27.01.1947 | 04.02.1963 | CIE | 9.00 |
| Clara St Junc - Streamstown St Junc | 27.01.1947 | 31.03.1963 g | CIE | 7.38 |

(g: last train ran on 18.03.1963.)

| Line | Date 1 | Date 2 | Operator | Miles |
|---|---|---|---|---|
| Tegral - Ballylinan | freight only | 01.04.1963 | CIE | 3.85 |
| Bagenalstown [+ 0.05] - Palace East | 02.02.1931 | 01.04.1963 h | CIE | 23.95 |

(h: last train ran on 25.03.63)

| Line | Date 1 | Date 2 | Operator | Miles |
|---|---|---|---|---|
| Enfield - Edenderry | 01.06.1931 | 01.04.1963 | CIE | 10.75 |
| Clonsilla - Navan East Junc | 27.01.1947 | 01.04.1963 | CIE | 23.55 |
| Tara Mines Junc - Oldcastle | 14.04.1958 | 01.04.1963 * | GNR/CIE * | 21.81 |
| Macmine Junc - New Ross | 01.04.1963 | 01.04.1963 | CIE | 18.74 |
| East Bridge St Junc - Donegal Quay | freight only | 03.06.1963 | UTA | 0.47 |
| Donegal Quay - Duffern Dock Junc | .1930 | 03.06.1963 | BHC | 0.96 |
| Greenisland - Monkstown | 09.09.1961 | 01.10.1963 | UTA | 1.78 |
| Warrenpoint - Goraghwood | 04.01.1965 | 04.01.1965 | UTA | 10.35 |
| Dungannon Junc - Coalisland | 04.01.1965 | 04.01.1965 | UTA | 5.00 |
| Brownstown - Portadown Junc | 01.10.1957 | 04.01.1965 * | GNR/UTA* | 0.89 |
| Londonderry (GN) - Portadown Junc | 15.02.1965 | 15.02.1965 | UTA | 75.39 |
| Market Branch Junc - Omagh Goods | freight only | 15.02.1965 | UTA | 0.50 |
| Newforge - Knockmore Junc | 29.04.1956 | .02.1965 | GNR/UTA* | 0.25 |
| Guinness Brewery - Dublin Heuston | freight only | 15.05.1965 | Guinness | 0.39 |
| Coleraine - Coleraine Harbour | 21.03.1924 | 01.10.1966 i | UTA | 0.39 |

(i: last train ran on 21.04.63.)

| Line | Date 1 | Date 2 | Operator | Miles |
|---|---|---|---|---|
| Ballinacourty Junc - Mallow | 26.03.1967 | 26.03.1967 | CIE | 49.45 |
| Patrickswell - Charleville S Junc | 31.12.1934 | 26.03.1967 | CIE | 17.50 |
| Thurles Junc - Clonmel Junc | 09.09.1963 | 26.03.1967 | CIE | 25.25 |
| Ballsbridge Junc - Royal Dublin Society | .1924 | .08.1971 | CIE | 0.23 |
| Fenit - Fenit Pier | freight only | .1973 | CIE | 0.66 |
| Limerick - Foynes Junc | 04.02.1963 | 02.10.1975 | CIE | 0.25 |
| Loughrea - Attymon Junc | 03.11.1975 | 03.11.1975 | CIE | 8.94 |
| Ardee - Dromin Junc | 03.06.1934 | 03.11.1975 | CIE | 4.82 |
| Listowel - Newcastle West | 04.02.1963 | 03.11.1975 | CIE | 23.59 |
| Newcastle West - Ballingrane Junc | 04.02.1963 | 03.11.1975 | CIE | 10.84 |

| | | | | |
|---|---|---|---|---|
| Claremorris Junc - Collooney Junc | 17.06.1963 | 03.11.1975 | CIE | 45.74 |
| Cork - Cork Albert Quay | . .1914 | 12.04.1976 | CIE | 0.71 |
| Grace Dieu Junc - Waterford South | 31.01.1908 | 05.09.1976 | CIE | 1.75 |
| Wicklow Junc - Morrough | 01.11.1976 | 01.11.1976 | CIE | 0.65 |
| Westport - Westport Quay | 16.09.1912 | . .1977 | CIE | 1.91 |
| Castleisland - Gortalea Junc | 24.02.1947 | 10.01.1977 | CIE | 4.25 |
| Listowel - Abberdorney | 04.02.1963 | 10.01.1977 | CIE | 11.25 |
| Curragh - Curragh Racecourse | 07.03.1977 | 07.03.1977 | CIE | 0.72 |
| Liffey Junc - North City Mills | freight only | . .1977 | CIE | 1.38 |
| Tralee Fenit Junc - Fenit | 31.12.1934 | 02.06.1978 | CIE | 7.85 |
| Tralee - Aberdorney | 04.02.1963 | 05.06.1978 | CIE | 8.38 |
| Dun Loaghaire Pier - Pier Junc | 11.10.1980 | 11.10.1980 | CIE | 0.22 |
| Suir Bridge Junc - Ballinacourty Junc | 26.03.1967 | 28.07.1982 | CIE | 25.61 |
| Ballinacourty Junc - Magnesite works | freight only | 28.07.1982 | CIE | 1.47 |
| Cobh Junc - Youghal | 04.02.1963 | 02.06.1988 | IE | 20.79 |
| Rosslare Harbour - Rosslare Pier | 14.09.1989 | 14.09.1989 j | IE | 0.30 |

(j: traversed by railtour on 19.10.1996, periodically used as siding.)

| | | | | |
|---|---|---|---|---|
| Silvermines Junc - Silvermines | freight only | 29.10.1993 | IE | 1.25 |
| Belfast Queens Quay - Ballymacarret Junc | 12.04.1976 | 28.11.1994 | NIR | 0.50 |
| New Ross - Waterford Abbey Junc | 01.04.1963 | 29.06.1995 | IE | 13.50 |
| Dundalk South Junc - East Junc | freight only | 31.03.1995 | IE | 0.47 |
| Dundalk East Junc - Barrack St | 01.01.1952 | 31.03.1995 | IE | 1.03 |
| Coniberry Junc - Coolnamona | 01.01.1963 | . .1995 | IE | 2.04 |
| Boyne Road - Cement Branch Junc | freight only | . .1997 | IE | 1.10 |
| Tara Mines Junc - Kingscourt | 27.01.1947 | 30.10.2001 | IE | 20.14 |
| Foynes Junc - Foynes | 04.02.1963 | 16.12.2001 | IE | 25.81 |
| Athenry - Claremorris | 08.04.1976 | 11.11.2002 k | IE | 33.33 |

(k: last known train 08.05.1999.)

distances in italics are approx.

| | |
|---|---|
| 5ft 3in gauge lines | 1628.14 |
| 3 ft gauge lines | 545.85 * |
| Note 1: Monorail | 9.25 |
| Total Mileage Closed = | 2183.24 |

# LINES CLOSED BUT STILL IN SITU

| Section | Date closed to passenger traffic | Date closed completely | Notes |
|---|---|---|---|
| Tralee - Fenit | 31.12.1934 | 05.06.1978 | 1 |
| Tara Junction - Kingscourt | 27.01.1947 | 30.10.2001 | |
| Glounthaune - Youghal | 04.02.1963 | .09.1989 | 2 |
| Limerick Check - Foynes | 04.02.1963 | 16.12.2001 | |
| Abbey Junction - New Ross | 01.04.1963 | 29.06.1995 | |
| Claremorris - Collooney Junction | 17.06.1963 | 03.11.1975 | 3 |
| Claremorris - Athenry | 05.04.1976 | 11.11.2002 | 4 |
| Athenry - Ennis | 05.04.1976 | 11.11.2002 | 5 |
| Mullingar - Athlone Midland | 11.05.1987 | - | 6 |
| Silvermines Junction - Silvermines | Freight only | 29.10.1993 | |

Notes:

1. Severed at Tralee.
2. Severed at Glounthaune. Approximately 3 miles of track has also been lifted between Youghal and Killeagh. The section from Glounthaune to Midleton is due to re-open in 2007.
3. Severed at Collooney Junction.
4. Severed at Athenry.
5. Athenry to Ennis is "Out of Use", the only expected use of this line is the yearly weed spraying train.
6. Mullingar to Athlone Midland is "Out of Use", the only expected use of this line is the yearly weed spraying train.

## LINES OPEN FOR FREIGHT TRAFFIC ONLY

| Section | Date closed to passenger traffic |
|---|---|
| Drogheda - Tara Mines | 14.04.58 |
| Limerick Check - Castlemungret | Freight only |
| Lisburn - Antrim | 29.06.03 * |

* Still in use by passenger trains for diversionary purposes only.

## SECTION 7 - PRESERVED STEAM LOCOMOTIVES

The following 5ft 3in and 3ft gauge steam locomotives, which were owned by constituent companies of NIR and IE, have been preserved.

| 1st No. | 2nd No. | Name | Builder | Works No. | Date Built | Status | Current Location |
|---|---|---|---|---|---|---|---|

### 5 ft 3 in Gauge Locomotives.

**GS&WR 2-2-2**
| 36 | | | BC&K | - | 1875 | PL | IE Cork Station. |

**CR (GS&WR Class 90) 0-6-4T Combined locomotive and carriage.**
| - | 90 | | GS&WR | - | 1875 | Su | Westrail, Tuam. |

Note: Carriage removed and rebuilt as 0-6-0T by GS&WR in 1915.

**GS&WR Class 101 (GSR Class J15) 0-6-0**
| 184 | | | GS&WR | - | 1880 | Su | RPSI Mullingar. |
| 186 | | | SS | 2838 | 1879 | M | RPSI Whitehead. |

**GNR Class JT 2-4-2T**
| 93 | | Sutton | Dundalk | 16 | 1895 | Se | UF&TM Cultra. |

Note: Name no longer carried.

**B&CDR (UTA Class I) 4-4-2T**
| 30 | 230 | | BP | 4231 | 1901 | Se | UF&TM Cultra. |

**GNR Class Q (Qs from 1914) 4-4-0**
| | | | | | | | |
|---|---|---|---|---|---|---|---|
| 131 | 131N | Uranus | NR | 5757 | 1901 | Ur | RPSI Whitehead. |

Note: Name removed in 1914.

**GNR Class S 4-4-0**
| | | | | | | | |
|---|---|---|---|---|---|---|---|
| 171 | 171N | Slieve Gullion | BP Rebuilt Dundalk 42 | 5629 | 1913 1938 | O | RPSI Whitehead. |

**D&SER (GSR Class 461) 2-6-0**
| | | | | | | |
|---|---|---|---|---|---|---|
| 15 | 461 | | BP | 6112 | 1922 | O | RPSI Whitehead. |

**LMS (NCC) Class U2 4-4-0**
| | | | | | | |
|---|---|---|---|---|---|---|
| 74 | | Dunluce Castle | NBL | 23096 | 1924 | Se | UF&TM Cultra. |

**GNR Class V 4-4-0**
| | | | | | | | |
|---|---|---|---|---|---|---|---|
| 85 | 85N | Merlin | BP | 6733 | 1932 | M | RPSI Whitehead. |

**GSR Class 800/B1A 4-6-0**
| | | | | | | |
|---|---|---|---|---|---|---|
| 800 | | Meadhbh | GSR | - | 1939 | Se | UF&TM Cultra. |

Note: Originally named Maeve.

**LMS (NCC) Class WT 2-6-2T**
| | | | | | | |
|---|---|---|---|---|---|---|
| 4 | | | Derby | - | 1947 | M | RPSI Whitehead. |

**SL&NC (UTA Class Z) 0-6-4T**
| | | | | | | | |
|---|---|---|---|---|---|---|---|
| - | 27 | Lough Erne | BP | 7242 | 1949 | Su | RPSI Whitehead. |

## 3 ft Gauge Locomotives.

**PT 0-4-0 Tram locomotives**
| | | | | | |
|---|---|---|---|---|---|
| 1 | | K | T56 | 1882 | Se | HCM&AG. |
| 2 | | K | T84 | 1883 | Se | UF&TM Cultra. |

**C&LR (GSR Class 1L) 4-4-0T**
| | | | | | | | |
|---|---|---|---|---|---|---|---|
| 2 | 2L | Kathleen | RS | 2613 | 1887 | Se | UF&TM Cultra. |
| 3 | 3L | Lady Edith | RS | 2614 | 1887 | Se | Scranton, USA. |

Note: Names removed in 1925.

**T&DLR (GSR Class 5T) 2-6-2T**
| | | | | | | |
|---|---|---|---|---|---|---|
| 5 | 5T | | HE | 555 | 1892 | Op | T&DSR. |

**WCR (GSR Class 5C) 0-6-2T**
| | | | | | | | |
|---|---|---|---|---|---|---|---|
| 5 | 5C | Slieve Callan | Dübs | 2890 | 1892 | Op | West Clare Railway. |

Note: name removed in 1925.

**CDRJC Class 5  2-6-4T**

| | | | | | | | |
|---|---|---|---|---|---|---|---|
| 16 | 4 | Meenglas | NW | 828 | 1907 | Se | FVR Londonderry. |
| 17 | 5 | Drumboe | NW | 829 | 1907 | Se | SDRRS Donegal Town. |
| 18 | 6 | Columbkille | NW | 830 | 1907 | Se | FVR Londonderry. |

Note: Originally named Donegal, Glenties and Killybegs respectively.

**CDRJC Class 5A  2-6-4T**

| | | | | | | | |
|---|---|---|---|---|---|---|---|
| 2A | 2 | Blanche | NW | 956 | 1912 | Se | UF&TM Cultra. |

Note: Name removed.

**Key to abbreviations used above:**

| | |
|---|---|
| B&CDR | Belfast & County Down Railway. |
| CDRJC | County Donegal Railway Joint Committee. |
| C&LR | Cavan & Leitrim Railway. |
| CR | Castleisland Railway. |
| D&SER | Dublin and South Eastern Railway. |
| GS&WR | Great Southern & Western Railway. |
| PT | Portstewart Tramway. |
| SL&NCR | Sligo Leitrim & Northern Counties Railway. |
| T&DLR | Tralee & Dingle Light Railway. |
| WCR | West Clare Railway. |

| | | | | |
|---|---|---|---|---|
| M | Operational - mainline registered. | | Se | Static exhibit. |
| Op | Operational - at location given. | | Su | Stored un-serviceable. |
| O | Undergoing overhaul (for mainline). | | Ur | Undergoing restoration. |
| PL | Plinthed. | | | |

| | | | | |
|---|---|---|---|---|
| BC&K | Bury, Curtis and Kennedy. | | NBL | North British Locomotive Co. |
| BP | Bayer Peacock. | | NR | Neilson Reid. |
| Dübs | Dübs. | | NW | Nasmyth Wilson. |
| HE | Hunslet Engine Company. | | RS | Robert Stephenson. |
| K | Kitson. | | SS | Sharp Stewart. |

| | |
|---|---|
| FVR Londonderry | Foyle Valley Railway, Londonderry (closed). |
| HCM&AG | Hull City Museum & Art Gallery, Humberside, England. |
| RPSI | Railway Preservation Society of Ireland. |
| SDRRS Donegal Town | South Donegal Railway Restoration Society. |
| T&DSR Blennerville | Tralee & Blennerville Steam Railway, Blennerville, Co. Kerry. |
| UF&TM Cultra | Ulster Folk & Transport Museum, Cultra, Co. Down. |
| Scranton, USA | Steamtown, Scranton, United States of America. |
| West Clare Railway | West Clare Railway, Moyasta Junction, Co. Clare. |

# SECTION 8 - PRESERVED COACHING STOCK

The following mainline registered coaches are operated by the Railway Preservation Society of Ireland. The Mark 2 carriages are currently being overhauled and fitted with vacuum brakes and steam heating to replace an older rake of timber framed coaches previously in use. A second rake of timber framed coaches is based in Dublin. Due to restrictions placed on the use of these timber framed coaches over Iarnród Éireann tracks it is expected these vehicles will eventually be replaced by a rake of former Iarnród Éireann Cravens coaches when they are taken out of service.

## Mark 2 coaches (based at Whitehead)

| RPSI No. | ex NIR No. | ex BR No. | Type as built |
|---|---|---|---|
| 170 | - | 5180 | Mk2 SO 1966. |
| 180 | - | 13475 | Mk2A FK 1968. |
| 181 | - | 13487 | Mk2B FK 1969, later BR SK 19487 then 977529. |
| 300 | 934 | - | Mk2B SO 1970, NIR 822 1970-1989. |
| 301 | - | 5207 | Mk2 SO 1966. |
| 302 | - | 5135 | Mk2 SO 1966. |
| 303 | 902 & 920 | 13509 | Mk2B SO 1969, FK on BR / NIR 1981-1991. |
| 304 | 923 | 13496 | Mk2B SO 1969, FK on BR / NIR1981-1989, NIR SK. |
| 305 | 935 | - | Mk2B SO 1970, NIR 823 1970-1989. |
| 460 | - | 9382 | Mk2 BSO 1966. |
| 462 | 916 | - | Mk2B DBSO 1970, NIR 812 1970-1992. |
| 463 | - | 14091 | Mk2 BFK 1966, later BR BSK 17091. |
| 547 | 547 | - | Mk2B Buffet 1970. |

Notes: 300, 303, 304, 305, 462 and 547 were acquired from Translink NI Railways (303 and 304 were originally purchased from British Rail by NIR). The remaining coaches have been acquired from various other operators / leasing companies.

## Timber framed coaches (based in Dublin).

| Number | Builder | Built at | Seats |
|---|---|---|---|
| 88 | GNR(I) | Dundalk, 1938 | 24S |
| 351 | GS&WR | Inchicore, 1902 | 18F |
| 1142 | GS&WR | Inchicore, 1921 | 42F |
| 1335 | GSR | Inchicore, 1937 | 56T |
| 1383 | CIE | Inchicore, 1955 | 82S |
| 1416 | CIE | Inchicore, 1955 | 72S |
| 1463 | CIE | Inchicore, 1958 | 64S |
| 1916 | CIE | Inchicore, 1958 | 48S |
| 2421 | CIE | Inchicore, 1956 | 39S |
| 2977 | CIE | Inchicore, 1935 | TPO |

351 was the former State Coach.

# SECTION 9 - FREIGHT TRAIN WORKINGS

All freight traffic in Ireland is operated by Iarnród Éireann. As there are no longer any cross-border liner services, freight traffic is now virtually non-existent in Northern Ireland. The Irish Republic has fared little better in recent years, with major reductions in liner and cement traffic, and the total loss of ammonia, fertiliser, grain, tar, molasses, scrap metal, coal and gypsum traffic.

The information in this section has been compiled from various sources and observations. It will be noted that the times shown only apply at the time of publication, and are for guidance only. Freight trains can often run early or late, or not at all, depending on availability of locomotives, crews, paths and completeness of trains.

The following abbreviations are used:
| | | | | | |
|---|---|---|---|---|---|
| M | Monday | S | | Saturday | |
| T | Tuesday | SUN | | Sunday | |
| W | Wednesday | O | | Only | |
| Th | Thursday | X | | Excepted | |
| F | Friday | | | | |

For Example: ThO = Thursdays Only, FX = Fridays Excepted.

# LINERS

This is the usual term applied to trains conveying containers. Beer products (including Guinness, Smithwicks ale and Budweiser lager) in kegs are also conveyed by such workings. The Sligo and Ballina trains will also convey oil tank cars, as dedicated oil trains have now been discontinued. North Wall Yard is usually closed on Sundays, so liner trains and transfers to and from Dublin Heuston do not work on that day.

| Route | Days Run | Dep. Time | Comments |
|---|---|---|---|
| North Wall – Dundalk | M – F | 21:30 | Beer |
| Dundalk – North Wall | T – S | 14:00 | Beer |

Generally worked by a 141 class locomotive.

| | | | |
|---|---|---|---|
| North Wall – Sligo | M – F | 19:20 | Oil/Beer/Containers |
| Sligo – North Wall | T – S | 02:00 | Oil/Beer/Containers |

Any container traffic is loaded/unloaded at Longford, as containers are conveyed to Sligo by road from Ballina. Generally worked by 071 class locomotives.

| | | | |
|---|---|---|---|
| North Wall – Ballina | M – F | 19:55 | Containers |
| Ballina – North Wall | T – S | 21:50 | Containers |

Ballina – North Wall service leaves at 22:20 FO. Trains normally formed of 18 bogie wagons, and worked by 071 class locomotives. The 071 class locomotive generally works the Ballina branch passenger service during the day after arrival from Dublin.

| | | | |
|---|---|---|---|
| North Wall – Claremorris | M – F | 20:45 | Normally Oil/Beer |
| Claremorris – North Wall | T – S | 04:10 | Normally Oil/Beer |

Normally worked by 071 class locomotives, but occasionally 201 class or 2 x 141 class locomotives are used.

| | | |
|---|---|---|
| North Wall – Limerick | M – F | 21:30 |
| Limerick – North Wall | T – S | 20:54 (21:33 FO) |

Generally, the 201 class locomotive off the 17:10 Dublin Heuston to Limerick passenger service works the up liner, whilst the 201 class locomotive off the down liner works the 07:50 Limerick to Dublin Heuston passenger service. These trains are formed on alternate nights of ordinary bogie container wagons and container pocket wagons.

| | | |
|---|---|---|
| North Wall – Cork | M – F | 12:00, 20:40, 23:20 |
| Cork – North Wall | T – S | 17:50, 20:25, 22:25 |

All trains normally worked by 201 class locomotives. Container pocket wagons work on the 12:00 down and 22:25 up trains.

| | | |
|---|---|---|
| North Wall – Waterford | M – F | 20:10 |
| Waterford – North Wall | T – S | 22:00 |

Attaches / detaches beer traffic at Kilkenny. Generally worked by a 201 or 071 class locomotive. The locomotive off the down 18:20 Dublin Heuston to Waterford passenger service works back to Dublin on the 22:00 up liner, while the locomotive off the 20:10 down liner works the 07:20 Waterford to Dublin Heuston passenger service.

| | | |
|---|---|---|
| Waterford – Ballina | T/Th/S | 07:50 |
| Ballina – Waterford | T/Th/S | 08:50 |

Generally formed of 18 bogie container wagons and worked by 071 class locomotives. Operated on behalf of Norfolk Lines, as required, and runs via Kildare both ways.

North Wall – Heuston Guinness Yard
Trains run several times a day, as required, to convey laden beer kegs to North Wall for incorporation into scheduled Liner trains. Generally worked by a 141 class locomotive.

## Wagons

Some 4-wheel flat wagons are still in service. These are in the 27xxx series, are vacuum-braked and were introduced between 1970 and 1973. There are four types of bogie flat wagons. The 30001 to 30218 series are 42' 9" long, vacuum-braked and were introduced between 1971 and 1978. They can carry 20' and 40' containers. The 30219 to 30278 series are 47' 6" long, vacuum-braked and were introduced in 1978, allowing 45' containers to be carried. The 30285 to 30294 series were converted from fertiliser wagons 35001 to 35010 to carry 40' containers in 2000. They are vacuum-braked and 42' 9" long. The 305xx series wagons are 62' 9_" long, air-braked and were introduced in 1984. The latest wagons are the 2001 Talgo-built container pocket wagons, numbered 36001 to 36024 and are 71' 10" long. In addition to air brakes, they also have vacuum through pipes, and can carry 45' long and 10' high containers. The oil tank wagons are all 4-wheel and vacuum-braked, and have a capacity of around 20 tons.

# BULK CEMENT

Trains are usually formed of about twenty 2-axle bulk cement wagons ("Bubbles"), unless otherwise stated. Cement factories are located at Mungret, near Limerick, and Platin, near Drogheda. Trip workings are operated as required (one for each train) from Mungret to Limerick and return, to provide wagons for the scheduled workings to and from Limerick. These are worked by 141 class locomotives. Similar trip workings to and from Platin are operated from Drogheda and North Wall (one for each train), and 2 x 141 class locomotives are based at Drogheda for this purpose. Trains work laden from Mungret/Limerick and Platin/North Wall. As these trains do not tend to operate to a schedule, no timings are given here.

| Route | Days Run | Dep. Time |
|---|---|---|
| North Wall – Tullamore | M – F | 04:00 or 06:00 |
| Tullamore – North Wall | M – F | 13:55 |

Generally worked by 071 class locomotives, but occasionally 2 x 141 class or a 201 class locomotive may be seen.

| | | |
|---|---|---|
| Limerick – Athy | T – F | 03:45 |
| Athy – Limerick | T – F | 12:40 |

Generally worked by one or two 141 class locomotives.

| | | |
|---|---|---|
| North Wall – Waterford | M – S | 03:40 |
| Waterford – North Wall | M – S | 12:50 or 14:05 |

Generally worked by 071 class locomotives, but occasionally 2 x 141 class or a 201 class locomotive may be seen.

| | | |
|---|---|---|
| Limerick – Cork | M – S | 04:10 |
| Cork – Limerick | M – S | 11:50 |

Generally worked by 2 x 141 class locomotives, and formed of bogie bulk cement wagons.

Limerick – Cork         M – F         10:50
Cork – Limerick         M – F         18:00
Generally worked by a 141 class locomotive, or 2 x 141 class locomotives. Bogie bulk cement wagons may occasionally be exchanged between this link and that above.

At the time of writing, a 121 class locomotive may appear in place of a 141 class locomotive on trains to and from Limerick.

### Wagons
The 4-wheel bulk cement wagons are numbered in the 25050 to 25199 series, are vacuum-braked, carry 20 tons and were introduced between 1964 and 1972. The bogie cement wagons are numbered 33001 to 33012, were introduced in 1979, are air-braked and carry 52 tons.

# TIMBER

Trains operate to bring cut logs from forestry areas in the north-west and west of Ireland to a Coillte (Irish Forestry Service) factory at Waterford. All trains are generally worked by 071 class locomotives, but the Westport and Ballina trains see substitutions by 201 class and pairs of 141 class locomotives. Trains indicated as being to or from Westport or Ballina will run to one or other location only, the selected location depending on the supply of timber. Sligo trains run via North Wall.

| Route | Days Run | Dep. Time |
| --- | --- | --- |
| Westport or Ballina – Waterford | M – Th | 16:40 |
| Waterford – Westport or Ballina | M – W | 12:10 |
| Ballina | SO | 08:35 |
| Sligo – Heuston Yard | SO | 12:00 or 14:05 |
| Heuston Yard – Waterford | SuO | 12:30 |
| Waterford – Sligo | FO | 06:00 or 07:45 |

The laden train stages at Heuston Guinness Yard overnight. The Sunday working represents one of the very few freight working that will be seen on that day.

The following trains may run instead of a Westport or Ballina train.
Sligo – Waterford         W or Th         14:05 (Depart North Wall approx. 19:00)
Waterford – Sligo         T or W          12:10

### Wagons
Two sets of twelve 62' 9½" bogie wagons are used for the traffic, these being bogie liner wagons fitted with cradles to carry the timber.

# SHALE

Shale is an aggregate used in the manufacture of cement. Laden trains run from Kilmastulla siding, controlled from Birdhill Signal Cabin on the Ballybrophy to Killonan line, to Limerick. Trains are generally worked by a single 141 class locomotive.

| Route | Days Run | Dep. Time |
|---|---|---|
| Kilmastulla – Limerick | M – F | 09:45, 12:55, 16:15 |
| Limerick – Kilmastulla | M – F | 08:17, 11:10, 14:50 |

**Wagons**
The dedicated wagons used for this traffic are numbered 31501 to 31528, carry 40 tons, are air-braked and were introduced in 1983.

## TARA MINES ORE TRAFFIC

Zinc ore is carried from Tara Mines, located west of Navan, to Alexandra Road at North Wall, from where it is exported for processing. Once the preserve of "A" class locomotives, the trains now rarely see anything other than an 071 class, with two usually based at Drogheda for this traffic.

| Route | Days Run | Dep. Time |
|---|---|---|
| Platin – Tara Mines | M – F | 07:00 |
| Tara Mines – Alexandra Rd. | M – F | 10:20 |
| Alexandra Rd. – Tara Mines | M – F | 15:08 |
| Tara Mines – Platin | M – F | 19:50 |
| Platin – Alexandra Rd. | M – F | 05:00 |
| Alexandra Rd. – Tara Mines | M – F | 08:40 |
| Tara Mines – Alexandra Rd. | M – F | 13:20 |
| Alexandra Rd. – Platin | M – F | 19:17 |

**Wagons**
The dedicated wagons used for this traffic are numbered 31001 to 31025, carry 62 tons, are vacuum-braked and were introduced in 1977.

## BEET

Sugar Beet is a root crop, and is harvested in the autumn. While rail-borne beet traffic was formerly very extensive, running to four factories, rationalisation in the industry has resulted in just one flow remaining. Beet from one of the main growing areas, South Wexford, is loaded at Wellingtonbridge, and is conveyed to the factory at Mallow, which is situated on the Tralee branch west of Killarney Junction. The traffic is seasonal, and normally runs between October and mid-December. If the harvest is difficult, usually as a result of poor weather conditions, the trains may run into early January.

Generally, three trains operate from Waterford to Mallow (via Clonmel) each day. Laden trains are formed of 25 4-wheel wagons, while the return empties are formed of up to 36 wagons. Therefore, the third return empty service may often be quite short, or even a light engine only. Due to the gradients east of Waterford, five trains each way normally operate, with smaller loads. As there is a single block section from Waterford to Wellingtonbridge, when an empty train arrives at Wellingtonbridge, a laden train usually departs. The service usually features two or three 071 class locomotives, and one or two pairs of 141 class locomotives.

**Wagons**
The 4-wheel wagons used on the service were converted from vacuum-braked container flat wagons, with the bodies of two 12-ton open wagons mounted on them. The conversions were carried out at Limerick Wagon Works in 1985, and are numbered in the series 285xx and 286xx. The open wagons which donated their bodies had previously been used for beet traffic, and were to a design introduced by O.V.S. Bulleid in the 1950's.

# APPENDIX 1 - FORMER UTA DIESEL LOCOMOTIVES

Note: The date to traffic relates to the date that the locomotives entered traffic with the LMS(NCC) or the B&CDR as appropriate.

## DIESEL SHUNTER                                                  0-4-0

**Built:** 1937 by Harland & Wolff, Belfast for their own use.
**Engine:** Harland Burmeister & Wain TR6 of 225 hp (168 kW).
**Transmission:** Mechanical.
**Transmission Type:** SLM 4 speed gearbox with Jackshaft.
**Maximum Tractive Effort:** 15000 lbf (67 kN).
**Continuous Tractive Effort:**
**Power At Rail:**
**Weight:** 28.31 tons.
**Length Over Buffers:** 23 ft 4 1/2 in (7.12 m).
**Wheel Diameter:** 3 ft 7 in (1092 mm).
**Maximum Speed:** 20 mph.
**Works Number:** H & W Order 11612.

| 1945 No. | 1951 No. | Month to Traffic | Month Stopped | Month Withdrawn | Month Cut Up | Cut Up Location |
|---|---|---|---|---|---|---|
| 20 | 16 | 01.45 | 02.66 | ? | .67 | ? |

Used by Harland & Wolff until 01.45, when it was loaned to LMS(NCC) and allocated number 20. Returned to Harland & Wolff 01.04.46. Returned to UTA (as successors to LMS(NCC)) as number 16 in 01.51 in exchange for number 2 ex. B&CDR.

## DIESEL SHUNTER (CLASS X)                            0-6-0

**Built:** 1936 by Harland & Wolff, Belfast, for LMS (NCC).
**Engine:** Harland Burmeister & Wain TR8 of 330 hp (246 kW).
**Transmission:** Hydraulic.
**Transmission Type:** Voith with Jackshaft.
**Maximum Tractive Effort:** 24000 lbf (107 kN).
**Continuous Tractive Effort:**
**Power At Rail:**                                    **Weight:** 49.00 tons.
**Length Over Buffers:** 32 ft 4 1/2 in (9.87 m).      **Wheel Diameter:** 4 ft 1 in (1245 mm).
**Maximum Speed:** 50 mph.                   **Works Number:** H & W Order 9825.

| No. | Month to Traffic | Month Stopped | Month Withdrawn | Month Cut Up | Cut Up Location |
|---|---|---|---|---|---|
| 17 | 12.37 | 03.66 | .70 | .70 | ? |

On loan until purchased by LMS(NCC) in 1941. Transferred to UTA 1948. Although passing to NIR in 1968, it had been out of use for some time before this date. Named "Harlandic'.

# DIESEL SHUNTER (CLASS X)  0-6-0

**Built:** 1933 by Harland & Wolff, Belfast, to shunt at Chester and Heysham Harbours.
**Original Engine:** Harland Burmeister & Wain of 150 hp (113 kW).
**Rebuilt:** 1945 by Harland & Wolff, Belfast, for LMS (NCC).
**Subsequent Engine:** Harland Burmeister & Wain TR6 of 225 hp (168 kW) at 1200 rpm.
**Transmission:** Hydraulic.
**Maximum Tractive Effort:** 15000 lbf (67 kN)
**Continuous Tractive Effort:**
**Power At Rail:**
**Weight:** 27.15 tons.
**Length Over Buffers:** 25 ft 4½ in (7.73 m).
**Wheel Diameter:** 3 ft 2 in (965 mm).
**Maximum Speed:** 10 mph.
**Works Number:** H & W Order 8627.

| No. | Month to Traffic | Month Stopped | Month Withdrawn | Month Cut Up | Cut Up Location |
|---|---|---|---|---|---|
| 22 | 01.46 | ? | 04.65 | 12.65 | ? |

Rebuilt and re-gauged from LMSR 7057, built by Harland & Wolff (order no. 2503) in 1933. Withdrawn by LMSR 01.44 and sold back to Harland & Wolff 01.45. Loaned to LMS(NCC) in 01.46 and later purchased by UTA (as successors to LMS(NCC)) 10.49.

# DIESEL ELECTRIC  1A-A1

**Built:** 1937 by Harland & Wolff, Belfast, for the Belfast & County Down Railway.
**Engine:** Harland Burmeister & Wain TR8 of 500 hp (373 kW).
**Transmission:** Electric.
**Traction Motors:** Laurence Scott & Electromotors Ltd. Two "Emcol" type.
**Maximum Tractive Effort:** 10000 lbf (44 kN).
**Continuous Tractive Effort:**
**Power At Rail:**
**Weight:** 48.00 tons.
**Length Over Buffers:** 36 ft 5½ in (11.11 m).  **Wheel Diameter:** 3 ft 7 in (1092 mm).
**Maximum Speed:** 60 mph.  **Works Number:** H & W Order 10170.
**Train Brakes:** Vacuum.

| 1st 1937 No. | 2nd 1937 No. | Month to Traffic | Month Stopped | Month Withdrawn | Month Cut Up | Cut Up Location |
|---|---|---|---|---|---|---|
| D2 | 28 | 12.37 | 05.73 | .74 | .75 | ? |

Originally only loaned to the B&CDR. Withdrawn by B&CDR 12.44 and then loaned by Harland & Wolff to LMS(NCC) in 07.45. Withdrawn for a second time (by UTA) 09.52, returning to Harland & Wolff. Ran on trials on GNR(I) 1957-61. Finally purchased by UTA on 01.11.62, retaining the number 28. Survived to NIR days before suffering a failure in 1973. Last reported dumped in Belfast in 1974.

# DIESEL ELECTRIC                                                    1-Bo

**Built:** 1933 by Harland & Wolff, Belfast, for the Belfast & County Down Railway.
**Engine:** Harland Burmeister & Wain TR4 of 270 hp (201 kW) at 850 rpm.
**Transmission:** Electric.
**Traction Motors:** Laurence Scott.
**Maximum Tractive Effort:** 9450 lbf (42 kN).
**Continuous Tractive Effort:**
**Power At Rail:**
**Weight:** 33.20 tons.
**Length Over Buffers:**
**Wheel Diameter:** 3 ft 7 in (1092 mm).
**Maximum Speed:** 50 mph.
**Works Number:** H & W Order 8252.
**Train Brakes:** Vacuum.

| 1933 No. | 1937 No. | UTA No. | Month to Traffic | Date Stopped | Month Withdrawn | Month Cut Up | Cut Up Location |
|---|---|---|---|---|---|---|---|
| D1 | 2 | 202 | 07.33 | 01.51 | 01.51 | 06.69 | Harland & Wolff |

Sold back to Harland & Wolff 01.51, who rebuilt it to an 0-4-0 shunting loco for their own use. It remained in their use until 10.67.

## APPENDIX 2 - FORMER DIESEL RAILBUSES, RAILCARS & MULTIPLE UNITS OF CIE, NIR & CONSTITUENT COMPANIES

Note: In addition to the vehicles contained within this section, there were other various CIE and UTA hauled coaches that were also wired to operate as un-powered trailers with either AEC or BUT built railcars. As these vehicles retained their hauled coach running numbers, they have not been classified as railcar vehicles for the purposes of this section.

## NCC RAILCARS

### DRIVING MOTOR BRAKE COMPOSITE (CLASS A)

**Built:** 1933 by LMS(NCC) at York Road Works, Belfast.
**Engines:** Two Leyland 10 litre petrol, each of 125 hp at 2000 rpm.
**Transmission:** Hydraulic. Two Lysholm Smith torque converters.
**Seats:** 6F, 55T.
**Length:** 57 ft (17.07 m).
**Width:** 9 ft 8 in (2.95 m).
**Weight:** 32 tons.
**Brakes:** Vacuum.
**Notes:** Re-engined in 1959 with two Leyland O600 of 125 hp (93 kW) at 1800 rpm.

| Vehicle No. | Month to Traffic | Date Stopped | Month Withdrawn | Disposal Location |
|---|---|---|---|---|
| 1 | 01.33 | 25.11.65 | 12.68 | RPSI Depot, Whitehead (P) |

# DRIVING MOTOR BRAKE COMPOSITE (CLASS B)

**Built:** 1934 by LMS(NCC), at York Road Works, Belfast.
**Engines:** Two Leyland of 125 hp (93 kW) each.
**Transmission:** Hydraulic. Two Lysholm Smith torque converters.
**Seats:** 5F, 75T.
**Length:** 60 ft (18.29 m).
**Width:** 9 ft (2.74 m).
**Weight:** 26 tons.
**Brakes:** Vacuum.

| Vehicle No. | Month to Traffic | Date Stopped | Month Withdrawn | Month Cut Up | Disposal Location |
|---|---|---|---|---|---|
| 2 | 06.34 | 04.54 | .57 | .57 | Belfast York Road |

Body survived as a shed until 1966.

# DRIVING MOTOR BRAKE COMPOSITE (CLASS C)

**Built:** 1935 (3) or 1938 (4) by LMS(NCC) at York Road Works, Belfast.
**Engines:** Two Leyland O600 of 125 hp (93 kW) each.
**Transmission:** Hydraulic. Two Lysholm Smith torque converters.
**Seats:** 12F, 60T.
**Length:** 62 ft (18.9 m).
**Weight:** 28 tons.
**Width:** 9 ft 6 in (2.9 m)
**Brakes:** Vacuum.
**Notes:** No. 3 was fitted with front end doors.

| Vehicle No. | Month to Traffic | Date Stopped | Month Withdrawn | Month Cut Up | Disposal Location |
|---|---|---|---|---|---|
| 3 | 07.36 | 07.07.56 | 07.57 | .57 | ? |
| 4 | .38 | 28.02.66 | 12.68 | 12.69 | Belfast York Road. |

No. 3 was destroyed by fire at Whitehead 07.07.56.
No. 4 was destroyed by fire on 18.11.69.

# TRAILER THIRD

**Built:** 1934 by LMS(NCC) at York Road Works, Belfast.
**Seats:** 100.
**Length:** 62 ft (18.9 m).
**Weight:** 17.5 tons.
**Width:** 9 ft 5 in (2.88 m).
**Brakes:** Vacuum.

| Vehicle No. | Month to Traffic | Date Stopped | Disposal Location |
|---|---|---|---|
| T1 | .34 | .59 | Renumbered in 1959 to 544 (qv). |
| T2 | .34 | .59 | Renumbered in 1959 to 545 (qv). |

# UTA DIESEL RAILCAR

## DRIVING MOTOR BRAKE COMPOSITE (CLASS D)

**Built:** 1936 by Metropolitan Cammell, Birmingham as a demonstration unit. Sold to UTA in February 1951, when it was regauged to 5 ft 3 in.
**Engine:** Ganz of 240 hp (179 kW) at 1250 rpm.
**Transmission:**
**Seats:** 18F, 38T.
**Length:** 64 ft (19.51 m).
**Width:** 8 ft 7 in (2.63 m).
**Weight:** 38 tons.
**Brakes:** Air.
**Notes:** Used in conjunction with trailer 515.

| Vehicle No. | Month to Traffic | Date Stopped | Month Withdrawn | Month Cut Up | Disposal Location |
|---|---|---|---|---|---|
| 5 | 04.51 | .63 | 05.65 | 05.65 | Belfast Maysfield Yard. |

# UTA DIESEL MECHANICAL MULTIPLE UNITS

## DRIVING MOTOR BRAKE COMPOSITE (CLASS E)

**Built:** 1937 by LMS(NCC) as J10 Class loco hauled coaches.
**Rebuilt:** 1951 by UTA.
**Engines:** Two AEC 9.6 litre of 125 hp (93 kW) each.
**Transmission:** Mechanical.
**Seats:** 8F, 65T.
**Length:** 61 ft 1 in (18.62 m).
**Width:** 9 ft 5 in (2.88 m).
**Weight:** 35 tons.
**Brakes:** Vacuum.
**Notes:** Used in conjunction with intermediate trailer 528. 7 was converted to DMBSO seating 79S in March 1958.

| Vehicle No. | Original No. | Month to Traffic | Date Stopped | Month Withdrawn | Month Cut Up | Disposal Location |
|---|---|---|---|---|---|---|
| 6 | 205 | 08.51 | 15.07.66 | 12.68 | 12.69 | Belfast York Road. |
| 7 | 208 | 08.51 | 15.07.66 | 12.68 | 12.69 | Belfast York Road. |

Both vehicles were destroyed by fire at Belfast York Road on 18.11.69. The remains of these vehicles were eventually disposed of in December 1969.

## TRAILER THIRD (COMPARTMENT)

**Built:** 1933 by LMS(NCC) as J7 Class loco hauled coach 279.
**Rebuilt:** 1951 by UTA.
**Length:**
**Weight:** 31 tons.
**Seats:** 120.
**Width:** 9 ft 5 in (2.88 m).
**Brakes:** Air.
**Notes:** Used in conjunction with power cars 6 & 7. Numbered 500 from July 1958 to August 1958.

| Vehicle No. | Month to Traffic | Date Stopped | Month Withdrawn | Month Cut Up | Disposal Location |
|---|---|---|---|---|---|
| 528 | 08.51 | .64 | 09.64 | .71 | ? |

Converted to hauled stock 09.64. Withdrawn as a hauled coach in 1967.

## UTA MULTI-ENGINED DIESEL MULTIPLE UNITS (MED)

**Notes:** All MED power cars and trailers 501-514 had air operated sliding doors, trailers 515-527 had slam doors.

## DRIVING MOTOR COMPOSITE (CLASS G)
## * DRIVING MOTOR BRAKE COMPOSITE (CLASS F)

**Built:** 1936-39 by LMS(NCC) as J10 Class loco hauled coaches.
**Rebuilt:** 1952-53 by UTA.
**Engines:** Two Leyland EO 600/177 of 125 hp (93 kW) at 1800 rpm.
**Transmission:** Hydraulic. Two Lysholm Smith torque converters. **Seats:** 12F, 60T (* 12F, 40T).
**Length:** 61 ft 1 in (18.62 m).
**Width:** 9 ft 5 in (2.88 m).
**Weight:** 35.75 tons.
**Brakes:** Air.
**Notes:** Used in conjunction with power cars 14-35 and trailers 501-514 & 515-527 in 3 or 4 (from 1956/7 onwards) car sets. All were re-engined with Leyland 680 165 hp (123 kW) engines between March and May 1956, and the DMBCO cars were converted at the same time to DMBTO seating 56T. The hydraulic transmissions were replaced by mechanical Wilson 4 speed gearboxes between August 1967 and May 1968.

| Vehicle No. | Original No. | Month to Traffic | Date Stopped | Month Withdrawn | Month Cut Up | Disposal Location |
|---|---|---|---|---|---|---|
| 8* | 206 | 03.52 | 02.76 | 02.76 | 02.78 | Magheramorne. |
| 9 | 201 | 03.52 | 06.75 | 06.75 | 02.78 | Magheramorne. |
| 10* | 207 | 03.52 | 10.77 | 05.79 | 09.80 | Crosshill Quarry (A). |
| 11 | 202 | 03.52 | 11.74 | 11.74 | 05.80 | Crosshill Quarry (A). |
| 12* | 204 | 04.53 | 10.73 | 10.73 | .74 | ? |
| 13 | 203 | 04.53 | 12.74 | 12.74 | 05.80 | Crosshill Quarry (A). |

10 was transferred to the RPSI reserve fleet on 04.05.79 to be refurbished with BR transmission parts. However, this project was soon abandoned. The bodyshell of this vehicle was then used as a storage shed at Nutts Corner Airport until September 1980.
12 was destroyed by a bomb at Belfast Great Victoria Street on 12.10.73.
12 and 13 originally entered traffic as non-powered vehicles in March 1952. Entered traffic as power cars on dates shown above.

# DRIVING MOTOR BRAKE COMPOSITE (CLASS F1)
# § DRIVING MOTOR COMPOSITE (CLASS G1)

**Built:** 1925-30 as J4 (†J5) Class loco hauled coaches.
**Rebuilt:** 1953-54 by UTA.
**Engines:** Two Leyland EO 600/177 of 125 hp (93 kW) at 1800 rpm.
**Transmission:** Hydraulic. Two Lysholm Smith torque converters.
**Seats:** 12F, 40T. § 12F, 59T. **Length:** 61 ft 1 in (18.62 m).
**Width:** 9 ft 5 in (2.88 m). **Weight:** 36 tons.
**Brakes:** Air.
**Notes:** Used in conjunction with power cars 8-13 & 24-35 and trailers 501-514 & 515-527 in 3 or 4 (from 1956/7 onwards) car sets. All were re-engined with Leyland 680 165 hp (123 kW) engines between June and November 1956, and DMCO cars 15 & 19 were converted at the same time to DMSO seating 75S. 17 was similarly converted in September 1958. The DMBCO cars were subsequently converted to DMBSO seating 56S, date unknown. The hydraulic transmissions were replaced by mechanical Wilson 4 speed gearboxes between December 1966 and December 1969.

| Vehicle No. | Original No. | Month to Traffic | Date Stopped | Month Withdrawn | Month Cut Up | Disposal Location |
|---|---|---|---|---|---|---|
| 14 | 248 | 11.53 | 02.77 | 02.77 | .78 | ? |
| 15§ | 246 | 11.53 | 02.77 | 02.77 | ? | ? |
| 16 | 250 | 12.53 | 01.75 | 01.75 | 05.80 | Crosshill Quarry (A). |
| 17§ | 254 | 12.53 | 11.74 | 11.74 | 05.80 | Crosshill Quarry (A). |
| 18 | 251 | 10.53 | 10.77 | 10.77 | .78 | ? |
| 19§ | 260† | 10.53 | 02.78 | 05.79 | 09.80 | Crosshill Quarry (A). |
| 20 | 252 | 01.54 | 08.77 | 11.77 | ? | ? |
| 21§ | 257† | 01.54 | 12.78 | 05.79 | 09.80 | Crosshill Quarry (A). |
| 22 | 253 | 02.54 | 11.77 | 01.78 | ? | ? |
| 23§ | 259† | 02.54 | 03.78 | 03.78 | 05.80 | Crosshill Quarry (A). |

19 and 21 were transferred to the RPSI reserve fleet on 04.05.79 to be refurbished with BR transmission parts. However, this project was soon abandoned. The bodyshells of these vehicles were then used as storage sheds at Nutts Corner Airport until September 1980.

# DRIVING MOTOR COMPOSITE (CLASS I)
# *DRIVING MOTOR BRAKE COMPOSITE (CLASS H)

**Built:** 1952-53 by UTA.
**Engines:** Two Leyland EO 600/177 of 125 hp (93 kW) at 1800 rpm.
**Transmission:** Hydraulic. Two Lysholm Smith torque converters.
**Seats:** 8F, 74T (* 8F, 50T). **Length:** 61 ft 3 in (18.67 m).
**Width:** 9 ft 5 in (2.88 m). **Weight:** 36 tons.
**Brakes:** Air.
**Notes:** The underframes for 24-30 were built by Metropolitan Cammell in 1950. The underframe for 31 was built by NCC. being spare from nos. 1-4. Used in conjunction with power cars 8-23 & 32-35 and trailers 501-514 & 515-527 in 3 or 4 (from 1956/7 onwards) car sets. All were re-engined with Leyland 680 165 hp (123 kW) engines during April and May 1956, and the DMBCO cars were converted at the same time to DMBTO seating 61T. These cars

were subsequently reconverted to DMBCO in September 1958, seating 8F, 46S. The DMCO cars were subsequently converted to DMSO seating 85S, date unknown. The hydraulic transmissions were replaced by mechanical Wilson 4 speed gearboxes between January 1968 and July 1969. Extra driving ends were fitted to 24 & 26 in December 1961 and 28 in January 1962 using equipment removed from 505-507.

| Vehicle No. | Month to Traffic | Date Stopped | Month Withdrawn | Month Disposed | Disposal Location |
|---|---|---|---|---|---|
| 24* | 08.52 | 12.76 | 12.76 | 05.80 | Crosshill Quarry (A). |
| 25 | 08.52 | 07.78 | .78 | 05.80 | Crosshill Quarry (A). |
| 26* | 10.52 | 07.78 | .78 | 05.80 | Crosshill Quarry (A). |
| 27 | 10.52 | 08.77 | 12.77 | 05.80 | Crosshill Quarry (A). |
| 28* | 12.52 | 04.78 | .78 | 05.80 | Crosshill Quarry (A). |
| 29 | 12.52 | 01.78 | 12.78 | 05.80 | Crosshill Quarry (A). |
| 30* | 03.53 | 04.78 | .78 | 05.80 | Crosshill Quarry (A). |
| 31 | 03.53 | 12.76 | 05.76 | 05.80 | Crosshill Quarry (A). |

## DRIVING MOTOR BRAKE COMPOSITE (CLASS J)
## *DRIVING MOTOR COMPOSITE (CLASS K)

**Built:** 1953 by UTA.
**Engines:** Two Leyland EO 600/177 of 125 hp (93 kW) at 1800 rpm.
**Transmission:** Hydraulic. Two Lysholm Smith torque converters.
**Seats:** 8F, 50T (* 8F, 74T). **Length:** 61 ft 3 in (18.67 m).
**Width:** 9 ft 5 in (2.88 m). **Weight:** 34 tons.
**Brakes:** Air.
**Notes:** Used in conjunction with power cars 8-31 and trailers 501-514 & 515-527 in 3 or 4 (from1956/7 onwards) car sets. All were re-engined with Leyland 680 165 hp (123 kW) engines between June 1956 and January 1957 and the DMCO cars were converted at the same time to DMSO seating 85S. The DMBCO cars were subsequently converted to DMBSO seating 61S, date unknown. The hydraulic transmissions were replaced by mechanical Wilson 4 speed gearboxes between July and December 1968.

| Vehicle No. | Month to Traffic | Date Stopped | Month Withdrawn | Month Disposed | Disposal Location |
|---|---|---|---|---|---|
| 32 | 06.53 | 12.78 | .78 | 05.80 | Crosshill Quarry (A). |
| 33* | 06.53 | 04.78 | .78 | 05.80 | Crosshill Quarry (A). |
| 34 | 07.53 | 11.77 | .78 | 05.80 | Crosshill Quarry (A). |
| 35* | 07.53 | 01.78 | 02.78 | 05.80 | Crosshill Quarry (A). |

## TRAILER THIRD

**Built:** 1952-54 by UTA. **Seats:** 91.
**Length:** 60 ft 4 in (18.39 m). **Width:** 9 ft 5 in (2.88 m).
**Weight:** 26 tons. **Brakes:** Air.
**Notes:** Used in conjunction with power cars 8-35. Originally numbered 201-214 (see below) prior to 1958. 504-509 were converted to DTSO between December 1957 and May 1958, seating 87S. 505-507 were reconverted to TSO in 1961, seating 93S, the driving equipment being subsequently fitted to 24, 26 & 28. The driving cabs were removed in 1963-64. 2 additional seats were fitted in 501-504 & 508-514 upon removal of their steam heating boilers in 1960-61, then seating 89 or 93S. The seating layout of 510 was further modified to seat 103S, date unknown.

| Vehicle No. | Original No. | Month to Traffic | Date Stopped | Month Withdrawn | Month Cut Up | Disposal Location |
|---|---|---|---|---|---|---|
| 501 | 201 | 08.52 | 12.77 | .78 | 05.80 | Crosshill Quarry (A). |
| 502 | 202 | 10.52 | 12.77 | .78 | 05.80 | Crosshill Quarry (A). |
| 503 | 203 | 12.52 | 02.78 | .78 | 05.80 | Crosshill Quarry (A). |
| 504 | 210 | 02.53 | 01.77 | .77 | 05.80 | Crosshill Quarry (A). |
| 505 | 211 | 03.53 | 06.77 | .77 | 05.80 | Crosshill Quarry (A). |
| 506 | 212 | 04.53 | 10.73 | 10.73 | 10.73 | ? |
| 507 | 213 | 06.53 | 09.76 | .76 | 05.80 | Crosshill Quarry (A). |
| 508 | 214 | 07.53 | 05.75 | 05.75 | 10.83 | Conv. to parcels van 631 |
| 509 | 204 | 07.53 | 12.78 | .78 | 05.80 | Crosshill Quarry (A). |
| 510 | 205 | 10.53 | 07.75 | 11.77 | 05.80 | Crosshill Quarry (A). |
| 511 | 206 | 10.53 | 11.75 | 11.75 | 01.85 | Conv. to parcels van 634 |
| 512 | 207 | 12.53 | 07.75 | 07.75 | 01.85 | Conv. to parcels van 632 |
| 513 | 208 | 02.54 | 10.75 | 10.75 | 01.85 | Conv. to parcels van 633 |
| 514 | 209 | 04.54 | 07.77 | .77 | 05.80 | Crosshill Quarry (A). |

506 was withdrawn following bomb damage suffered at Marino on 11.10.73.
After being withdrawn as parcels vans, 631-634 were sent to Crosshill Quarry (A), 631 in October 1983 and the others in January 1985.

## TRAILER BRAKE THIRD

**Built:** 1953 by UTA.
**Length:** 60 ft 4 in (18.39 m).
**Weight:** 24 tons.
**Seats:** 80.
**Width:** 9 ft 5 in (2.88 m).
**Brakes:** Air, vacuum piped.
**Notes:** Originally built as a trailer for railcar 5. Numbered 215 prior to 1958. Modified for MED use in 1963 after railcar 5 was withdrawn. Gangway ends were fitted in March 1968, seating ?? S. The seating layout was further modified in January 1972, seating 68S. Converted to a Parcels Van in April 1973 without further renumbering.

| Vehicle No. | Month to Traffic | Date Stopped | Month Withdrawn | Month Disposed | Disposal Location |
|---|---|---|---|---|---|
| 515 | 06.53 | 04.73 | 11.77 | 05.80 | Crosshill Quarry (A). |

## TRAILER STANDARD (COMPARTMENT)

**Built:** 1925-38 by LMS, transferred to LMS(NCC) in 1941 as J11 Class loco hauled coaches.
**Rebuilt:** 1956 by UTA.
**Length:** 57 ft 1 in (17.40 m).
**Weight:** 30 tons (* 28 tons).
**Seats:** 108.
**Width:** 9 ft (2.74 m).
**Brakes:** Air.
**Notes:** 519 was converted to TSO seating 72S in May 1968. 523 was converted to TSO seating 64S in August 1968. The 28 ton vehicles had wooden bodies, the others steel. 518 was dual fitted for MED/MPD use in August 1962.

| Vehicle No. | NCC No. | LMS No. | Month to Traffic | Date Stopped | Month Withdrawn | Month Cut Up | Disposal Location |
|---|---|---|---|---|---|---|---|
| 516 | 169 | 12952 | 06.56 | 06.70 | 06.70 | ? | ? |
| 517* | 173 | 11013 | 12.56 | 06.73 | 06.73 | ? | ? |
| 518* | 174 | 11057 | 11.56 | 12.70 | 12.70 | ? | ? |

| | | | | | | | | |
|---|---|---|---|---|---|---|---|---|
| 519* | 176 | 11211 | 05.56 | 04.78 | .78 | 05.80 | Antrim. |
| 520 | 177 | 11386 | 05.56 | 09.70 | 09.70 | 09.70 | Queens Quay |
| 521 | 181 | 11539 | 05.56 | 06.70 | 06.70 | ? | ? |
| 522 | 186 | 11767 | 06.56 | 09.70 | 09.70 | 09.70 | Queens Quay |
| 523 | 187 | 11847 | 06.56 | 10.77 | .77 | 05.80 | Antrim. |
| 524 | 189 | 11956 | 12.56 | 06.73 | 06.73 | ? | ? |
| 525* | 191 | 10878 | 06.56 | 09.70 | 09.70 | ? | ? |

## TRAILER STANDARD

**Built:** 1929-30 by LMS(NCC) as J5 Class loco hauled coaches.
**Rebuilt:** 1956-57 by UTA.  **Seats:** 80.
**Length:** 57 ft 1 in (17.40 m).  **Width:** 9 ft 4 in (2.85 m).
**Weight:** 28 tons.  **Brakes:** Air, vacuum piped.
**Notes:** Converted to dual MED/MPD TSO in August 1962. 526 was transferred to the RPSI reserve fleet on 04.05.79 to be refurbished. However, this project was soon abandoned but the vehicle was retained for preservation by the RPSI.

| Vehicle No. | Original No. | Month to Traffic | Date Stopped | Month Withdrawn | Month Cut Up | Disposal Location |
|---|---|---|---|---|---|---|
| 526 | 255 | 03.57 | 06.76 | 05.79 | ? | RPSI, Whitehead. |
| 527 | 261 | 10.56 | 05.77 | 11.77 | 02.78 | Magheramorne. |

526 was damaged by fire on 22.05.96 and later scrapped.

## UTA MULTIPURPOSE DIESEL MULTIPLE UNITS (MPD)

## DRIVING MOTOR BRAKE STANDARD (CLASS L)

**Built:** 1951 by UTA as J17 Class loco hauled coaches.
**Rebuilt:** 1957-58 by UTA.
**Engine:** Leyland O900 of 275 hp (205 kW) at 1800 rpm.
**Transmission:** Hydraulic. Schneider torque converter.  **Seats:** 48.
**Length:** 57 ft 9 in (17.61 m).  **Width:** 9 ft 5 in (2.88 m).
**Weight:** 39 tons.  **Brakes:** Air, vacuum piped.
**Notes:** 36, 37 & 39 were re-engined with an AEC AH1100/6 260 hp (194 kW) engine in May 1966, June 1966 and December 1965 respectively. 38 was re-engined with a Rolls Royce C6.TFLH Mark IV engine of 260 hp (194 kW) at 1800 rpm in September 1964.

| Vehicle No. | Original No. | Month to Traffic | Date Stopped | Month Withdrawn | Month Cut Up | Disposal Location |
|---|---|---|---|---|---|---|
| 36 | 321 | 09.57 | .77 | 04.78 | 06.78 | Magheramorne. |
| 37 | 322 | 09.57 | 07.68 | 07.68 | 03.70 | York Road. |
| 38 | 323 | 12.57 | 08.76 | 12.77 | .78 | Magheramorne. |
| 39 | 326 | 01.58 | 07.78 | 07.78 | 09.80 | Crosshill Quarry (A) |

37 was withdrawn following fire damage suffered at Ballymena on 24.07.68 whilst working the 07:10 Portrush to Belfast York Road service.
The bodyshell of 39 was used as a storage shed at Nutts Corner Airport until September 1980.

## DRIVING MOTOR STANDARD (CLASS M)

**Built:** 1951 by UTA as J17 Class loco hauled coaches.
**Rebuilt:** 1957 by UTA.
**Engine:** Leyland O900 of 275 hp (205 kW) at 1800 rpm
**Transmission:** Hydraulic, Schneider torque converter.
**Seats:** 54 (40), 51(41).
**Width:** 9 ft 5 in (2.88 m).
**Brakes:** Air, vacuum piped.
**Length:** 57 ft 9 in (17.61 m).
**Weight:** 39 tons.
**Notes:** Both were re-engined with an AEC AH1100/6 260 hp (194 kW) at 1800 rpm engine in November 1966 and 1970 respectively.

| Vehicle No. | Original No. | Month to Traffic | Date Stopped | Month Withdrawn | Month Cut Up | Disposal Location |
|---|---|---|---|---|---|---|
| 40 | 324 | 12.57 | 12.73 | 12.73 | 02.78 | Magheramorne. |
| 41 | 325 | 11.57 | 07.75 | 07.75 | 02.78 | Magheramorne. |

40 was withdrawn following collision damage at Larne Town 12.73

## DRIVING MOTOR COMPOSITE (COMPARTMENT) (CLASS N)

**Built:** 1951 by UTA as F7 Class loco hauled coaches.
**Rebuilt:** 1957-58 by UTA.
**Engine:** Leyland O900 of 275 hp (205 kW) at 1800 rpm.
**Transmission:** Hydraulic. Schneider torque converter.
**Seats:** 18F, 24S.
**Length:** 57 ft 9 in (17.61 m).
**Width:** 9 ft 5 in (2.88 m).
**Weight:** 40 tons.
**Brakes:** Air, vacuum piped.
**Notes:** Both were re-engined with an AEC AH1100/6 260 hp (194 kW) at 1800 rpm engine in 1970 and 1969 respectively.

| Vehicle No. | Original No. | Month to Traffic | Date Stopped | Month Withdrawn | Month Cut Up | Disposal Location |
|---|---|---|---|---|---|---|
| 42 | 341 | 11.57 | .75 | 03.78 | 09.80 | Crosshill Quarry (A). |
| 43 | 342 | 01.58 | 10.73 | 10.73 | 02.78 | Magheramorne. |

The bodyshell of 42 was used as a storage shed at Nutts Corner Airport until September 1980.
43 was withdrawn following fire damage 10.73.

## DRIVING MOTOR BRAKE COMPOSITE (COMPARTMENT) (CLASS O)

**Built:** 1951 by UTA as K6 Class loco hauled coach body 331 and underframe 303 (44) and coach 332 (45).
**Rebuilt:** 1958-59 by UTA.
**Engine:** Leyland O900 of 275 hp (205 kW) at 1800 rpm.
**Transmission:** Hydraulic. Schneider torque converter.
**Seats:** 12F/24S.
**Length:** 57 ft 9 in (17.61 m).
**Width:** 9 ft 5 in (2.88 m).
**Weight:** 44 tons.
**Brakes:** Air, vacuum piped.
**Notes:** Both were re-engined with a Rolls Royce C6.TFLH Mark IV engine of 260 hp (194 kW) at 1800 rpm in November 1967 and April 1968 respectively.

| Vehicle No. | Month to Traffic | Date Stopped | Month Withdrawn | Month Cut Up | Disposal Location |
|---|---|---|---|---|---|
| 44 | 10.58 | 07.75 | 08.76 | .78 | Magheramorne. |
| 45 | 11.59 | 04.77 | 03.78 | 10.78 | Magheramorne. |

## DRIVING MOTOR BRAKE COMPOSITE (COMPARTMENT) (CLASS P)

**Built:** 1933 by LMS(NCC) as H2/J16* Class loco hauled coaches.
**Rebuilt:** 1958-59 by UTA.
**Engine:** Leyland O900 of 275 hp (205 kW) at 1800 rpm.
**Transmission:** Hydraulic. Schneider torque converter.
**Seats:** 16F, 60S.
**Width:** 9 ft 5 in (2.88 m).
**Length:** 57 ft 9 in (17.61 m).
**Weight:** 40 tons.
**Brakes:** Air, vacuum piped.
**Notes:** 46 was re-engined with a Rolls Royce C6.TFLH Mark IV engine of 260 hp (194 kW) at 1800 rpm in July 1969. 47 & 48 were re-engined with an AEC AH1100/6 260 hp (194 kW) at 1800 rpm engine in March 1970 and November 1970 respectively. 46, 47 & 48 were converted to DMBSoC seating 16F, 44S at the same time.

| Vehicle No. | Original Nos. | Month to Traffic | Date Stopped | Month Withdrawn | Month Cut Up | Disposal Location |
|---|---|---|---|---|---|---|
| 46 | 280/331* | 12.58 | 04.78 | .78 | ? | ? |
| 47 | 281/301* | 02.59 | 05.77 | 05.77 | .78 | Magheramorne. |
| 48 | 282/302* | 02.59 | 06.76 | 06.76 | .78 | Magheramorne. |

Note: First former number relates to the body used and the second to the frame used.
47 was withdrawn following a collision at Carrickfergus on 07.05.77.

## DRIVING MOTOR BRAKE STANDARD (COMPARTMENT) (CLASS Q)

**Built:** 1951 by UTA as K6 Class loco hauled coach 351.
**Rebuilt:** 1959 by UTA.
**Engine:** Leyland O900 of 275 hp (205 kW) at 1800 rpm.
**Transmission:** Hydraulic. Schneider torque converter.
**Seats:** 84.
**Width:** 9 ft 5 in (2.88 m).
**Brakes:** Air, vacuum piped.
**Length:** 57 ft 9 in (17.61 m).
**Weight:** 40 tons.
**Notes:** Re-engined with an AEC AH1100/6 260 hp (194 kW) at 1800 rpm engine in December 1970. Converted to DMBSO seating 68S at the same time.

| Vehicle No. | Month to Traffic | Date Stopped | Month Withdrawn | Month Cut Up | Disposal Location |
|---|---|---|---|---|---|
| 49 | 01.59 | 08.77 | 05.79 | 09.83 | Crosshill Quarry (A). |

Engine removed and converted to form part of a loco hauled excursion set for use with 101 class locomotives 05.79. Withdrawn as loco hauled coach 04.81.

## DRIVING MOTOR BRAKE STANDARD (COMPARTMENT) (CLASS R)

**Built:** 1933 by LMS(NCC) as J7 Class loco hauled coaches.
**Rebuilt:** 1959 by UTA.
**Engine:** Leyland O900 of 275 hp (205 kW) at 1800 rpm.
**Transmission:** Hydraulic. Schneider torque converter.
**Seats:** 96.
**Width:** 9 ft 5 in (2.88 m).
**Brakes:** Air, vacuum piped.
**Length:** 60 ft 9 in (18.53 m).
**Weight:** 43 tons.
**Notes:** Re-engined with Rolls Royce C6.TFLH Mark IV engines of 260 hp (194 kW) at 1800 rpm in October 1969, March 1969, April 1969 and December 1968 respectively. All were converted to DMBSO seating 78S at the same time.

| Vehicle No. | Original No. | Month to Traffic | Date Stopped | Month Withdrawn | Month Cut Up | Disposal Location |
|---|---|---|---|---|---|---|
| 50 | 274 | 03.59 | 09.77 | 09.77 | 02.78 | Magheramorne. |
| 51 | 275 | 03.59 | 02.80 | 02.80 | ? | ? |
| 52 | 276 | 03.59 | 09.80 | 09.80 | ? | ? |
| 53 | 277 | 04.59 | 07.74 | 07.74 | 07.74 | York Road. |

50 was withdrawn following fire damage 09.77.

# DRIVING MOTOR BRAKE COMPOSITE (CLASS S)

**Built:** 1931 by LMS(NCC) as I3/J16* Class loco hauled coaches.
**Rebuilt:** 1959 by UTA.
**Engine:** Leyland O900 of 275 hp (205 kW) at 1800 rpm.
**Transmission:** Hydraulic. Schneider torque converter.
**Seats:** 12F, 55S (54), 10F, 50S (55).
**Width:** 9 ft 5 in (2.88 m).
**Brakes:** Air, vacuum piped.
**Length:** 57 ft 9 in (17.61 m).
**Weight:** 40 tons.
**Notes:** 54 was re-engined with a Rolls Royce C6.TFLH Mark IV engine of 260 hp (194 kW) at 1800 rpm in August 1969. 55 was re-engined with an AEC AH1100/6 260 hp (194 kW) at 1800 rpm engine in October 1965.

| Vehicle No. | Original Nos. | Month to Traffic | Date Stopped | Month Withdrawn | Month Cut Up | Disposal Location |
|---|---|---|---|---|---|---|
| 54 | 54/304* | 04.59 | 04.77 | 10.77 | .78 | Magheramorne. |
| 55 | 55/305* | 05.59 | 01.74 | 12.77 | 07.78 | Magheramorne. |

Note: First former number relates to the body used and the second to the frame used.

# DRIVING MOTOR BRAKE COMPOSITE (CLASS T)

**Built:** 1944 by LMS(NCC) as A5 Class loco hauled coach 5.
**Rebuilt:** 1959 by UTA.
**Engine:** Leyland O900 of 275 hp (205 kW) at 1800 rpm.
**Transmission:** Hydraulic. Schneider torque converter.
**Seats:** 12F, 60S.
**Width:** 9 ft 5 in (2.88 m).
**Brakes:** Air, vacuum piped.
**Length:** 60 ft 9 in (18.53 m).
**Weight:**
**Notes:** Re-engined with an AEC AH1100/6 260 hp (194 kW) at 1800 rpm engine in April 1964.

| Vehicle No. | Month to Traffic | Date Stopped | Month Withdrawn | Month Cut Up | Disposal Location |
|---|---|---|---|---|---|
| 56 | 08.59 | 07.66 | 07.66 | ? | ? |

Withdrawn following fire damage suffered at Brookmount on 30.06.66.

# DRIVING MOTOR BRAKE STANDARD (CLASS U)

**Built:** 1932-35 by LMS(NCC) as J6/F8/J16† Class loco hauled coaches.
**Rebuilt:** 1959 by UTA.
**Engine:** Leyland O900 of 275 hp (205 kW) at 1800 rpm.
**Transmission:** Hydraulic. Schneider torque converter.
**Seats:** 70.
**Width:** 9 ft 5 in (2.88 m).
**Brakes:** Air, vacuum piped.
**Length:** 57 ft 9 in (17.61 m)
**Weight:** 40 tons.
**Notes:** All except 58 were re-engined with a Rolls Royce C6.TFLH Mark IV engine of 260 hp (194 kW) at 1800 rpm as follows: 57 in June 1968, 59 in October 1968, 60 in December 1967, 61 in March 1968 and 62 in January 1968.

| Vehicle No. | Original No(s). | Month to Traffic | Date Stopped | Month Withdrawn | Month Cut Up | Disposal Location |
|---|---|---|---|---|---|---|
| 57 | 265/361* | 05.59 | 05.77 | 05.77 | 02.78 | Magheramorne. |
| 58 | 266/306† | 06.59 | 07.59 | 07.59 | 08.59 | ? |
| 59 | 267 | 06.59 | 06.78 | .80 | 09.80 | ? |
| 60 | 268 | 07.59 | 02.78 | 02.78 | 10.78 | Magheramorne. |
| 61 | 269 | 07.59 | 12.78 | 05.79 | 09.83 | Crosshill Quarry (A). |
| 62 | 270 | 07.59 | 07.77 | 07.77 | 09.80 | Crosshill Quarry (A). |

**Note:** First former number relates to the body used and the second to the frame used.
57 was withdrawn following a collision at Carrickfergus on 07.05.77.
58 was withdrawn following a collision with a motor car at Downhill accommodation crossing on 18.07.59.
61 had its engine removed and was converted to form part of a loco hauled excursion set for use with 101 class locomotives 05.79. Withdrawn as loco hauled coach 04.81.
The bodyshell of 62 was used as a storage shed at Nutts Corner Airport until September 1980.

## DRIVING MOTOR BRAKE STANDARD (CLASS V)

**Built:** 1938 by LMS(NCC) as I4 Class loco hauled coaches.
**Rebuilt:** 1961-62 by UTA.
**Engine:** Leyland O900 of 275 hp (205 kW) at 1800 rpm.
**Transmission:** Hydraulic. Schneider torque converter.
**Seats:** 70.  **Length:** 61 ft 6 in (18.75 m).
**Width:** 9 ft 5 in (2.88 m).  **Weight:** 43 tons.
**Brakes:** Air, vacuum piped.
**Notes:** Re-engined with Rolls Royce C6.TFLH Mark IV engines of 260 hp (194 kW) at 1800 rpm in February 1969, May 1968 and June 1968 respectively. These vehicles had a driving cab at both ends.

| Vehicle No. | Original No. | Month to Traffic | Date Stopped | Month Withdrawn | Month Disposed | Disposal Location |
|---|---|---|---|---|---|---|
| 63 | 252 | 11.61 | 04.81 | .81 | 10.83 | Crosshill Quarry (A). |
| 64 | 254 | 12.61 | 05.83 | .84 | 08.85 | Crosshill Quarry (A). |
| 65 | 256 | 02.62 | 04.81 | .81 | 10.83 | Crosshill Quarry (A). |

Coaches 252, 254 & 256 were previously 37, 38 & 39 respectively.

## DRIVING TRAILER STANDARD (COMPARTMENT)

**Built:** 1951 by UTA as H2*/J16 Class loco hauled coaches.
**Rebuilt:** 1959 by UTA.
**Seats:** 56.  **Length:** 57 ft 9 in (17.61 m).
**Width:** 9 ft 5 in (2.88 m).  **Weight:** 30 tons.
**Brakes:** Air, vacuum piped.

| Vehicle No. | Original Nos. | Month to Traffic | Date Stopped | Month Withdrawn | Month Cut Up | Disposal Location |
|---|---|---|---|---|---|---|
| 529 | 303/280* | 02.59 | .77 | .77 | 07.78 | Magheramorne. |
| 530 | 301/281* | 04.59 | .77 | .78 | .79 | ? |
| 531 | 302/282* | 06.59 | .76 | .77 | ? | ? |

| | | | | | | | |
|---|---|---|---|---|---|---|---|
| 532 | 304/254 | 04.59 | .78 | 04.78 | - | RPSI Whitehead. | |
| 533 | 305/255 | 04.59 | 11.77 | 04.78 | - | Body to 583. | |
| 534 | 306/256 | 05.59 | .76 | 10.76 | - | Converted to 728 (qv). | |

**Note:** First former number relates to the body used and the second to the frame used. After withdrawal the bodyshell of 533 was fitted to the underframe of 583, whose body had been destroyed by fire. The underframe of 533 was converted to a conflat wagon.

## DRIVING TRAILER STANDARD (COMPARTMENT)

**Built:** 1937/39 by LMS(NCC) as J11 Class loco hauled coaches.
**Rebuilt:** 1959 by UTA.
**Length:** 57 ft 9 in (17.61 m).
**Weight:** 30 tons.
**Seats:** 96.
**Width:** 8 ft 11 in (2.72 m).
**Brakes:** Air, vacuum piped.
**Notes:** Rebuilt to TSO seating 64S in March and June 1971 respectively, length then reduced to 57 ft 1 in (17.40 m).

| Vehicle No. | NCC No. | LMS No. | Month to Traffic | Date Stopped | Month Withdrawn | Month Disposed | Disposal Location |
|---|---|---|---|---|---|---|---|
| 535 | 188 | 11939 | 06.59 | ? | 05.79 | 09.83 | Crosshill Quarry (A). |
| 536 | 195 | 12160 | 07.59 | ? | 05.79 | 09.83 | Crosshill Quarry (A). |

Converted to form part of a loco hauled excursion set for use with 101 class locomotives 05.79. Withdrawn as loco hauled coaches 04.81.

## DRIVING TRAILER STANDARD (COMPARTMENT)

**Built:** 1933 by LMS(NCC) as K2 Class loco hauled coaches.
**Rebuilt:** 1959 by UTA.
**Seats:** 102.
**Width:** 9 ft 5 in (2.88 m).
**Brakes:** Air, vacuum piped.
**Length:** 57 ft 9 in (17.61 m).
**Weight:** 31 tons.
**Notes:** Rebuilt to TSO seating 68S in April 1970, March 1969 and August 1971 respectively.

| Vehicle No. | Original No. | Month to Traffic | Date Stopped | Month Withdrawn | Month Cut Up | Disposal Location |
|---|---|---|---|---|---|---|
| 537 | 271 | 07.59 | 04.75 | .78 | 02.78 | Magheramorne. |
| 538 | 272 | 08.59 | ? | 12.80 | 09.83 | ? |
| 539 | 273 | 09.59 | ? | 05.79 | 09.83 | Crosshill Quarry (A). |

539 was converted to form part of a loco hauled excursion set for use with 101 class locomotives 05.79. Withdrawn as loco hauled coach 04.81.

## DRIVING TRAILER STANDARD

**Built:** 1935 by LMS(NCC) at Derby C & W Works as J6 Class loco hauled coaches.
**Rebuilt:** 1959 by UTA.
**Length:** 57 ft 9 in (17.61 m).
**Weight:** 29 tons.
**Seats:** 85.
**Width:** 9 ft 5 in (2.88 m).
**Brakes:** Air, vacuum piped.

| Vehicle No. | Original No. | Month to Traffic | Date Stopped | Month Withdrawn | Month Disposed | Disposal Location |
|---|---|---|---|---|---|---|
| 540 | 229 | 10.59 | ? | 05.79 | 09.83 | Crosshill Quarry (A). |
| 541 | 231 | 10.59 | ? | 05.79 | 09.83 | Crosshill Quarry (A). |

Converted to form part of a loco hauled excursion set for use with 101 class locomotives 05.79. Withdrawn as loco hauled coaches 04.81.

## DRIVING TRAILER COMPOSITE

**Built:** 1931 by LMS(NCC) as I3 Class loco hauled coach 57.
**Rebuilt:** 1959 by UTA.
**Seats:** 12F, 65S.  **Length:** 57 ft 9 in (17.61m).
**Width:** 9 ft 5 in (2.88 m).  **Weight:** 29 tons.
**Brakes:** Air, vacuum piped.

| Vehicle No. | Month to Traffic | Date Stopped | Month Withdrawn | Month Disposed | Disposal Location |
|---|---|---|---|---|---|
| 542 | 10.59 | ? | 05.79 | 09.83 | Crosshill Quarry (A). |

Converted to form part of a loco hauled excursion set for use with 101 class locomotives 05.79. Withdrawn as loco hauled coach 04.81.

## DRIVING TRAILER COMPOSITE (COMPARTMENT)

**Built:** 1951 by UTA as F8/J6* Class loco hauled coach body 361 and underframe 265*.
**Rebuilt:** 1959 by UTA.
**Seats:** 32F, 36S.  **Length:** 57 ft 9 in (17.61 m).
**Width:** 9 ft 5 in (2.88 m)  **Weight:** 31 tons.
**Brakes:** Air, vacuum piped.  **Note:** Rebuilt to TSO seating ??S in 1972.

| Vehicle No. | Month to Traffic | Date Stopped | Month Withdrawn | Month Cut Up | Disposal Location |
|---|---|---|---|---|---|
| 543 | 05.59 | .74 | .74 | 10.74 | Belfast York Road. |

The cutting up date above relates to the body only. The underframe was converted to a Conflat wagon.

## TRAILER THIRD

Renumbered from NCC Trailer Thirds T1 & T2 respectively (qv).

| Vehicle No. | Month to Traffic | Date Stopped | Month Withdrawn | Month Cut Up | Disposal Location |
|---|---|---|---|---|---|
| 544 | ? | ? | .67 | .68 | ? |
| 545 | ? | ? | ? | .78 | - |

545 was converted to signals van 3109 in 1970.

# TRAILER BUFFET FIRST

**Built:** 1924 by LMS(NCC) as B2 Class loco hauled coach 88.
**Rebuilt:** 1960 by UTA.
**Seats:** 32F.  **Length:** 57 ft (17.37 m).
**Width:** 9 ft 6 in (2.90 m).  **Weight:** 31.5 tons.
**Brakes:** Air, vacuum piped.
**Notes:** Declassified to standard class April 1964. Modified for operation with MPD/70 Class vehicles in August 1966.

| Vehicle No. | Month to Traffic | Date Stopped | Month Withdrawn | Month Cut Up | Disposal Location |
|---|---|---|---|---|---|
| 548 | 05.60 | 07.70 | 10.72 | 10.72 | ? |

# TRAILER BUFFET FIRST

**Built:** 1934 by LMS(NCC) as B4 Class loco hauled coach 90.
**Rebuilt:** 1957 by UTA.
**Seats:** 32F.  **Length:** 60 ft 1 in (18.31 m).
**Width:** 9 ft 6 in (2.90 m).  **Weight:** 30 tons.
**Brakes:** Air, vacuum piped.
**Notes:** Declassified to standard class April 1964.

| Vehicle No. | Month to Traffic | Date Stopped | Month Withdrawn | Month Cut Up | Disposal Location |
|---|---|---|---|---|---|
| 549 | 05.57 | 07.66 | 06.70 | 06.70 | ? |

# TRAILER BUFFET FIRST

**Built:** 1950 by UTA as B5 Class loco hauled coach 87. (Built to LMS(NCC) order).
**Rebuilt:** 1957 by UTA.
**Seats:** 30F.  **Length:** 60 ft 1 in (18.31 m).
**Width:** 9 ft 5¼ in (2.88 m).  **Weight:** 31 tons.
**Brakes:** Air, vacuum piped.
**Notes:** Declassified to standard class seating 34S in April 1964. Modified for operation with 70 Class vehicles in May 1966.

| Vehicle No. | Month to Traffic | Date Stopped | Month Withdrawn | Disposal Location |
|---|---|---|---|---|
| 550 | 10.57 | .73 | .78 | RPSI Depot, Whitehead (P). |

Converted back to loco hauled coach 87 by the RPSI.

# TRAILERS FOR EX-GNR(I) AEC/BUT RAILCARS

## TRAILER BUFFET STANDARD

**Built:** 1936 by GNR(I) as B8 Class loco hauled coach 266.
**Rebuilt:** 1958 by UTA.  **Seats:** 27.
**Length:** 58 ft 0³/₄ in (17.70 m).  **Width:** 9 ft 6 in (2.90 m).
**Weight:** 32 tons.  **Brakes:** Vacuum.
**Note:** Modified for use with UTA BUT railcars 121-135.

| Vehicle No. | Month to Traffic | Date Stopped | Month Withdrawn | Month Cut Up | Disposal Location |
|---|---|---|---|---|---|
| 551 | 05.58 | .70 | .73 | 06.73 | Antrim. |

## TRAILER BUFFET COMPOSITE

**Built:** 1938 by GNR(I) as B6 Class loco hauled coach 88.
**Rebuilt:** 1957 by UTA.  **Seats:** 12F, 18S.
**Length:** 58 ft 0³/₄ in (17.70 m).  **Width:** 9 ft 6 in (2.90 m).
**Weight:** 32.5 tons.  **Brakes:** Vacuum.
**Notes:** Converted to TBSO seating 30S in March 1962. Modified for use with UTA BUT railcars 121-135.

| Vehicle No. | Month to Traffic | Date Stopped | Month Withdrawn | Disposal Location |
|---|---|---|---|---|
| 552 | 12.57 | .72 | .73 | RPSI Dublin (P). |

Converted back to loco hauled coach 88 by the RPSI.

## TRAILER BUFFET STANDARD

**Built:** 1942 by GNR(I) as B9 Class loco hauled coach 124.
**Rebuilt:** 1957 by UTA.  **Seats:** 24.
**Length:** 58 ft 0³/₄ in (17.70 m).  **Width:** 9 ft 6 in (2.90 m).
**Weight:** 30 tons.  **Brakes:** Vacuum.
**Note:** Modified for use with UTA BUT railcars 121-135.

| Vehicle No. | Month to Traffic | Date Stopped | Month Withdrawn | Month Cut Up | Disposal Location |
|---|---|---|---|---|---|
| 553 | 06.57 | 02.65 | ? | 04.71 | ? |

## TRAILER BUFFET STANDARD

**Built:** 1950 by GNR(I) as B4 Class loco hauled coach 403.
**Rebuilt:** 1957 by UTA.
**Length:** 60 ft 0¾ in (18.31 m).
**Weight:** 31 tons.
**Seats:** 24.
**Width:** 9 ft 6 in (2.90 m).
**Brakes:** Vacuum.
**Notes:** Modified for use with UTA AEC railcars 111-120. Modified for dual use with 70 class vehicles in July 1969.

| Vehicle No. | Month to Traffic | Date Stopped | Month Withdrawn | Month Cut Up | Disposal Location |
|---|---|---|---|---|---|
| 554 | 11.57 | 07.70 | .70 | 05.73 | Antrim. |

## TRAILER BUFFET STANDARD

**Built:** 1943 by GNR(I) as K23 Class loco hauled coach 188. Later converted to K15 Class.
**Rebuilt:** 1950 by UTA.
**Length:** 58 ft 0¾ in (17.70 m).
**Weight:** 29.5 tons.
**Seats:** 48.
**Width:** 9 ft 6 in (2.90 m).
**Brakes:** Vacuum.
**Notes:** Bar removed and re-seated to 72S in June 1967. Modified for use with UTA AEC railcars 111 - 120.

| Vehicle No. | Month to Traffic | Date Stopped | Month Withdrawn | Month Cut Up | Disposal Location |
|---|---|---|---|---|---|
| 555 | 06.50 | .70 | .72 | 06.73 | Antrim. |

## TRAILER BUFFET STANDARD

**Built:** 1951 by GNR(I) as K23 Class loco hauled coach 127. Later converted to K15 Class.
**Rebuilt:** 1958 by UTA.
**Length:** 58 ft 0¾ in (17.70 m).
**Weight:** 29.5 tons.
**Seats:** 47.
**Width:** 9 ft 6 in (2.90 m).
**Brakes:** Vacuum.
**Notes:** Bar removed and re-seated to 72S in 1966. Modified for use with UTA BUT railcars 121 - 135. Modified in May 1969 for operation with 70 Class vehicles.

| Vehicle No. | Month to Traffic | Date Stopped | Month Withdrawn | Month Cut Up | Disposal Location |
|---|---|---|---|---|---|
| 556 | 10.58 | 05.69 | 05.69 | - | Converted to 70 Class TSK 727 (qv). |

## TRAILER FIRST (COMPARTMENT)

**Built:** 1949 by GNR(I) as C2 Class loco hauled coach 227.
**Rebuilt:** 1957 by UTA.
**Length:** 60 ft 0¾ in (18.31 m).
**Weight:** 32.5 tons.
**Seats:** 36.
**Width:** 9 ft 6 in (2.90 m).
**Brakes:** Vacuum.
**Notes:** Converted to TCK seating 18F, 24S in March 1961. Modified for use with UTA BUT railcars 121 - 135.

| Vehicle No. | Month to Traffic | Date Stopped | Month Withdrawn | Month Cut Up | Disposal Location |
|---|---|---|---|---|---|
| 561 | 09.57 | 06.71 | 09.75 | ? | RPSI Depot, Whitehead. |

Damaged by fire on 22.05.96 and later scrapped.

## TRAILER BRAKE FIRST (COMPARTMENT)

**Built:** 1948 by GNR(I) as D5 Class loco hauled coach 231.
**Rebuilt:** 1957 by UTA.
**Length:** 60 ft 0³/₄ in (18.31 m).
**Weight:** 34.75 tons.
**Seats:** 18.
**Width:** 9 ft 6 in (2.90 m).
**Brakes:** Vacuum.
**Note:** Modified for use with UTA BUT railcars 121 - 135.

| Vehicle No. | Month to Traffic | Date Stopped | Month Withdrawn | Month Cut Up | Disposal Location |
|---|---|---|---|---|---|
| 562 | 12.57 | 11.74 | 02.75 | ? | RPSI Depot, Whitehead. |

Damaged by fire on 22.05.96 and later scrapped.

## TRAILER COMPOSITE (COMPARTMENT)

**Built:** 1935-39 by GNR(I) as F16 Class loco hauled coaches.
**Rebuilt:** 1957-58 by UTA.
**Length:** 58 ft 0³/₄ in (17.70 m).
**Weight:** 31.5 tons.
**Seats:** 24F, 24S.
**Width:** 9 ft 6 in (2.90 m).
**Brakes:** Vacuum.
**Notes:** 571 was converted to TSK seating 56S date unknown. 572 was converted to TBFK seating 18F date unknown. Modified for use with UTA BUT railcars 121 - 135.

| Vehicle No. | Original No. | Month to Traffic | Date Stopped | Month Withdrawn | Month Cut Up | Disposal Location |
|---|---|---|---|---|---|---|
| 571 | 20 | 12.57 | 06.71 | .73 | ? | ? |
| 572 | 29 | 09.58 | 06.71 | .73 | ? | ? |
| 573 | 89 | 01.58 | 04.71 | .75 | 05.75 | Antrim. |

## TRAILER STANDARD

**Built:** 1948 by GNR(I) as K15 Class loco hauled coach 145.
**Rebuilt:** 1962 by UTA.
**Length:** 58 ft 0³/₄ in (17.70 m).
**Weight:** 29 tons.
**Seats:** 70.
**Width:** 9 ft 6 in (2.90 m).
**Brakes:** Vacuum.
**Notes:** Formerly UTA 416 1959-1962. Modified for use with UTA AEC railcars 111 - 120.

| Vehicle No. | Month to Traffic | Date Stopped | Month Withdrawn | Month Cut Up | Disposal Location |
|---|---|---|---|---|---|
| 580 | 02.62 | 07.71 | .72 | ? | ? |

## TRAILER STANDARD

**Built:** 1941-47 by GNR(I) as K15 Class loco hauled coaches.
**Rebuilt:** 1951 (581) or 1957-58 (582-4) by UTA.
**Length:** 58 ft 0³/₄ in (17.70 m).
**Weight:** 29 tons.
**Seats:** 70.
**Width:** 9 ft 6 in (2.90 m).
**Brakes:** Vacuum.
**Notes:** 581 & 582 modified for use with UTA AEC railcars 111 - 120; 583 & 584 modified for use with UTA BUT railcars 121 - 135.

| Vehicle No. | Original No. | Month to Traffic | Date Stopped | Month Withdrawn | Month Cut Up | Disposal Location |
|---|---|---|---|---|---|---|
| 581 | 98 | 01.51 | 06.71 | .71 | .95 | RPSI Depot, Whitehead. |
| 582 | 186 | 10.58 | 06.70 | .72 | 06.73 | Antrim. |
| 583 | 176 | 06.57 | 08.72 | ? | - | RPSI Depot, Whitehead (P). |
| 584 | 177 | 07.57 | 06.71 | ? | 05.75 | Antrim. |

The original body of 583 was destroyed by fire on 23.03.78 and the body ex. 533 was subsequently fitted to the underframe.

## DRIVING TRAILER STANDARD

**Built:** 1954 by GNR(B) as AEC Driving Trailer K31 Class.
**Length:** 60 ft 0³/₄ in (18.31 m).
**Weight:** 29.5 tons.
**Notes:** Modified for use with UTA AEC railcars 111 - 120.
**Seats:** 72.
**Width:** 9 ft 6 in (2.90 m).
**Brakes:** Vacuum.

| Vehicle No. | Original No. | Month to Traffic | Date Stopped | Month Withdrawn | Month Cut Up | Disposal Location |
|---|---|---|---|---|---|---|
| 585 | 8 | 03.54 | 03.71 | 04.71 | ? | ? |
| 586 | 9 | 04.54 | 09.72 | 06.73 | - | RPSI Depot, Whitehead (P) |

586 had its cab removed and was converted to loco hauled coach 9 by the RPSI.

## TRAILER BRAKE STANDARD

**Built:** 1937/39 by GNR(I) as L12 Class loco hauled coaches.
**Rebuilt:** 1958 by UTA
**Length:** 58 ft 0³/₄ in (17.70 m).
**Weight:** 31.5 tons.
**Note:** Modified for use with UTA BUT railcars 121 - 135.
**Seats:** 21.
**Width:** 9 ft 6 in (2.90 m).
**Brakes:** Vacuum.

| Vehicle No. | Original No. | Month to Traffic | Date Stopped | Month Withdrawn | Month Cut Up | Disposal Location |
|---|---|---|---|---|---|---|
| 591 | 53 | 04.58 | 09.72 | .74 | ? | ? |
| 592 | 94 | 01.58 | 07.74 | .74 | .80 | ? |

## TRAILER BRAKE STANDARD

**Built:** 1940 by GNR(I) as L13 Class loco hauled coach 115.
**Rebuilt:** 1950 by UTA.
**Length:** 58 ft 0³/₄ in (17.70 m).
**Weight:** 31.25 tons.
**Seats:** 39.
**Width:** 9 ft 6 in (2.90 m).
**Brakes:** Vacuum.
**Note:** Modified for use with UTA AEC railcars 111 - 120.

| Vehicle No. | Month to Traffic | Date Stopped | Month Withdrawn | Month Cut Up | Disposal Location |
|---|---|---|---|---|---|
| 593 | 11.50 | .70 | 06.73 | ? | ? |

## TRAILER BRAKE STANDARD

**Built:** 1946 by GNR(I) as L14 Class loco hauled coaches.
**Rebuilt:** 1958 by UTA.
**Length:** 58 ft 0³/₄ in (17.70 m).
**Weight:** 28 tons.
**Seats:** 21.
**Width:** 9 ft 6 in (2.90 m).
**Brakes:** Vacuum.
**Note:** Modified for use with UTA BUT railcars 121 - 135.

| Vehicle No. | Original No. | Month to Traffic | Date Stopped | Month Withdrawn | Month Cut Up | Disposal Location |
|---|---|---|---|---|---|---|
| 594 | 175 | 06.58 | 04.74 | ? | 07.80 | Crumlin. |
| 595 | 189 | 07.58 | 08.72 | ? | 11.94 | RPSI Depot, Whitehead. |

595 had been in use as a Permanent Way Department Brake Van immediately prior to withdrawal.

# UTA / NIR DIESEL ELECTRIC MULTIPLE UNITS (DE)

## DRIVING MOTOR STANDARD (CLASS W)

**Built:** 1966-68 by UTA.
**Engine:** English Electric 4SRKT turbocharged of 550 hp (410 kW) at 850 rpm.
**Transmission:** Electric.
**Traction Motors:** Two EE 538 of 220 hp (164 kW) mounted on power car bogie remote from the engine.
**Seats:** 44.
**Length:** 64 ft 6 in (19.66 m).
**Width:** 9 ft 5 in (2.88 m).
**Weight:** 61.8 tons.
**Brakes:** Air, vacuum piped.
**Notes:** From 1976 onwards all vehicles were re-seated to seat 53. The power equipment from these cars is now fitted to the Castle Class power cars.

| Vehicle No. | Month to Traffic | Date Stopped | Month Withdrawn | Month Disposed | Disposal Location |
|---|---|---|---|---|---|
| 71 | 07.66 | 05.84 | 01.85 | 08.85 | Crosshill Quarry (A). |
| 72 | 07.66 | 10.85 | 10.85 | 08.86 | Crosshill Quarry (A). |

| 73 | 10.66 | 05.85 | 05.85 | 08.85 | Crosshill Quarry (A). |
| 74 | 10.66 | 05.83 | 04.84 | 01.85 | Crosshill Quarry (A). |
| 75 | 11.66 | 04.86 | 04.86 | 08.86 | Crosshill Quarry (A). |
| 76 | 02.67 | 04.84 | 09.84 | 01.85 | Crosshill Quarry (A). |
| 77 | 04.67 | 04.86 | 04.86 | 08.86 | Crosshill Quarry (A). |
| 78 | 09.68 | 05.79 | 05.79 | 05.80 | Crosshill Quarry (A). |

**Names**

| 71 | RIVER BUSH  | 75 | RIVER MAINE |
| 72 | RIVER FOYLE | 76 | RIVER INVER |
| 73 | RIVER ROE   | 77 | RIVER BRAID |
| 74 | RIVER LAGAN | 78 | RIVER BANN  |

72 was painted in Sealink livery for a time immediately prior to withdrawal.
75 & 77 were withdrawn after suffering vandal damage on 01.04.86.
78 was withdrawn after suffering fire bomb damage at Belfast York Road on 25.05.79.

## TRAILER BRAKE FIRST (COMPARTMENT)

**Built:** 1930 by LMS(NCC) as J11 Class loco hauled coach 373.
**Rebuilt:** 1966 by UTA (new body).
**Length:** 57 ft 4 in (17.48 m).
**Weight:** 30 tons.
**Seats:** 24.
**Width:** 9 ft 5 in (2.88 m).
**Brakes:** Air, vacuum piped.
**Notes:** Converted to DBSO seating 58S in December 1977.

| Vehicle No. | Month to Traffic | Date Stopped | Month Withdrawn | Month Disposed | Disposal Location |
|---|---|---|---|---|---|
| 701 | 06.66 | 10.85 | 04.86 | 08.86 | Crosshill Quarry (A). |

This vehicle was painted in Sealink livery for a time immediately prior to withdrawal.

## TRAILER BRAKE COMPOSITE (COMPARTMENT)

**Built:** 1929 by LMS(NCC) as J11 Class loco hauled coach 371.
**Rebuilt:** 1966 by UTA (new body).
**Length:** 57 ft 4 in (17.48 m).
**Weight:** 30 tons.
**Seats:** 12F, 16S.
**Width:** 9 ft 5 in (2.88 m).
**Brakes:** Air, vacuum piped.

| Vehicle No. | Month to Traffic | Date Stopped | Month Withdrawn | Month Disposed | Disposal Location |
|---|---|---|---|---|---|
| 702 | 09.66 | .79 | .84 | 01.85 | Crosshill Quarry (A). |

## TRAILER BRAKE STANDARD (COMPARTMENT)

**Built:** 1928 by LMS(NCC) as J11 Class loco hauled coach either 363, 365,367 or 369.
**Rebuilt:** 1966 by UTA (new body).
**Length:** 57 ft 4 in (17.48 m).
**Weight:** 30 tons.
**Seats:** 32.
**Width:** 9 ft 5 in (2.88 m).
**Brakes:** Air, vacuum piped.
**Notes:** Converted to DTBSO seating 58S in November 1977.

| Vehicle No. | Month to Traffic | Date Stopped | Month Withdrawn | Month Disposed | Disposal Location |
|---|---|---|---|---|---|
| 703 | 03.67 | .01.85 | ? | 01.85 | Crosshill Quarry (A). |

## DRIVING TRAILER BRAKE COMPOSITE (COMPARTMENT)

**Built:** 1928 by LMS(NCC) as J11 Class loco hauled coach either 363, 365,367 or 369.
**Rebuilt:** 1966 by UTA (new bodies). **Seats:** 12F, 24S.
**Length:** 57 ft 4 in (17.48 m). **Width:** 9 ft 5 in (2.88 m).
**Weight:** 30 tons. **Brakes:** Air, vacuum piped.
**Notes:** Both vehicles were converted to DTBSO seating 63S in 1976.

| Vehicle No. | Month to Traffic | Date Stopped | Month Withdrawn | Month Disposed | Disposal Location |
|---|---|---|---|---|---|
| 711 | 05.66 | 05.85 | 05.85 | 08.85 | Crosshill Quarry (A). |
| 712 | 10.66 | 03.83 | 03.83 | 10.83 | Crosshill Quarry (A). |

712 was withdrawn after an accident at Hilden on 25.03.83.

## DRIVING TRAILER BRAKE STANDARD (COMPARTMENT)

**Built:** 1924 by LMS(NCC) as F2 Class loco hauled coaches 278 & 280 respectively.
**Rebuilt:** 1968-69 by UTA (new bodies). **Seats:** 40.
**Length:** 57 ft 1 in (17.40 m). **Width:** 9 ft (2.74 m).
**Weight:** 29 tons. **Brakes:** Air, vacuum piped.
**Notes:** 713 was converted to DTBSO seating 63S in July 1977. 714 was converted to DTBSO seating 49S in May 1978.

| Vehicle No. | Original No. | Month to Traffic | Date Stopped | Month Withdrawn | Month Cut Up | Disposal Location |
|---|---|---|---|---|---|---|
| 713 | 278 | 11.68 | 04.84 | .84 | 01.03 | Downpatrick. |
| 714 | 280 | 10.69 | 07.79 | 07.79 | 07.80 | Magheramorne. |

713 was scrapped at Downpatrick following an arson attack on 26.12.02.
714 was withdrawn after an accident at Dunloy on 09.07.79.

## TRAILER STANDARD (COMPARTMENT)

**Built:** (721) 1928 by LMS(NCC) as J11 Class loco hauled coach either 363, 365,367 or 369.
(722/724) 1925 by LMS(NCC) as J11 Class loco hauled coaches either 357 or 359.
(723/725) 1932 by LMS(NCC) as J11 Class loco hauled coaches 377 & 379 respectively.
**Rebuilt:** 1966 by UTA (new bodies). **Seats:** 56.
**Length:** 57 ft 4 in (17.48 m). **Width:** 9 ft 5 in (2.88 m).
**Weight:** 30 tons. **Brakes:** Air, vacuum piped.

| Vehicle No. | Month to Traffic | Date Stopped | Month Withdrawn | Month Disposed | Disposal Location |
|---|---|---|---|---|---|
| 721 | 03.66 | 04.86 | 04.86 | 08.86 | Crosshill Quarry (A). |
| 722 | 03.66 | 05.79 | 05.79 | 05.80 | Crosshill Quarry (A). |
| 723 | 03.66 | 03.84 | ? | 08.85 | Crosshill Quarry (A). |
| 724 | 05.66 | 04.86 | 04.86 | 08.86 | Crosshill Quarry (A). |
| 725 | 03.66 | 04.86 | 04.86 | 08.86 | Crosshill Quarry (A). |

721, 724 & 725 were withdrawn after suffering vandal damage on 01.04.86.
722 was withdrawn after suffering fire bomb damage at Belfast York Road on 25.05.79.
725 was painted in Sealink livery for a time immediately prior to withdrawal.

## TRAILER STANDARD (COMPARTMENT)

**Built:** 1932 by LMS(NCC) as J6 Class loco hauled coach 362 (previously 263).
**Rebuilt:** 1969 by NIR.                              **Seats:** 64.
**Length:** 57ft (17.37 m).                            **Width:** 9ft 6 in (2.90 m).
**Weight:** 29 tons.                                   **Brakes:** Air, vacuum piped.
**Notes:** Converted to TSO seating 70S in July 1976.

| Vehicle No. | Month to Traffic | Date Stopped | Month Withdrawn | Month Cut Up | Disposal Location |
|---|---|---|---|---|---|
| 726 | 03.69 | 03.83 | 03.83 | 10.83 | ? |

This vehicle was withdrawn after an accident at Hilden on 25.03.83.

## TRAILER STANDARD (COMPARTMENT)

**Built:** 1951 by GNR(I) as K23 Class loco hauled coach. Subsequently modified to K15 Class, and then converted in 1958 to DMU Trailer Buffet Standard 556.
**Rebuilt:** 1969 by NIR.                              **Seats:** 72.
**Length:** 58ft (17.68 m).                            **Width:** 9 ft (2.74 m).
**Weight:** 29.5 tons.                                 **Brakes:** Air, vacuum piped.

| Vehicle No. | Month to Traffic | Date Stopped | Month Withdrawn | Month Cut Up | Disposal Location |
|---|---|---|---|---|---|
| 727 | 05.69 | .80 | .82 | 11.94 | RPSI Depot, Whitehead. |

## TRAILER BRAKE STANDARD

**Built:** 1951 by UTA as J16 Class loco hauled coach (using body ex. 306 and frame ex. 256). Converted 1959 to DMU Driving Trailer Standard 534.
**Rebuilt:** 1976 by NIR.                              **Seats:** 70.
**Length:** 57ft (17.37 m).                            **Width:** 9 ft 5 in (2.88 m).
**Weight:** 29 tons.                                   **Brakes:** Air, vacuum piped.

| Vehicle No. | Month to Traffic | Date Stopped | Month Withdrawn | Month Cut Up | Disposal Location |
|---|---|---|---|---|---|
| 728 | 10.76 | 04.86 | 04.86 | - | Downpatrick (P). |

This vehicle was withdrawn after suffering vandal damage on 01.04.86.

## DN&GR RAILBUSES
### DRIVING MOTOR BRAKE THIRD

Converted to rail use: 1935
Transmission: Mechanical.
Length:
Weight:

Engine:
Seats:
Width:
Brakes:

| DN&GR No. | Month to Traffic | Month Withdrawn | Month Cut Up | Disposal Location |
|---|---|---|---|---|
| 1 | .35 | .48 | - | GNR(I) No. 3 (q.v.). |
| 2 | .35 | .48 | - | GNR(I) No. 4 (q.v.). |

## GNR(I) RAILBUSES
### DRIVING MOTOR BRAKE THIRD

Built:
Transmission: Mechanical.
Length:
Weight:
Notes: Former road buses converted or rail use.

Engine: D - Gardner 4LW of 60 hp.
Seats:
Width:
Brakes:

| 1st No. | 2nd No. | 3rd No. | 4th No. | Month to Traffic | Month Withdrawn | Month Cut Up | Disposal Location |
|---|---|---|---|---|---|---|---|
| D | D1 | | | 09.34 | .39 | - | Sold to SLNCR as A[2]. |
| E | E2 | 1 | 8178 | 10.34 | .63 | - | UF&TM Cultra (P). |
| F | F3[1] | | | 01.35 | .44 | ? | ? |
| | F3[2] | 2 | | .44 | ? | ? | ? |

Notes: F3[1] was with withdrawn following an accident in Dundalk 26.04.44. Another road bus was converted as a replacement carrying the same number.
F3[2] to CIE in 1958.
1 is preserved at Ulster Folk and Transport Museum at Cultra.
8178 was a departmental number, to UTA in 1958.

## DRIVING MOTOR BRAKE THIRD

Converted to rail use: 1935  
Transmission: Mechanical.  
Length:  
Weight:  
Notes: Former road buses converted or rail use.

Engine:  
Seats:  
Width:  
Brakes:

| 1st No. | 2nd No. | Month to Traffic | Month Withdrawn | Month Cut Up | Disposal Location |
|---|---|---|---|---|---|
| 3 |  | .48 | .55 | .55 | ? |
| 4 | 8177 | .48 | .61 | ? | ? |

Notes: Formerly DN&GR Nos. 1 & 2 respectively.  
8177 was a departmental number, to CIE in 1958.

# GNR(I) RAILCARS

## DRIVING MOTOR BRAKE THIRD

Built: 1932 by GNR(I) at Dundalk Works  
Transmission: Mechanical.  
Length: 40 ft (12.19 m).  
Weight: 18$^{3/4}$ tons.  
Engine: AEC of 130 hp (97 kW).  
Seats: 32 (later 50, then 48).  
Width: 9 ft 7$^{1/4}$ in (2.93 m).  
Brakes: Vacuum.  

Notes: This vehicle was re-engined with a Gardner 6LW of 102 hp (75 kW) engine, date unknown.

| GNR(I) Vehicle No. | UTA Vehicle No. | Month to Traffic | Date Stopped | Month Withdrawn | Month Cut Up | Disposal Location |
|---|---|---|---|---|---|---|
| A | 101 | 07.32 | 10.63 | 05.64 | c.1970 | Sold to contractor. |

Noted in use by the contractor lifting the Clonsilla to Navan line, and also the Londonderry to Portadown line (1966-67).

## DRIVING MOTOR BRAKE THIRD

Built: 1932 Chassis by Kerr-Stuart & Co., Stoke on Trent: Works No. KS 4464/29.  
Bodywork by GNR(I) at Dundalk Works.  
Transmission: Electric.  
Length: 42 ft (12.80 m).  
Weight: 21 tons.  
Engine: Gleniffer 120 hp (90 kW).  
Seats: 32 (later 40, then 38).  
Width: 9 ft 6 in (2.90 m).  
Brakes: Vacuum.

| GNR(I) Vehicle No. | UTA Vehicle No. | Month to Traffic | Date Stopped | Month Withdrawn | Month Cut Up | Disposal Location |
|---|---|---|---|---|---|---|
| B | - | .32 | 10.46 | 10.46 | .56 | converted to hauled stock. |

Note: engine removed in 10.46, then used as a coach No. 500 between 1948 and 1949.

# DRIVING MOTOR BRAKE THIRD

**Built:** 1934 Chassis by Walker Bros. Wigan. Bodywork by GNR(I) at Dundalk Works.
**Engine:** Gardner 6LW of 96 hp (72 kW).
**Transmission:** Mechanical. Four speed gearbox     **Seats:** 50.
**Length:** 48 ft 1³/₄ in (14.67m)     **Weight:**
**Width:** 8ft (2.44m)     **Brakes:** Vacuum.

| GNR(I) Vehicle No. | CIE Vehicle No. | Month to Traffic | Date Stopped | Month Withdrawn | Month Cut Up | Disposal Location |
|---|---|---|---|---|---|---|
| C1 | § | 11.34 | .59 | 09.61 | ? | ? |

Note: Originally numbered C. To CIE in 1958.

# DRIVING MOTOR BRAKE COMPOSITE

**Built:** 1935 Chassis by Walker Bros. Wigan. Bodywork by GNR(I) at Dundalk Works.
**Engine:** Gardner 6LW of 96 hp (72 kW).
**Transmission:** Mechanical. Four speed gearbox.
**Seats:** * 52T (* 48T from 1948), 6F, 8S, 32T.     **Width:**
**Length:** 48 ft 11¹/₄ in (14.92 m)     **Brakes:** Vacuum.
**Weight:** 15 tons.     **Maximum Speed:** 48 mph.

| GNR(I) Vehicle No. | UTA/CIE § Vehicle No. | Month to Traffic | Date Stopped | Month Withdrawn | Month Cut Up | Disposal Location |
|---|---|---|---|---|---|---|
| C2 * | § | 06.35 | ? | 09.61 | ? | ? |
| C3 | 102 | 06.35 | ? | .59 | 12.61 | Queens Quay. |

Note: Ran back to back as a two car set until 08.37, as such, only the leading power bogie would be in use. C2 to CIE in 1958.

# DRIVING MOTOR BRAKE COMPOSITE

**Built:** 1936 Chassis by Walker Bros. Wigan. Bodywork by GNR(I) at Dundalk Works.
**Engine:** Gardner 6L3 of 153 hp (114 kW) at 1200 rpm.
**Transmission:** Mechanical. Wilson four speed gearbox.     **Seats:** 8F, 50S, 101T
**Length:** 124 ft 5 in (over both vehicles).     **Width:** 9 ft 6 in (2.90 m).
**Weight:**     **Brakes:** Vacuum.

| GNR(I) Vehicle No. | UTA/CIE § Vehicle No. | Month to Traffic | Date Stopped | Month Withdrawn | Month Cut Up | Disposal Location |
|---|---|---|---|---|---|---|
| D | 103 | 05.36 | ? | 12.62 | 09.63 | ? |
| E | § | 06.36 | ? | 10.61 | ? | Queens Quay. |

E to CIE in 1958, and then sold to the UTA 10.61. It was not renumbered into UTA stock, but cannibalised to repair 104.

## DRIVING MOTOR BRAKE COMPOSITE

**Built:** 1938 by GNR(I) at Dundalk Works.
**Engine:** Two Gardner 6LW of 102 hp (76 kW).
**Transmission:** Hydraulic. Wilson five speed gearbox.　　**Seats:** 8F, 51S, 105T.
**Length:** 124 ft 9 in (over both vehicles).　　**Width:**
**Weight:** 41½ tons.　　**Brakes:** Vacuum.

| GNR(I) Vehicle No. | UTA/CIE § Vehicle No. | Month to Traffic | Date Stopped | Month Withdrawn | Month Cut Up | Disposal Location |
|---|---|---|---|---|---|---|
| F | 104 | 03.38 | .63 | 11.65 | .70 | Sold to contractor. |
| G | § | 04.38 | 01.65 | ? | .68 | ? |

F was sold to an un-named contractor. It was noted in use by the contractor lifting the Clonmel to Thurles line in July 1970.
G to CIE in 1958, and then sold to the UTA 10.61 and renumbered 105. Subsequently destroyed by fire in 1968.

## GNR(I) AEC MULTIPLE UNITS
## DRIVING MOTOR BRAKE COMPOSITE

**Built:** 1950-53 by GNR(I) at Dundalk Works, (built from kits supplied by Park Royal Vehicles, London).
**Engine:** Two AEC A215 of 125 hp (93 kW) at 1800 rpm.
**Transmission:** Mechanical. SCG 5 speed gearbox.　　**Seats:** 12F, 32S.
**Length:** 62 ft 6 in (19.05 m).　　**Width:** 9 ft 6 in (2.90 m).
**Weight:** 38.25 tons (* 39.5 tons).　　**Brakes:** Vacuum.
**Notes:** Gangwayed at inner end only. * fitted with Spanner train heating boiler.

| GNR(I) Vehicle No. | UTA/CIE § Vehicle No. | Month to Traffic | Date Stopped | Month Withdrawn | Month Cut Up | Disposal Location |
|---|---|---|---|---|---|---|
| 600 * | 600N § | 06.50 | ? | ? | .75 | Mullingar Scrapyard. |
| 601 | 601N § | 06.50 | ? | ? | .75 | Mullingar Scrapyard. |
| 602 * | 112 † | 07.50 | 11.70 | ? | 05.75 | Antrim. |
| 603 | 111 † | 07.50 | 10.69 | ? | ? | Antrim. |
| 604 * | 604N § | 08.50 | ? | ? | .75 | Mullingar Scrapyard. |
| 605 | 605N § | 08.50 | ? | ? | .75 | Mullingar Scrapyard. |
| 606 * | 114 † | 09.50 | 09.72 | .74 | - | Conv. to parcels van 622. |
| 607 | 113 † | 09.50 | 07.71 | 09.73 | .77 | Mullingar Scrapyard. |
| 608 * | 608N § | 10.50 | ? | ? | .75 | Mullingar Scrapyard. |
| 609 | 609N § | 10.50 | ? | ? | .75 | Mullingar Scrapyard. |
| 610 * | 116 † | 11.50 | 07.71 | 09.73 | .77 | Mullingar Scrapyard. |
| 611 | 115 † | 11.50 | 09.72 | 05.75 | 05.75 | Antrim. |
| 612 * | 6l2N § | 12.50 | ? | ? | .75 | Mullingar Scrapyard. |
| 613 | 6l3N § | 12.50 | ? | ? | .75 | Mullingar Scrapyard. |
| 614 *1 | - | 12.50 | ? | .52 | .52 | ? |
| 614 *2 | 118 † | 09.53 | 07.72 | 05.75 | .75 | Antrim. |

| | | | | | | |
|---|---|---|---|---|---|---|
| 615 | 117 † | 12.50 | 07.71 | 05.75 | .75 | Antrim. |
| 616 * | 616N § | 01.51 | ? | ? | .75 | Mullingar Scrapyard. |
| 617 | 617N § | 01.51 | ? | ? | .75 | Mullingar Scrapyard. |
| 618 * | 120 † | 04.51 | 08.72 | .74 | - | Conv. to parcels van 621. |
| 619 | 119 † | 04.51 | 07.71 | ? | .75 | Antrim. |

† Used in conjunction with trailer vehicles 554/55/80/81/82/85/86/93.
After withdrawal as parcels vans, 621 & 622 were cut up at Ballymena in 1983.
The original 614 was withdrawn as a result of fire damage sustained at Drogheda on 11.09.52, a replacement vehicle was built in 1953.
113 and 116 were sold to CIE for spares in 1977.

## GNR(B) BUT MULTIPLE UNITS

## DRIVING MOTOR STANDARD

**Built:** 1957-58/62 by GNR(B) at Dundalk Works, (built from kits supplied by Park Royal Vehicles, London).
**Engine:** Two BUT A230 of 150 hp (112 kW) at 1800 rpm.
**Transmission:** Mechanical. SCG 4 speed gearbox.   **Seats:** 56.
**Length:** 65 ft 6 in (19.96 m).   **Width:** 9 ft 5 in (2.88 m).
**Weight:** 41 tons.   **Brakes:** Vacuum.
**Notes:** Through gangwayed.

| GNR(B) Vehicle No. | UTA/CIE § Vehicle No. | Month to Traffic | Date Stopped | Month Withdrawn | Month Disposed | Disposal Location |
|---|---|---|---|---|---|---|
| 701 | 121 † | 06.57 | 09.72 | .75 | 05.80 | Crosshill Quarry (A). |
| 702 | 122 † | 06.57 | 11.74 | .75 | 05.80 | Crosshill Quarry (A). |
| 703 | 123 † | 06.57 | 08.72 | .75 | 05.80 | Crosshill Quarry (A). |
| 704 | 704N § | 06.57 | ? | ? | .73 | Mullingar Scrapyard. |
| 705 | 124 † | 07.57 | 07.72 | .75 | 05.80 | Crosshill Quarry (A). |
| 706 | 706N § | 08.57 | ? | ? | ? | Mullingar Scrapyard. |
| 707 | 125 † | 09.57 | 07.72 | .75 | 05.80 | Crosshill Quarry (A). |
| 708 | 708N § | 09.57 | ? | ? | .73 | Mullingar Scrapyard. |
| 709 | 126 † | 10.57 | 08.72 | .75 | 05.80 | Crosshill Quarry (A). |
| 710 | 710N § | 10.57 | ? | ? | ? | Mullingar Scrapyard. |
| 711 | 127 † | 01.58 | 08.72 | .75 | 05.80 | Crosshill Quarry (A). |
| 712 | 712N § | 01.58 | ? | ? | ? | Mullingar Scrapyard. |
| 713 | 128 † | 03.58 | 08.72 | .75 | 05.80 | Crosshill Quarry (A). |
| 714 | 714N § | 03.58 | ? | ? | ? | Mullingar Scrapyard. |
| 715 | $129^1$ † | 05.58 | 05.60 | .60 | ? | ? |
|  | $129^2$ † | 04.62 | 11.74 | .75 | 05.80 | Crosshill Quarry (A). |
| 716 | 716N § | 05.58 | ? | ? | ? | Mullingar Scrapyard. |

† Used in conjunction with trailer vehicles 551/52/53/56/61/62/71/72/73/83/84/91/92/94/95.
The original 129 was destroyed by fire at Castlebellingham on 12.05.60 whilst working the 1445 Dublin to Belfast service. A replacement body was built on the original frame in early 1962.
121-129 were converted to hauled stock in 1975 (engines removed), withdrawn 09.78.

# DRIVING MOTOR COMPOSITE

**Built:** 1958 by GNR(B) at Dundalk Works, (built from kits supplied by Park Royal Vehicles, London).
**Engine:** Two BUT A230 of 150 hp (112 kW) at 1800 rpm.
**Transmission:** Mechanical. SCG 4 speed gearbox.
**Seats:** 16F, 40S (* 12F, 40S). **Length:** 65 ft (19.81 m).
**Width:** 9 ft 5 in (2.88 m). **Weight:** 38.25 tons.
**Brakes:** Vacuum.
**Note:** Gangwayed at inner end only.

| GNR(B) Vehicle No. | UTA/CIE § Vehicle No. | Month to Traffic | Date Stopped | Month Withdrawn | Month Cut Up | Disposal Location |
|---|---|---|---|---|---|---|
| 901 | 131 † | 07.58 | 07.74 | .74 | 05.75 | Antrim. |
| 902 * | 132 † | 07.58 | 07.74 | .74 | 03.75 | Antrim. |
| 903 * | 133 † | 08.58 | 03.72 | 03.72 | ? | ? |
| 904 | 904N § | 08.58 | ? | ? | ? | Mullingar Scrapyard. |
| 905 | 134 † | 09.58 | 07.72 | .74 | 03.75 | Antrim. |
| 906 | 906N § | 09.58 | ? | .74 | ? | Mullingar Scrapyard. |
| 907 * | 135 † | 10.58 | 09.72 | .74 | 03.75 | Antrim. |
| 908 | 908N § | 10.58 | 01.60 | 01.60 | 05.69 | Mullingar Scrapyard. |

† Used in conjunction with trailer vehicles 551/52/53/56/61/62/71/72/73/83/84/91/92/94/95.
133 was withdrawn following bomb damage suffered at Great Victoria Street on 27.03.72.
908N was destroyed by fire at Finaghy on 28.01.60

# GSR BATTERY ELECTRIC STOCK "DRUMM TRAINS"

## DRIVING MOTOR BRAKE THIRD

**Built:**
**Rebuild:** 1929 by GSR, Inchicore Works, Dublin. **Batteries:** 60 cells producing 110v.
**Transmission:** Electric 2 x 30 hp traction motors. **Seats:**
**Length:** **Width:**
**Weight:** **Brakes:**
**Note:** Experimental battery powered vehicle converted from coach 386, fitted with driving cabs at each end.

| Vehicle No. | Month to Traffic | Month Withdrawn | Month Cut Up | Disposal Location |
|---|---|---|---|---|
| 386 | 08.29 | ? | ? | ? |

# DRIVING MOTOR BRAKE SECOND

**Built:** 1931 by GSR Inchicore Works, Dublin.
**Batteries:** 272 cells producing 600v.
**Transmission:** Electric, 2 BTH 300hp traction motors.  **Seats:** 140.
**Length:** 126 ft (38.40 m).  **Width:**
**Weight:**  **Brakes:**
**Notes:** Two car articulated, the centre bogies being the power bogie. Length and seating details refer to a two car set.

| Vehicle No. | Month to Traffic | Converted to hauled stock | Month Withdrawn | Month Cut Up | Disposal Location |
|---|---|---|---|---|---|
| 2500 | 12.31 | .49 | 09.57 | ? | Inchicore Works. |
| 2501 | 12.31 | .49 | 09.57 | ? | Inchicore Works. |
| 2502 | .32 | .54 | 02.64 | ? | Inchicore Works. |
| 2503 | .32 | .54 | 02.64 | ? | Inchicore Works. |

2500 + 2501 ran as Set "A", 2502 + 2503 ran as set "B".

# DRIVING MOTOR BRAKE SECOND

**Built:** 1938 by CIE Inchicore Works, Dublin.
**Batteries:** 272 cells producing 600v.
**Transmission:** Electric 2 BTH 300hp traction motors.  **Seats:** 140.
**Length:** 126 ft (38.40 m).  **Width:**
**Weight:**  **Brakes:**
**Notes:** Two car articulated, the centre bogies being the power bogie. Length and seating details refer to a two car set.

| Vehicle No. | Month to Traffic | Converted to hauled stock | Month Withdrawn | Month Cut Up | Disposal Location |
|---|---|---|---|---|---|
| 2504 | .39 | 09.57 | ? | ? | Inchicore Works. |
| 2505 | .39 | 09.57 | ? | ? | Inchicore Works. |
| 2506 | .39 | 02.64 | ? | ? | Inchicore Works. |
| 2507 | .39 | 02.64 | ? | ? | Inchicore Works. |

2504 + 2505 ran as Set "C", 2506 + 2507 ran as set "D".

## CIE RAILBUS, RAILCAR & MULTIPLE UNIT STOCK
## DRIVING MOTOR BRAKE THIRD

**Built:** 1933 by AEC, London, for the Dublin United Tramway Company.
**Engine:**
**Transmission:** Mechanical.   **Seats:**
**Length:**   **Width:**
**Weight:**   **Brakes:**
**Note:** Converted for rail use from an A class AEC Regal bus in 1952.

| Vehicle No. | Bus No. | Month to Traffic | Month Withdrawn | Month Cut Up | Disposal Location |
|---|---|---|---|---|---|
| 2508 | TP17 | .52 | 10.61 | ? | ? |

## DRIVING MOTOR BRAKE THIRD

**Built:** 1947 by Walker Brothers, Wigan for the Sligo, Leitrim & Northern Counties Railway.
**Engines:** Gardner 6LW Duo-directional of 117 hp (87 kW) at 1700 rpm.
**Transmission:** Mechanical. Wilson epicyclic gearbox.   **Seats:** 59.
**Length:** 47 ft 1½ in (14.36 m).   **Width:** 9 ft 6 in (2.90 m).
**Weight:** 18.6 tons.   **Brakes:** Vacuum.
**Notes:** Formerly SL&NCR railcar "B", being purchased by CIE in October 1958 from the liquidator of the SL&NCR. This vehicle is articulated, with a four wheel bogie underneath the driving cab which also contains the power unit, and another four wheel bogie under the passenger section. Fitted with manually operated sliding doors.

| Vehicle No. | Date to Traffic | Date Withdrawn | Month Reinstated | Date Withdrawn | Store Location |
|---|---|---|---|---|---|
| 2509 | 09.07.47 | 01.10.57 | 07.59 | 18.09.71 | Inchicore Works (P). |

This vehicle was latterly used as an Inspection Saloon and route learning vehicle based at Limerick Junction, and was stored there for a number of years prior to moving to Mallow in 1986. It was subsequently moved to Inchicore Works on 11/03/00.

## DRIVING MOTOR BRAKE COMPOSITE

**Built:** 1951-54 by AEC/Park Royal Vehicles, London.
**Engines:** Two AEC A215 of 125 hp (93 kW) at 1800 rpm.
**Transmission:** Mechanical. SCG 5 speed gearbox.   **Seats:** 12F, 32T (Mainline style).
**Length:** 62 ft 6 in (19.05 m).   **Width:** 9 ft 6 in (2.90 m).
**Weight:** 38.5 tons.   **Brakes:** Vacuum.
**Works Numbers:** ACV 8031 022-069.
**Notes:** † Fitted with Spanner Swirlyflow 500 lbs/hr boiler.
\* Converted to suburban DMBSO seating 70S in 1970-72.
§ Converted to suburban DMSO seating 91S in 1970-72.
+ Converted to suburban DMSO seating 83S in 1970-72.
‡ Converted to suburban DMBSO seating 78S in 1970-72.

¶ Converted to suburban DMSO seating 85S in 1970-72.
$ Converted to suburban DMSO seating 90S in 1970-72.

| Vehicle No. | Month Delivered | Month Withdrawn | Month Cut Up | Disposal Location |
|---|---|---|---|---|
| 2600 †* | 03.52 | .73 | - | Converted to push/pull DSO 6109. |
| 2601 § | 03.52 | .75 | ? | Mullingar Scrapyard. |
| 2602 †* | 03.52 | .72 | - | Converted to push/pull CSO 6203 |
| 2603 § | 03.52 | .75 | ? | Mullingar Scrapyard. |
| 2604 †* | 01.53 | .73 | - | Converted to push/pull DSO 6108. |
| 2605 + | 01.53 | .72 | - | Converted to push/pull SO 6302 |
| 2606 †* | 01.53 | .71 | - | Converted to push/pull CSO 6201 |
| 2607 * | 01.53 | .72 | - | Converted to push/pull SO 6309 |
| 2608 †* | 01.53 | .72 | - | Converted to push/pull DSO 6104 |
| 2609 § | 01.53 | .73 | - | Converted to push/pull SO 6327 |
| 2610 †* | 02.53 | .72 | - | Converted to push/pull CSO 6204 |
| 2611 * | 02.53 | .73 | - | Converted to push/pull SO 6325 |
| 2612 † | 02.53 | 08.57 | ? | Mullingar Scrapyard. |
| 2613 * | 02.53 | .73 | - | Converted to push/pull SO 6323 |
| 2614 †‡ | 02.53 | .61 | - | Converted MS 2666 (qv). |
| 2615 + | 02.53 | .72 | - | Converted to push/pull SO 6318 |
| 2616 †* | 03.53 | .75 | - | Mullingar Scrapyard. |
| 2617 | 03.53 | .61 | - | Converted MS 2667 (qv). |
| 2618 †* | 03.53 | .72 | - | Converted to push/pull DSO 6103 |
| 2619 $ | 03.53 | .72 | - | Converted to push/pull SO 6306 |
| 2620 †* | 03.53 | .73 | - | Converted to push/pull DSO 6112 |
| 2621 + | 04.53 | .72 | - | Converted to push/pull SO 6304 |
| 2622 †‡ | 04.53 | .73 | - | Converted to push/pull DSO 6110 |
| 2623 § | 04.53 | .73 | - | Converted to push/pull SO 6331 |
| 2624 †‡ | 05.53 | .73 | - | Converted to push/pull DSO 6111 |
| 2625 § | 05.53 | .73 | - | Converted to push/pull SO 6326 |
| 2626 †¶ | 05.53 | .72 | - | Converted to push/pull DSO 6102 |
| 2627 $ | 05.53 | .72 | - | Converted to push/pull SO 6313 |
| 2628 †‡ | 06.53 | .73 | - | Converted to push/pull CSO 6210 |
| 2629 $ | 06.53 | .73 | - | Converted to push/pull SO 6328 |
| 2630 †‡ | 06.53 | .73 | - | Converted to push/pull CSO 6206 |
| 2631 $ | 06.53 | .72 | ? | Mullingar Scrapyard. |
| 2632 †* | 07.53 | .72 | - | Converted to push/pull CSO 6202 |
| 2633 * | 07.53 | .72 | ? | Converted to push/pull CSO 6212 |
| 2634 †* | 08.53 | .73 | - | Converted to push/pull DSO 6106 |
| 2635 ¶ | 08.53 | .73 | - | Converted to push/pull SO 6330 |
| 2636 †* | 09.53 | .72 | ? | Mullingar Scrapyard. |
| 2637 § | 09.53 | .72 | - | Converted to push/pull SO 6314 |
| 2638 †* | 10.53 | .72 | - | Converted to push/pull DSO 6105 |
| 2639 $ | 10.53 | .72 | - | Converted to push/pull SO 6310 |
| 2640 †* | 11.53 | .73 | - | Converted to push/pull DSO 6107 |
| 2641 § | 11.53 | .72 | - | Converted to push/pull SO 6317 |
| 2642 †* | 12.53 | .75 | ? | Mullingar Scrapyard. |
| 2643 * | 12.53 | .73 | - | Converted to push/pull CSO 6211 |
| 2644 †‡ | 01.54 | .73 | - | Converted to push/pull CSO 6209 |

| 2645 + | 01.54 | .72 | - | Converted to push/pull SO 6303 |
| 2646 †* | 02.54 | .71 | - | Converted to push/pull DSO 6101 |
| 2647 + | 02.54 | .71 | - | Converted to push/pull SO 6301 |

2612 was destroyed by fire at Multyfarnham in August 1957.
2614 and 2617 were re-built as Motor Standard following accident damage (qv).
2636 was withdrawn following derailment damage at Dromin Junction on 12.12.70.

## DRIVING MOTOR BRAKE COMPOSITE (§ DRIVING MOTOR BRAKE THIRD)

**Built:** 1954 by AEC/Park Royal Vehicles, London.
**Engines:** Two AEC of 125 hp (93 kW) at 1800 rpm.
**Transmission:** Mechanical. SCG 5 speed gearbox
**Length:** 62 ft 6 in (19.05 m).
**Weight:** 38.5 tons.
**Works Numbers:** ACV 8031 070-081.
**Seats:** 12F, 36T (2648-2657), 96T (2658-2659).
**Width:** 9 ft 6 in (2.90 m).
**Brakes:** Vacuum.
**Notes:** † Fitted with Clarkson Vapour boiler. Later replaced by Spanner Swirlyflow boiler, dates unknown.

| Vehicle No. | Month Delivered | Month Withdrawn | Month Cut Up | Disposal Location |
|---|---|---|---|---|
| 2648 † | 03.54 | .75 | ? | Mullingar Scrapyard. |
| 2649 | 03.54 | .73 | - | Converted to push/pull SO 6332 |
| 2650 † | 04.54 | .73 | - | Converted to push/pull CSO 6208 |
| 2651 | 04.54 | 09.75 | ? | Mullingar Scrapyard. |
| 2652 † | 05.54 | .73 | - | Converted to push/pull CSO 6207 |
| 2653 | 05.54 | .73 | - | Converted to push/pull SO 6322 |
| 2654 † | 06.54 | .75 | ? | Mullingar Scrapyard. |
| 2655 | 06.54 | .73 | - | Converted to push/pull SO 6324 |
| 2656 † | 07.54 | .61 | - | Converted to MS 2668 (qv). |
| 2657 | 07.54 | .72 | - | Converted to push/pull SO 6311 |
| 2658 †§ | 09.54 | .72 | - | Converted to push/pull CSO 6205 |
| 2659 § | 09.54 | .73 | - | Converted to push/pull SO 6329 |

2648 to 2656 were re-seated 80S in 1957.
2648, 2650, 2652 and 2654 were re-seated 78S in 1962-63.
2649, 2651, 2653 and 2655 were re-seated 94S in 1962-63.
2656 was re-built as Motor Standard following accident damage.
2657 was re-seated 70S in 1970.
2658 was re-seated 83S in 1971.
2658 & 2659 were used exclusively on the isolated Waterford to Tramore line until its closure on 31.12.60. 2657 was re-seated in 1955 to 96S to join 2658 & 2659, which were delivered new to the line.

## DRIVING MOTOR BRAKE COMPOSITE (*DRIVING MOTOR STANDARD)

**Built:** 1956 by CIE at Inchicore Works, Dublin to a Bullied design.
**Engines:** Two AEC of 125 hp (93 kW) at 1800 rpm.
**Transmission:** Mechanical. SCG 5 speed gearbox.  **Seats:** 12F, 32T.
**Length:** 62 ft 6 in (19.05 m).  **Width:** 9 ft 6 in (2.90 m).
**Weight:**  **Brakes:** Vacuum.
**Notes:** The DMBCO vehicles were converted to MBS in 1961 seating 52S. The DMSO vehicles were converted to MS in 1961, seating 64S.

| Vehicle No. | Month Delivered | Month Withdrawn | Month Cut Up | Disposal Location |
|---|---|---|---|---|
| 2660 | 02.57 | .72 | - | Converted to push/pull SO 6312 |
| 2661* | 02.57 | .72 | - | Converted to push/pull SO 6320 |
| 2662 | 02.57 | .72 | - | Converted to push/pull SO 6319 |
| 2663* | 03.57 | .72 | - | Converted to push/pull SO 6305 |
| 2664 | 04.57 | .72 | - | Converted to push/pull SO 6316 |
| 2665* | 04.57 | .72 | - | Converted to push/pull SO 6307 |

## MOTOR STANDARD (NON DRIVING)

**Built:** 1952-54 by AEC/Park Royal Vehicles, London as DMBCO vehicles.
**Rebuilt:** 1961 by CIE at Inchicore Works, Dublin.
**Engines:** Two AEC of 125 hp (93 kW) at 1800 rpm.
**Transmission:** Mechanical. SCG 5 speed gearbox.  **Seats:** 52 (* 64).
**Length:** 62 ft 6 in (19.05 m).  **Width:** 9 ft 6 in (2.90 m).
**Weight:**  **Brakes:** Vacuum.

| Vehicle No. | Original No. | Month to Traffic | Month Withdrawn | Month Cut Up | Disposal Location |
|---|---|---|---|---|---|
| 2666 | 2614 | .61 | .73 | - | Converted to push/pull SO 6321 |
| 2667* | 2617 | 09.61 | .72 | - | Converted to push/pull SO 6315 |
| 2668 | 2656 | 09.61 | .72 | - | Converted to push/pull SO 6308 |

# WEST CLARE RAILCARS AND TRAILERS

## DRIVING MOTOR BRAKE THIRD

**Built:** 1952 by CIE Inchicore Works, Dublin (bodywork), mechanical parts supplied by Walker Brothers, Wigan.
**Engine:** Gardner 6LW of 107 hp (80 kW) at 1700rpm.
**Transmission:**  **Seats:** 41.
**Length:**  **Width:**
**Weight:** 11.00 tons  **Brakes:** Vacuum.
**Maximum Speed:** $38_{1/2}$ mph.  **Gauge:** 3 ft 0 in.

| Vehicle No. | Month to Traffic | Date Withdrawn | Month Disposed | Disposal Location |
|---|---|---|---|---|
| 3386 | 18.03.52 | 31.01.61 | .62 | Bord na Móna, Boora, Co. Offaly. |
| 3387 | 17.03.52 | 31.01.61 | .62 | Bord na Móna, Oweninny, Co. Mayo. |
| 3388 | .05.52 | 31.01.61 | .62 | Bord na Móna, Derrygreenagh, Co. Offaly. |
| 3389 | .03.52 | 31.01.61 | .62 | Bord na Móna, Littleton, Co. Tipperary. |

The cabs, power unit and bogies were delivered to Inchicore Works in 09.51. Originally numbered 286 to 289, subsequently numbered 386 to 389 respectively, then again as shown above.
All had power bogies removed before sale to Bord na Móna.
3387 and 3388 are believed to still exist at the locations shown (as a flat wagons).

## TRAILER THIRD

**Built:** 1951-52 by CIE at Inchicore Works, Dublin.
**Length:**                                         **Seats:** 43.
**Weight:**                                         **Width:**
**Gauge:** 3 ft 0 in.                               **Brakes:** Vacuum.
**Note:** Built on former Tralee and Dingle coach underframes 1, 6 and 8 respectively.

| Vehicle No. | Month to Traffic | Date Withdrawn | Month Disposed | Cut Up/Disposal Location |
|---|---|---|---|---|
| 46c | .52 | 31.01.61 | .62 | Bord na Mona, Boora, Co. Offally. |
| 47c | .52 | 31.01.61 | .62 | Cavan & Leitrim Railway, Dromod. |
| 48c | .52 | 31.01.61 | .62 | Cavan & Leitrim Railway, Dromod. |

46c, body scrapped at Boora, bogies in use under 3386.
47c is in use as a passenger carriage at Dromod, Co. Leitrim.
The body of 48c was scrapped at Blackwater 10.93, with the underframe and bogies removed to Dromod, Co. Leitrim
In addition, three trailer luggage vans, nos. 200c, 201c & 202c were converted from former Clougher Valley goods wagons, nos.187c, 188c & 190c respectively. However, as they were not passenger carrying vehicles, they have not been included for the purposes of this book.

# SL&NCR RAILBUSES

## DRIVING MOTOR BRAKE THIRD

**Built:**
**Engine:** A[1] Petrol of 40 hp, re-engined 1938 with Gardner 4LW. 2A Gardner 4LW.
**Transmission:** Mechanical.                       **Seats:** A[1] - 32.
**Length:**                                         **Width:**
**Weight:**                                         **Brakes:**
**Note:** Converted for rail use from road buses.

| Vehicle No. | Bus No. | Month to Traffic | Month Withdrawn | Month Cut Up | Disposal Location |
|---|---|---|---|---|---|
| A[1] | ? | 06.35 | 03.39 | ? | ? |
| A[2] | GNR D1 | .39 | 10.57 | ? | ? |
| 2A | GNR ? | 04.38 | 10.57 | ? | ? |

Notes: A[2] was re-bodied with a secondhand bus body in 1950. A[2] and 2A were withdrawn upon closure of the SL&NCR on 01.10.57.

# APPENDIX 3 - FORMER CIE PUSH/PULL VEHICLES

**Note:** The authors recognise that much information is still required to make this section as complete as the rest of the book. If any readers can help with any of the missing information please contact the authors at the publishers address for inclusion in future editions.

It should be noted that some of these vehicles were re-seated on a number of occasions and full details are not available.

## CIE/PARK ROYAL                    DRIVING OPEN STANDARD

**Built:** 1951-53 by AEC/Park Royal Vehicles, London as DMU vehicles.
**Rebuilt:** 1972-74 by CIE at Inchicore Works, Dublin.
**Bogies:** AEC Design.                        **Seats:** 58.
**Length:** 62 ft 6 in (19.05 m).              **Brakes:** Vacuum.
**Width:** 9 ft 6 in (2.90 m).                 **Weight:** 30 tons.

| Vehicle No. | Ex DMU Number | Month Converted | Date Withdrawn | Month Cut Up | Disposal/Store Location |
|---|---|---|---|---|---|
| 6101 | 2646 | 12.72 | .10.76 | ? | Mullingar Scrapyard. |
| 6102 | 2626 | 12.72 | 21.10.74 | ? | Mullingar Scrapyard. |
| 6103 | 2618 | 02.73 | 26.11.83 | ? | Mullingar Scrapyard. |
| 6104 | 2608 | 04.73 | .10.76 | ? | Mullingar Scrapyard. |
| 6105 | 2638 | 05.73 | .04.83 | 06.83 | Mullingar Scrapyard. |
| 6106 | 2634 | 06.73 | .04.85 | ? | Mullingar Scrapyard. |
| 6107 | 2640 | 08.73 | 14.09.87 | 07.89 | Dundalk. |
| 6108 | 2604 | 10.73 | 06.07.82 | 06.83 | Mullingar Scrapyard. |
| 6109 | 2600 | 12.73 | 02.09.81 | ? | Mullingar Scrapyard. |
| 6110 | 2622 | 02.74 | .04.85 | ? | Mullingar Scrapyard. |
| 6111 | 2624 | 04.74 | 14.09.87 | - | Inchicore Works. |
| 6112 | 2620 | 03.74 | 26.05.80 | ? | Mullingar Scrapyard. |

6101 & 6104 were both withdrawn following fire damage, date unknown.
6102 was withdrawn following an accident at Gormanston on 21.10.74.
6111 is at Inchicore Works for possible preservation.

## CIE/PARK ROYAL　　CONNECTOR OPEN STANDARD

**Built:** 1951-53 by AEC/Park Royal Vehicles, London as DMU vehicles.
**Rebuilt:** 1972-74 by CIE at Inchicore Works, Dublin.
**Bogies:** AEC Design.　　　　　　　　　　　　**Seats:** 58.
**Length:** 62 ft 6 in (19.05 m).　　　　　　　　**Brakes:** Vacuum.
**Width:** 9 ft 6 in (2.90 m).　　　　　　　　　　**Weight:** 30 tons.

| Vehicle No. | Ex DMU Number | Month Converted | Date Withdrawn | Month Cut Up | Disposal/Store Location |
|---|---|---|---|---|---|
| 6201 | 2606 | 12.72 | .11.83 | ? | Mullingar Scrapyard. |
| 6202 | 2632 | 12.72 | . .85 | ? | Mullingar Scrapyard. |
| 6203 | 2602 | 06.73 | 14.09.87 | ? | Mullingar Scrapyard. |
| 6204 | 2610 | 02.73 | .10.76 | ? | Mullingar Scrapyard. |
| 6205 | 2658 | 04.73 | .11.83 | ? | Mullingar Scrapyard. |
| 6206 | 2630 | 05.73 | 14.09.87 | 07.89 | Dundalk. |
| 6207 | 2652 | 08.73 | 26.10.83 | ? | Mullingar Scrapyard. |
| 6208 | 2650 | 12.73 | .04.85 | ? | Mullingar Scrapyard. |
| 6209 | 2644 | 12.73 | 26.10.83 | ? | Mullingar Scrapyard. |
| 6210 | 2628 | 02.74 | .11.83 | ? | Mullingar Scrapyard. |
| 6211 | 2643 | 04.74 | .11.83 | ? | Mullingar Scrapyard. |
| 6212 | 2633 | 06.74 | .05.80 | ? | Mullingar Scrapyard. |

6204 was withdrawn following fire damage, date unknown.

## CIE/PARK ROYAL　　INTERMEDIATE OPEN STANDARD

**Built:** 1951-53 by AEC/Park Royal Vehicles, London as DMU vehicles.
**Rebuilt:** 1972 by CIE at Inchicore Works, Dublin.
**Bogies:** AEC Design.　　　　　　　　　　　　**Seats:** 70.
**Length:** 62 ft 6 in (19.05 m).　　　　　　　　**Brakes:** Vacuum.
**Width:** 9 ft 6 in (2.90 m).　　　　　　　　　　**Weight:** 30 tons.

| Vehicle No. | Ex DMU Number | Month Converted | Date Withdrawn | Month Cut Up | Disposal Location |
|---|---|---|---|---|---|
| 6301 | 2647 | 12.72 | . .85 | ? | Mullingar Scrapyard. |
| 6302 | 2605 | 12.72 | . .85 | ? | Mullingar Scrapyard. |
| 6303 | 2645 | 12.72 | .07.82 | ? | Mullingar Scrapyard. |
| 6304 | 2621 | 12.72 | 26.10.83 | ? | Mullingar Scrapyard. |

## CIE/PARK ROYAL　　INTERMEDIATE OPEN STANDARD

**Built:** 1956 by CIE at Inchicore Works, Dublin as DMU DMBS.
**Rebuilt:** 1973 by CIE at Inchicore Works, Dublin.
**Bogies:** AEC Design.　　　　　　　　　　　　**Seats:** 66.
**Length:** 62 ft 6 in (19.05 m).　　　　　　　　**Brakes:** Vacuum.
**Width:** 9 ft 6 in (2.90 m).　　　　　　　　　　**Weight:** 30 tons.

| Vehicle No. | Ex DMU Number | Month Converted | Date Withdrawn | Month Cut Up | Disposal Location |
|---|---|---|---|---|---|
| 6305 | 2663 | 02.73 | .10.76 | ? | Mullingar Scrapyard. |

Withdrawn following fire damage, date unknown.

## CIE/PARK ROYAL — INTERMEDIATE OPEN STANDARD

Details as 6301-4.

| Vehicle No. | Ex DMU Number | Month Converted | Date Withdrawn | Month Cut Up | Disposal Location |
|---|---|---|---|---|---|
| 6306 | 2619 | 04.73 | .11.83 | ? | Mullingar Scrapyard. |

## CIE/PARK ROYAL — INTERMEDIATE OPEN STANDARD

Details as 6305.

| Vehicle No. | Ex DMU Number | Month Converted | Date Withdrawn | Month Cut Up | Disposal Location |
|---|---|---|---|---|---|
| 6307 | 2665 | 02.73 | .10.76 | ? | Mullingar Scrapyard. |

Withdrawn following fire damage, date unknown.

## CIE/PARK ROYAL — INTERMEDIATE OPEN STANDARD

**Built:** 1954 by AEC/Park Royal Vehicles, London as DMU DMCO.
**Rebuilt:** 1973 by CIE at Inchicore Works, Dublin.
**Bogies:** AEC Design.   **Seats:** 66.
**Length:** 62 ft 6 in (19.05 m).   **Brakes:** Vacuum.
**Width:** 9 ft 6 in (2.90 m).   **Weight:** 30 tons.

| Vehicle No. | Ex DMU Number | Month Converted | Date Withdrawn | Month Cut Up | Disposal Location |
|---|---|---|---|---|---|
| 6308 | 2668 | 05.73 | .11.83 | ? | Mullingar Scrapyard. |

## CIE/PARK ROYAL — INTERMEDIATE OPEN STANDARD

Details as 6301-4.

| Vehicle No. | Ex DMU Number | Month Converted | Date Withdrawn | Month Cut Up | Disposal Location |
|---|---|---|---|---|---|
| 6309 | 2607 | 04.73 | .11.83 | ? | Mullingar Scrapyard. |
| 6310 | 2639 | 10.73 | . .85 | ? | Mullingar Scrapyard. |
| 6311 | 2657 | 10.73 | 14.09.87 | 07.89 | Dundalk. |

## CIE/PARK ROYAL — INTERMEDIATE OPEN STANDARD

Details as 6305.

| Vehicle No. | Ex DMU Number | Month Converted | Date Withdrawn | Month Cut Up | Disposal Location |
|---|---|---|---|---|---|
| 6312 | 2660 | 05.73 | . .85 | ? | Mullingar Scrapyard. |

## CIE/PARK ROYAL — INTERMEDIATE OPEN STANDARD

Details as 6301-4.

| Vehicle No. | Ex DMU Number | Month Converted | Date Withdrawn | Month Cut Up | Disposal Location |
|---|---|---|---|---|---|
| 6313 | 2627 | 08.73 | .04.85 | ? | Mullingar Scrapyard. |
| 6314 | 2637 | 06.73 | . .85 | ? | Mullingar Scrapyard. |

## CIE/PARK ROYAL — INTERMEDIATE OPEN STANDARD

Details as 6308.

| Vehicle No. | Ex DMU Number | Month Converted | Date Withdrawn | Month Cut Up | Disposal Location |
|---|---|---|---|---|---|
| 6315 | 2667 | 06.74 | . .85 | ? | Mullingar Scrapyard. |

## CIE/PARK ROYAL — INTERMEDIATE OPEN STANDARD

Details as 6305.

| Vehicle No. | Ex DMU Number | Month Converted | Date Withdrawn | Month Cut Up | Disposal Location |
|---|---|---|---|---|---|
| 6316 | 2664 | 02.74 | 14.09.87 | ? | Mullingar Scrapyard. |

## CIE/PARK ROYAL — INTERMEDIATE OPEN STANDARD

Details as 6301-4.

| Vehicle No. | Ex DMU Number | Month Converted | Date Withdrawn | Month Cut Up | Disposal Location |
|---|---|---|---|---|---|
| 6317 | 2641 | 12.73 | .11.83 | ? | Mullingar Scrapyard. |
| 6318 | 2615 | 06.73 | .11.82 | ? | Mullingar Scrapyard. |

## CIE/PARK ROYAL — INTERMEDIATE OPEN STANDARD

Details as 6305.

| Vehicle No. | Ex DMU Number | Month Converted | Date Withdrawn | Month Cut Up | Disposal Location |
|---|---|---|---|---|---|
| 6319 | 2662 | 04.74 | .04.85 | ? | Mullingar Scrapyard. |
| 6320 | 2661 | 05.74 | .11.83 | ? | Mullingar Scrapyard. |

## CIE/PARK ROYAL INTERMEDIATE OPEN STANDARD

Details as 6308.

| Vehicle No. | Ex DMU Number | Month Converted | Date Withdrawn | Month Cut Up | Disposal Location |
|---|---|---|---|---|---|
| 6321 | 2666 | 05.74 | .11.83 | ? | Mullingar Scrapyard. |

## CIE/PARK ROYAL INTERMEDIATE OPEN STANDARD

Details as 6301-4.

| Vehicle No. | Ex DMU Number | Month Converted | Date Withdrawn | Month Cut Up | Disposal Location |
|---|---|---|---|---|---|
| 6322 | 2653 | .73 | . .84 | ? | Dundalk. |
| 6323 | 2613 | 12.73 | 26.10.83 | ? | Mullingar Scrapyard. |
| 6324 | 2655 | 08.73 | .08.82 | 06.83 | Mullingar Scrapyard. |
| 6325 | 2611 | 04.74 | .11.83 | ? | Mullingar Scrapyard. |
| 6326 | 2625 | 02.74 | 16.02.82 | ? | Mullingar Scrapyard. |
| 6327 | 2609 | 06.74 | . .86 | ? | Mullingar Scrapyard. |
| 6328 | 2629 | 04.74 | . .85 | ? | Mullingar Scrapyard. |
| 6329 | 2659 | 06.74 | . .85 | ? | Mullingar Scrapyard. |
| 6330 | 2635 | 02.74 | 26.10.83 | ? | Mullingar Scrapyard. |
| 6331 | 2623 | .74 | . .84 | ? | Mullingar Scrapyard. |
| 6332 | 2649 | .74 | . .84 | ? | Mullingar Scrapyard. |

## APPENDIX 4 - DISPOSAL OF ASBESTOS CONTAMINATED VEHICLES

In the late 1970s new regulations were introduced controlling the handling and disposal of asbestos contaminated vehicles which had previously been broken up without special precautions. The two railway companies were faced with the problem of disposing of many redundant vehicles which were found to contain blue asbestos between the outer and inner skins of the vehicle bodies and roofs. Neither of the two companies possessed the special facilities required by law to dispose of these contaminated vehicles and therefore a feasibility study was undertaken by NIR, (who owned most of the affected vehicles), to decide the safest and most economic way to resolve the problem. Six different schemes were explored, each of which is detailed below, together with the final recommendations made.

### Scheme A - Shallow Water Disposal.

This scheme involved the transportation of the vehicles from either Stormont Wharf or Albert Quay by ship to Beaufort Dyke, which is 8 to 10 miles east north east of the Copeland Islands, for dumping at sea. However, the Water Pollution Control Branch at Stormont reported that dumping was not possible under the Oslo Convention Annexe 2, in that bulky material cannot be dumped on the Continental Shelf. Any dumping at sea must be in water at least 6000 feet deep and must be at least 150 miles from the nearest land.

## Scheme B - Stripping at Antrim Goods Yard.

This scheme involved the dismantling of the affected vehicles under controlled conditions by outside contractors at the former goods yard at Antrim. The cost of providing the special facilities required by law, including the construction of a sealed building in which the eventual stripping of the asbestos would take place, proved to be too expensive and the whole scheme was found to be too long and complex.

## Scheme C - Deep water disposal.

Following the conclusions reached in scheme A, the possibility of deep water dumping of the vehicles was explored. However, the application was refused by the Department of the Environment as alternative land based methods were available.

## Scheme D - Burning under controlled circumstances.

No facilities existed for the controlled burning of contaminated vehicles in Ireland and the nearest available licensed facility was that at the premises of King & Sons Ltd., Newmarket (now Mayer Parry Ltd.). The possibility of transporting these vehicles by sea from Belfast to Felixstowe and then conveying them by rail to Newmarket was explored, but the different track and loading gauges precluded this option. An alternative option of conveying the vehicles by road on low loaders from Felixstowe was found to be impracticable as road access to the yard was limited. The cost of sea transport was also very high and therefore this scheme was abandoned.

## Scheme E - Burial in abandoned tunnel.

The abandoned Lisummon Tunnel on the former route from Markethill to Goraghwood was found to be in a satisfactory condition following an inspection by the permanent way department. Reinstatement of the line for the short distance from Goraghwood to the tunnel mouth was planned so that the vehicles could be delivered directly to the site. Upon completion the tunnel mouths would be plugged with concrete and the line back to Goraghwood lifted. This scheme met with approval, but scheme F below ultimately was found to be more cost effective and required little capital outlay.

## Scheme F - Burial in Crosshill Quarry, Co. Antrim.

The scheme ultimately adopted. The former quarry at Crosshill, Co. Antrim was found to be an ideal site for the burial of the contaminated vehicles, being only a short distance from the railway line at Crumlin. The vehicles were "shrink wrapped" at York Road prior to delivery to a specially laid siding at Crumlin station for final transportation by road to the quarry. The quarry was partially filled with water, with depths varying between 40 and 80 feet. In addition to the vehicles shown in the text, the following CIE vehicles were also dumped in the quarry in February 1985: 1497, 1498, 1499, 1500, 1631, 1924, 1925, 1927, 1929, 1930, 2402.

# APPENDIX 5 - ACCOMMODATION

Additional information to update this section occasionally appears in "The Irish Mail", the journal of the Irish Traction Group - see advert for details.

## Belfast
"Helga Lodge", Cromwell Road, Botanic, Belfast. 028 9032 4820
Directions: Turn left outside Botanic station and continue for approx. 100 metres. Turn second left into Cromwell Road and "Helga Lodge" is almost immediately on the right hand side. (Walking time less than 5 minutes).

## Cork
"Oaklands", 51 Lower Glanmire Road, Cork. 00353 21-500578
Directions: Turn right outside the main station gates and proceed along Lower Glanmire Road for approx. 100 metres. "Oaklands" is on the right hand side (Walking time less than 5 minutes).

"Tivoli House", 143 Lower Glanmire Road, Cork. 00353 21 -506605
Directions: Turn right outside the main station gates and proceed along Lower Glanmire Road for approx. 400 metres. "Tivoli House" is on the left hand side, just before the railway bridge. (Walking time 5 minutes).

## Dublin
"Kingsbridge", 14 Parkgate Street, Dublin. 00353 1 6773263
Directions: Leave Heuston Station by the LUAS bus pick up/set down exit. Turn first left and cross the River Liffey. "Kingsbridge" is almost directly opposite across Parkgate Street. (Walking time less than 5 minutes).

## Limerick
"Boylans", 22 Davis Street, Limerick. 00353 61 418916
Directions: Leave the station by the main exit and cross the main road. Proceed along Davis Street and "Boylans" is approx. 100 metres further along on the right. (Walking time less than 5 minutes).

## Waterford
"Portree", Mary Street, Waterford. 00353 51 874574.
Leave the station and cross the river bridge, turn 1st right, take 1st left, The Portree is straight ahead, by the Brewery. (Walking time 5 minutes).

## Carrick-On-Suir (for Irish Traction Group base)
'Fatima House', John Street, Carrick-On-Suir, Co. Tipperary. 00 353 51 640298 Directions: Proceed along the station approach and turn left at the end. Continue across the park to the traffic lights and turn right along the main road past the Garda Station. "Fatima House" is approximately 300 metres along on the right hand side. (Walking time less than 10 minutes).

All sections of line are single except
for the following which are double :

Bangor - Bray ;
West Road Jn - Island Bridge Jn ;
Heuston - Cobh ;
Limerick - Killonan Jn ;
Howth Jn - Howth ;
Newcomen Jn - Maynooth ;
Yorkgate - Carrickfergus ;
Bleach Green Jn - Monkstown ;
Waterford West - Abbey Jn

C & LR   Cavan & Leitrim Railway
D & AR   Downpatrick & Ardglass Railway
IE       Iarnród Éireann
ITG      Irish Traction Group
NIR      Northern Ireland Railways
RPSI     Railway Preservation Society of Ireland
T & DSR  Tralee & Dingle Steam Railway
WSVR     Waterford & Suir Valley Railway

(c) R Fraser

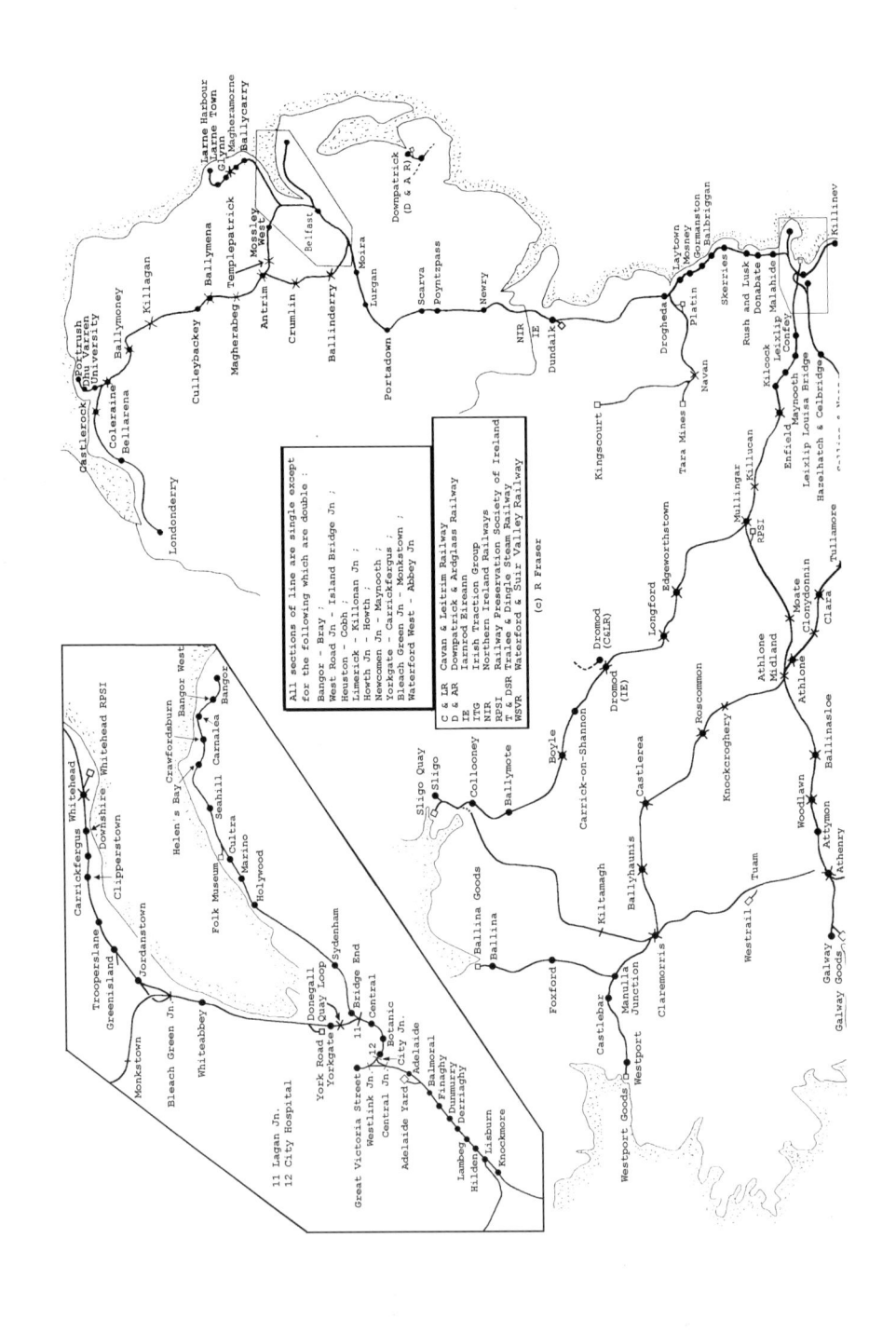

11 Lagan Jn.
12 City Hospital